5 STEPS TO A 5™

AP English Literature and Composition

2023

5 STEPS TO A 5™

AP English Literature and Composition

2023

Michael Hartnett
Barbara L. Murphy

Mc
Graw
Hill

New York   Chicago   San Francisco   Athens   London   Madrid
Mexico City   Milan   New Delhi   Singapore   Sydney   Toronto

CONTENTS

STEP 4

Review the Knowledge You Need to Score High

PREFACE

Welcome to our latest revised AP Literature class. As we said in the earlier versions of this book, we are first and foremost teachers who have taught Advanced Placement to literally thousands of students who successfully took the AP exam. With this guide, we hope to share with you what we know as well as what we have learned from our own students.

We see you as a student in our class—only quieter! Our philosophy has always been NOT to teach only for the AP test. Instead, our goal has always been to develop those insights, appreciations, and skills that lead to advanced levels of facility with literature and composition. These are the very same skills which will enable you to do well on the AP Literature exam. Our aim is to remove your anxiety and to improve your comfort level with the test. We believe that you are already motivated to succeed; otherwise, you would not have come this far. And, obviously, you would not have purchased this prep book.

Since you are already in an English class, this book is going to supplement your literature course readings, analysis, and writing. We are going to give you the opportunity to practice processes and techniques that we know from experience REALLY WORK! If you apply the techniques and processes presented in this book, we are confident you can succeed in both the course and on the exam.

We have listened to comments and suggestions from both instructors and students of AP English Literature, and keeping their thoughts in mind, this revised text has more interactive activities and practice to help hone those skills needed to do well in class and on the AP Literature exam. In addition, there are special review questions and activities related to specific chapters that McGraw Hill has available on its website devoted to the *5 Steps* series. There you can test how well you have internalized the material in the chapter.

Let's begin.

ACKNOWLEDGMENTS

Our love and appreciation to Allan and to Leah for their constant support and encouragement. Our very special thanks to our professional mentors who have guided us throughout our careers: Steven Piorkowski and Howard Damon. To the following for their support and suggestions: Diane Antonucci, Richard Andres, Mary Moran, Mike Thier, Mark Misthal, Dave Martin, Edward Stern, Christine Scarf, John Smales, and Michael Hartnett—thank you.

The authors wish to acknowledge the participation, insights, and feedback provided us by the following colleagues and students:

Islip High School:
  Teacher: Marge Grossgold
  Students: Caitlin Rizzo and Katelyn Zawyrucha

Jericho High School:
  Teachers: Diane Antonucci, Michael Hartnett
  Students: Tara Arschin, Samantha Brody, Jenna Butner, Julie Ivans, Grace Kwak, Ari Weiss, Erica Ross, David Swidler, and Sherli Yeroushalmi

Massapequa High School:
  Teachers: Sue Bruno and Rosemary Verade
  Student: Margaretta Dimos

Solomon Schechter School:
  Teachers: Dennis Young and Miriam Fischer
  Students: Yadin Duckstein, Ari Lucas, and Jonathan Kotter

Wantagh High School:
  Teachers: Sherry Skolnick and Pat Castellano
  Student: Lauren Manning

Also, our thanks to Danielle Tumminio and Andrew Brotman.

CREDITS

ABOUT THE AUTHORS

Michael Hartnett has been a high school AP Literature teacher and college professor for more than 30 years. He received his PhD in Literature from the State University of New York at Stony Brook. He is the author of six published novels, the latest being *Death Canal* (Black Rose Writing, 2022), and he has also worked as an editor for the literary magazine *Confrontation*. Michael is the coauthor of the *5 Minutes to a 5* section of *5 Steps to a 5: AP English Literature*, Elite Edition.

Barbara L. Murphy taught AP Language and other college-level courses at Jericho High School for over 26 years. She is a long-time reader of the AP English Language exam and is a consultant for the College Board's AP Language and Composition and Building for Success divisions, for which she has conducted workshops, conferences, and Summer Institutes.

After earning her BA from Duquesne University and her MA from the University of Pittsburgh, Ms. Murphy did her doctoral course work at Columbia University. She also holds professional certifications in still photography and motion picture production and is one of the founding members of the women's film company Ishtar Films.

So much of the primary planning, organization, choice of texts, and activities in this book is due to the knowledge, determination, love of students, and bountiful sense of humor of Estelle M. Rankin, original coauthor of *5 Steps to a 5: AP English Literature*.

Ms. Murphy and Ms. Rankin are also the coauthors of McGraw Hill's *5 Steps to a 5: AP English Language*, *Writing the AP English Essay*, and *Writing an Outstanding College Application Essay*.

INTRODUCTION: THE FIVE-STEP PROGRAM

Some Basics

Consider this section as a map of the new territory you are going to explore. We will provide the general directions, and you can decide when, where, and how you will follow this map.

Reading

We believe that reading should be an exciting interaction between you and the writer. You have to bring your own context to the experience, and you must feel comfortable reaching for and exploring ideas. You are an adventurer on a journey of exploration, and we will act as your guides. We will set the itinerary, but you will set your own pace. You can feel free to "stop and smell the roses" or to explore new territory.

The Journey

On any journey, each traveler sees something different on new horizons. So, too, each student is free to personalize his or her own literary experience, provided he or she tries at all times to strive for excellence and accuracy.

Critical Thinking

There are no tricks to critical thinking. Those who claim to guarantee you a score of 5 with gimmicks are doing you a disservice. No one can guarantee a 5; however, the reading and writing skills you will review, practice, and master will give you the very best chance to do your very best. You will have the opportunity to learn, to practice, and to master the critical thinking processes that can empower you to achieve your highest score.

The Beginning

It is our belief that if you focus on the beginning, the rest will fall into place. Once you purchase this book and decide to work your way through it, you are beginning your journey to the AP Literature exam. We will be with you every step of the way.

Why This Book?

We believe we have something unique to offer you. For over 25 years we have addressed the needs of AP students just like you. And we've been fortunate to learn from these students. Therefore, the content of this book reflects genuine student concerns and needs. **This is a student-oriented book**. We will not overwhelm you with pompous language, mislead you with inaccurate information and tasks, or lull you into a false sense of confidence with easy shortcuts. We stand behind every suggestion, process, and question we present. There is no "busywork" in this book.

We know you will not do every activity. Therefore, think of this book as a resource and guide to accompany you on your AP Literature journey to the exam. This book is designed to serve many purposes. It will:

- Clarify requirements for the AP English Literature exam.
- Provide you with test practice.
- Show you rubrics (grading standards) on which you can model and evaluate your own work.
- Anticipate and answer your questions.
- Enrich your understanding and appreciation of literature.
- Help you pace yourself.
- Make you aware of the Five Steps to Mastering the AP English Literature exam.

Organization of the Book

We know that your primary concern is to obtain information about the AP Literature exam. So, we begin at the beginning with an overview of the AP exam in general. We then introduce you to our Diagnostic/Master exam, which we use throughout the book to show you the ins and outs of an AP Literature test. In separate chapters you will become familiar with both sections of the exam. We will lead you through the multiple-choice questions and explain how you should answer them. Then we will take you through the essay questions and discuss approaches to writing these essays.

Because you must be fluent in the language and processes of literary analysis and composition, we provide a Comprehensive Review section in both prose and poetry. This review is not a mere listing of terms and concepts. Rather, it is a series of practices that will hone your analytical and writing skills. But, do not fear. You will find terms and concepts clearly delineated within their contexts. We also provide annotated suggestions for high-interest prose and poetry readings.

A separate section of the book contains practice exams. Here is where you will test your skills and knowledge. You may be sure that the prose and poetry selections included in each exam are on the AP level. The multiple-choice questions provide you with practice in responding to typical types of questions asked in past AP exams. The essay questions are designed to cover the techniques and terms required by the AP exam. The free-response essays are both challenging and specific, yet they are broad enough to suit all curricula. After taking each test, you can check yourself against the explanations of every multiple-choice question and the ratings of the sample student essays.

The final section is one that you should not pass over. It presents a Suggested Reading Guide, a General Bibliography, a Glossary of Terms that may be of importance to you, and a list of websites related to the AP Literature exam.

Introduction to the Five-Step Preparation Program

The **Five-Step Program** is a powerful program designed to provide you with the best possible skills, strategies, and practice to help lead you to that perfect 5 on the Advanced Placement English Literature exam that is administered each May to more than 350,000 high school students. Each of the five steps will provide you with the opportunity to get closer and closer to the 5, which is the gold medal to all AP students.

Step 1: Set Up Your Study Program

- Useful information about the Advanced Placement program and exams
- Three alternative study schedules and advice for determining which is best for you

Step 2: Determine Your Test Readiness

- A first look at the overall exam, to be repeated in greater detail later

Step 3: Develop Strategies for Success

- Learn about the test itself
- Learn to read multiple-choice questions
- Learn how to answer multiple-choice questions, including whether or not to guess
- Learn how to deconstruct the essay prompts
- Learn how to plan the essay

Step 4: Review the Knowledge You Need to Score High

- Practice activities that will hone your skills in close reading
- Practice activities in critical thinking
- Practice activities in critical/analytical writing

Step 5: Build Your Test-Taking Confidence

- Two practice exams that test how well honed your skills are
- Rubrics for self-evaluation

Finally, at the back of the book you'll find additional resources to aid your preparation. These include:

- A comprehensive review of literary analysis
- A glossary of terms
- A bibliography for further reading
- A list of websites related to the AP English Literature exam

The Graphics Used in This Book

To emphasize particular skills and strategies, we use several icons throughout this book. An icon in the margin will alert you that you should pay particular attention to the accompanying text. We use three icons:

This icon points out a very important concept or fact that you should not pass over.

This icon calls your attention to a problem-solving strategy that you may want to try.

This icon indicates a tip that you might find useful.

Boldfaced and *italicized* words indicate important terms as well as those that are included in the Glossary at the back of the book.

Throughout the book you will find margin notes and boxes. We want you to pay close attention to these areas because they can provide tips, hints, strategies, and explanations that will help you reach your full potential.

5 STEPS TO A 5™

AP English Literature and Composition

2023

STEP 1

Set Up Your Study Program

CHAPTER 1

What You Should Know About the AP Literature Exam

IN THIS CHAPTER

Summary: Information about the AP English Literature and Composition exam and its scoring

Key Ideas
- ✪ Learn answers to frequently asked questions
- ✪ Learn how your final score is calculated
- ✪ Learn tips for successfully taking the exam

The College Board has introduced changes that will be reflected in the AP English Literature exam.

You should be aware of the following:

The rating of the exam will remain 1, 2, 3, 4, 5.

Multiple choice will comprise 45% of the final score, with the essay section of the exam comprising 55%.

- There are **no changes** to MC questions.
- There are **no changes** to the types of prompts (FRQ): poetry + prose + free response
- There is **renewed emphasis** on skills development in consideration of prose + poetry + longer works

- The **<u>MAJOR CHANGE</u> is in the method of rating essays**
  - From holistic to analytic
  - **From 9 points to 6 points**
  - 6 points
    - ✓ 1 point for thesis/claim
    - ✓ 4 points for appropriate evidence and commentary
    - ✓ 1 point for syntax, diction, and/or complexity

Background on the Advanced Placement Exam

"AP" does not stand for "Always Puzzling." The following should help lift the veil of mystery associated with the AP exam.

What Is the Advanced Placement Program?

The Advanced Placement program was begun by the College Board in 1955 to construct standard achievement exams that would allow highly motivated high school students the opportunity to be awarded advanced placement as freshmen in colleges and universities in the United States. Today, there are more than 39 courses and exams with over 2.7 million students from every state in the nation, and from foreign countries, taking the annual exams in May.

As is obvious, the AP programs are designed for high school students who wish to take college-level courses. The AP Literature course and exam are designed to involve high school students in college-level English studies in both literature and composition.

Who Writes the AP Literature Exam?

According to the folks at the College Board, the AP Literature exam is created by college and high school English instructors called the AP Development Committee. The committee's job is to ensure that the annual AP Literature exam reflects what is being taught and studied in college-level English classes in high schools.

This committee writes a large number of multiple-choice questions that are pretested and evaluated for clarity, appropriateness, and a range of possible answers. The committee also generates a pool of essay questions, pretests them, and chooses those questions that best represent the full range of the scoring scale to allow the AP readers to evaluate the essays fairly.

It is important to remember that the AP Literature exam is thoroughly evaluated after it is administered each year. This way, the College Board can use the results to make course suggestions and to plan future tests.

What Are the Advanced Placement Scores, and Who Receives Them?

Once you have taken the exam and it has been scored, your test will be assigned one of five numbers by the College Board:

- 5 indicates you are extremely well qualified.
- 4 indicates you are well qualified.
- 3 indicates you are qualified.
- 2 indicates you are possibly qualified.
- 1 indicates you are not qualified to receive college credit.

A score of 5, 4, 3, 2, or 1 will be reported to your college or university first, to your high school second, and to you third. All this reporting is usually completed by the middle to end of July.

Reasons for Taking the Advanced Placement Exam

At some point during the year, every AP student asks the ultimate question: Why am I taking this exam?

Good question. Why put yourself through a year of intensive study, pressure, stress, and preparation? To be honest, only you can answer that question. Over the years, our students have indicated to us that there are several prime reasons why they were willing to take the risk and to put in the effort:

- For personal satisfaction
- To compare themselves with other students across the nation
- Because colleges look favorably on the applications of students who elect to enroll in AP courses
- To receive college credit or advanced standing at their colleges or universities
- Because they love the subject
- So that their families will really be proud of them

There are plenty of other reasons, but no matter what the other reasons might be, the top reason for your enrolling in the AP Lit course and taking the exam in May should be to feel good about yourself and the challenges you have met.

What You Need to Know About the AP Lit Exam

Let's answer a few of the nitty-gritty questions about the exam and its scoring.

If I Don't Take an AP Lit Course, Can I Still Take the AP Lit Exam?

Yes. Even though the AP Lit exam is designed for the student who has had a year's course in AP Literature, there are high schools that do not offer this type of course, yet there are students in these high schools who have also done well on the exam. However, if your high school does offer an AP Lit course, by all means take advantage of it and the structured background it will provide you.

How Is the Advanced Placement Literature Exam Organized?

The exam has two parts and is scheduled to last 3 hours. The first section is a set of multiple-choice questions based on a series of prose passages and poems. You will have 1 hour to complete this part of the test. The second section of the exam is a 2-hour essay-writing segment consisting of three different essays: one on prose, one on poetry, and one free-response based on a major work of literary complexity.

After you complete the multiple-choice section and hand in your test booklet and scan sheet, you will be given a brief break. Note that you will not be able to return to the multiple-choice questions when you return to the examination room.

Must I Check the Box at the End of the Essay Booklet That Allows the AP People to Use My Essays as Samples for Research?

No. This is simply a way for the College Board to make certain that it has your permission if it decides to use one or more of your essays as a model. Checking the box will not affect your grade.

How Is My AP Lit Exam Scored?

Let's look at the basics first. The multiple-choice section counts for 45 percent of your total score, and the essay section counts for 55 percent. Next comes a four-part calculation: the raw scoring of the multiple-choice section, the raw scoring of the essay section, the calculation of the composite score, and the conversion of the composite score into the AP grade of 5, 4, 3, 2, or 1.

How Is the Multiple-Choice Section Scored?

The scan sheet with your answers is run through a computer that counts the number of correct answers. Questions left blank and questions answered incorrectly are treated the same and get no points. There is no "guessing penalty," which would involve the deduction of a fraction of a point for answering a question but getting it wrong.

How Is My Essay Section Scored?

Each of your essays is read by a different, trained AP reader. The AP/College Board people have developed a highly successful training program for these readers. This factor, together with many opportunities for checks and double checks of essays, ensures a fair and equitable reading of each essay.

The scoring guides are carefully developed by a chief faculty consultant, a question leader, table leaders, and content experts. All faculty consultants are then trained to read and score just *one* essay question on the exam. They actually become experts in that one essay question. No one knows the identity of any writer. The identification numbers and names are covered, and the exam booklets are randomly distributed to the readers in packets of 25 randomly chosen essays. Table leaders and the question leader review samples of each reader's scores to ensure that quality standards are consistent.

Each essay is scored as 6, 5, 4, 3, 2, 1, plus 0, with 6 the highest possible score. Once your essay is given a number from 6 to 1, the next set of calculations is completed using a formula developed to account for the score of each essay. This is the raw score for the essay section of the exam.

$$(\text{pts.} \times 3.055) + (\text{pts.} \times 3.055) + (\text{pts.} \times 3.055) = \text{essay raw score}$$
$$\text{Essay 1} \qquad\qquad \text{Essay 2} \qquad\qquad \text{Essay 3}$$

How Is My Composite Score Calculated?

The total composite score for the AP Lit test is 150. Of this score, 55 percent is the essay section; that equals 82.5 points. The multiple-choice section is 45 percent of the composite score, which equals 67.5 points. Each of your three essays is graded on a 6-point scale; therefore, each point is worth 4.58. Divide the number of multiple-choice questions by 67.5.

If you add together the raw scores of each of the two sections, you will have a composite score.

"Over the years, in comparison to students who fight the material, I've found students who receive the 4s and 5s are those who truly allow themselves to relate to the literature covered in the class."
—Pat K.
    AP teacher

How Is My Composite Data Turned into the Score That Is Reported to My College?

Keep in mind that the total composite scores needed to earn a 5, 4, 3, 2, or 1 are different each year. This is determined by a committee of AP/College Board/Educational Testing Service directors, experts, and statisticians. The score is based on items such as:

• AP distribution over the past three years
• Comparability studies
• Observations of the chief faculty consultant
• Frequency distributions of scores on each section and the essays
• Average scores on each exam section and essays

However, over the years a trend is apparent which indicates the number of points required to achieve a specific score:

• 150–100 points = 5
• 99–86 = 4
• 85–67 = 3

Scores of 2 and 1 fall below this range. You do not want to go there.

What Should I Bring to the Exam?

You should bring:

• Several pencils with erasers
• Several *black* pens (black ink is easier to read than other colors)
• A watch
• Something to drink—water is best
• A quiet snack
• Tissues

Is There Anything Else I Should Be Aware Of?

You should be aware of the following:

• Allow plenty of time to get to the test site.
• Wear comfortable clothing.
• Eat a light breakfast or lunch.
• Remind yourself that you are well prepared and that the test is an enjoyable challenge and a chance to share your knowledge. Be proud of yourself! You worked hard all year. Now is your time to shine.

Is There Anything Special I Should Do the Night Before the Exam?

We certainly don't advocate last-minute cramming. If you've been following the guidelines, you won't have to cram. But there may be a slight value to some last-minute review. Spend the night before the exam relaxing with family or friends. Watch a movie; play a game; gab on the phone, blog, or Twitter. Then find a quiet spot. While you're unwinding, flip through your own notebook and review sheets. Recall some details from the full-length works you've prepared and think of your favorite scenes. By now, you're bound to be ready to drift off. Pleasant dreams.

How to Plan Your Time

IN THIS CHAPTER

Summary: Assess your own study patterns and preparation plans.

Key Ideas
- ✪ Explore three approaches
- ✪ Choose a calendar that works for you

Three Approaches to Preparing for the AP Literature Exam

No one knows your study habits, likes, and dislikes better than you do. So you are the only one who can decide which approach you want and/or need to adopt to prepare for the Advanced Placement Literature exam. Look at the brief profiles below. These may help you to place yourself in a particular prep mode.

You're a full-year prep student (Approach A) if:

1. You're the kind of person who likes to plan for a vacation or the prom a year in advance.

2. You'd never think of missing a practice session, whether it's your favorite sport, musical instrument, or activity.

3. You like detailed planning and everything in its place.

4. You feel you must be thoroughly prepared.

5. You hate surprises.

6. You're always early for appointments.

You're a one-semester prep student (Approach B) **if:**

1. You begin to plan for your vacation or the prom 4–5 months before the event.

2. You are willing to plan ahead so that you will feel comfortable in stressful situations, but you are okay with skipping some details.

3. You feel more comfortable when you know what to expect, but a surprise or two does not floor you.

4. You're always on time for appointments.

You're a 4–6 week prep student (Approach C) **if:**

1. You accept or find a date for the prom a week before the big day.

2. You work best under pressure and tight deadlines.

3. You feel very confident with the skills and background you've gained in your AP Literature class.

4. You decided late in the year to take the exam.

5. You like surprises.

6. You feel okay if you arrive 10–15 minutes late for an appointment.

CALENDARS FOR PREPARING
FOR THE AP LITERATURE EXAM

This is a personal journey, and each of you will have particular time constraints.
Choose the calendar that will work best for you.

Calendar for Approach A:
Yearlong Preparation for the AP Literature Exam

Although its primary purpose is to prepare you for the AP Literature exam you
will take in May, this book can enrich your study of literature, your analytical
skills, and your writing skills.

SEPTEMBER–OCTOBER (Check off the
activities as you complete them.)

_____ Determine the student mode into which
you place yourself.

_____ Carefully read Chapters 1 and 2.

_____ Pay close attention to the walk through
the Diagnostic/Master exam.

_____ Take a close look at the AP Central
website(s).

_____ Skim the Comprehensive Review section.

_____ Buy a highlighter.

_____ Flip through the entire book. Break in
the book. Write in it. Highlight it.

_____ Get a clear picture of what your own
school's AP Literature curriculum is.

_____ Review the Bibliography and establish a
pattern of outside reading in the literary
genres (pp. 247–249).

_____ Begin to use the book as a resource.

NOVEMBER (The first 10 weeks have elapsed.)

_____ Write the free-response essay in the
Diagnostic/Master exam.

_____ Compare your essay with the sample
student essays.

_____ Refer to the section on the free-response
essay.

_____ Take five of our prompts and write solid
opening paragraphs.

DECEMBER

_____ Maintain notes on literary works you
studied in and out of class.

_____ Refine your analytical skills.

_____ Write the prose passage or poetry essay in
the Diagnostic/Master exam. (This will
depend on the organization of your own
curriculum.)

_____ Compare your essay with sample student
essays.

JANUARY (20 weeks have elapsed.)

_____ Write the third essay in the Diagnostic/
Master exam. (This will depend on the
one you did previously.)

_____ Compare your essay with sample student
essays.

FEBRUARY

_____ Take the multiple-choice section of the
Diagnostic/Master exam.

_____ Carefully go over the explanations of the
answers to the questions.

_____ Score yourself honestly.

_____ Make a note of terms, concepts, and types
of questions that give you difficulty.

_____ Review troublesome terms in the Glossary.

MARCH (30 weeks have elapsed.)

_____ Form a study group.
_____ Outline or create a chart for full-length works that would be appropriate for the free-response essay.
_____ Choose a favorite poem and create an essay question to go with it, or use one of our suggested prompts.
_____ Choose a prose passage or essay and create an essay question to go with it, or choose one of our suggested prompts.
_____ Write the poetry essay.
_____ Write the prose essay.
_____ Compare essays and rate them with your study group. (Use our rubrics.)

APRIL

_____ Take Practice Test 1 in the first week of April.
_____ Evaluate your strengths and weaknesses.
_____ Study appropriate chapters to correct your weaknesses.

_____ Practice creating multiple-choice questions of different types with your study group.
_____ Develop and review worksheets for and with your study group.

MAY—First Week (THIS IS IT!)

_____ Highlight only those things in the Glossary you are still unsure of. Ask your teacher for clarification. Study!
_____ Thoroughly prepare three to five complete, full-length works; include several quotations that you can work into various responses.
_____ Write at least three times a week under timed conditions.
_____ Take Practice Test 2.
_____ Score yourself.
_____ Give yourself a pat on the back for how much you have learned and improved over the past 9 months.
_____ Go to the movies. Call a friend.
_____ Get a good night's sleep. Fall asleep knowing you are well prepared.

GOOD LUCK ON THE TEST.

> **KEY IDEA** Make certain you become familiar with and make good use of AP Central's APCLASSROOM site at https://myap.collegeboard.org/login?.

Calendar for Approach B:
Semester-Long Preparation for the AP Literature Exam

Working under the assumption that you've completed one semester of literature studies, apply those skills you've learned to prepare for the May exam.

You have plenty of time to supplement your course work by taking our study recommendations, maintaining literary notations, doing outside readings, and so on.

We divide the next 16 weeks into a workable program of preparation for you.

JANUARY–FEBRUARY (Check off the activities as you complete them.)

_____ Carefully read Chapters 1 and 2.
_____ Write the three essays in the Diagnostic/Master exam.
_____ Compare your essays with the sample student essays.
_____ Complete the multiple-choice section of the Diagnostic/Master exam.
_____ Carefully go over the answers and explanations of the answers.
_____ Take a close look at the Bibliography for suggestions on possible outside readings.

MARCH (10 weeks to go.)

_____ Form a study group.
_____ Outline or create a chart for full-length works that would be appropriate for the free-response essay.
_____ Choose a favorite poem and create an essay question to go with it, or use one of our suggested prompts.
_____ Choose a prose passage or essay and create an essay question to go with it, or choose one of our suggested prompts.
_____ Write the poetry essay.
_____ Write the prose essay.
_____ Compare essays and rate them with your study group. (Use our rubrics.)

APRIL

_____ Take Practice Test 1 in the first week of April.
_____ Evaluate your strengths and weaknesses.
_____ Study appropriate chapters to correct your weaknesses.
_____ Practice creating multiple-choice questions of different types with your study group.
_____ Develop and review worksheets for and with your study group.

MAY First Week (THIS IS IT!)

_____ Highlight only those things in the Glossary you are still unsure of. Ask your teacher for clarification. Study!
_____ Thoroughly prepare at least three to five complete, full-length works; include several quotations that you can work into various questions.
_____ Write at least three times a week under timed conditions.
_____ Take Practice Test 2.
_____ Score yourself.
_____ Give yourself a pat on the back for how much you have learned and improved over the past 9 months.
_____ Go to the movies. Call a friend.
_____ Get a good night's sleep. Fall asleep knowing you are well prepared.

GOOD LUCK ON THE TEST.

Make certain you become familiar with and make good use of AP Central's APCLASSROOM site at https://myap.collegeboard.org/login?.

"One of the first steps to success on the AP exam is knowing your own study habits."
—Margaret R.
AP English
teacher

Calendar for Approach C:
4–6 Week Preparation for the AP Literature Exam

At this point, we are going to assume that you have been developing your literary, analytical, and writing skills in your English class for more than 6 months. You will, therefore, use this book primarily as a specific guide to the AP Literature exam.

Remember, there is a solid review section in this text to which you should refer.

Given the time constraints, now is not the time to try to expand your AP Literature background. Rather, it is the time to limit and refine what you already know.

APRIL

_____ Skim through Chapters 1 and 2.

_____ Carefully go over the "rapid reviews."

_____ Strengthen, clarify, and correct areas you are weak in after taking the Diagnostic/ Master exam.

_____ Write a minimum of three sample opening paragraphs for each of the three types of essays.

_____ Write a minimum of two timed essays for each type of essay on the exam.

_____ Complete Practice Test 1.

_____ Score yourself and analyze your errors.

_____ Refer to appropriate chapters to correct your weaknesses.

_____ Refer to the Bibliography.

_____ If you feel unfamiliar with specific poetic forms, refer to the list of suggested, appropriate works.

_____ Create review sheets for three to five solid, full-length works.

_____ Skim and highlight the Glossary.

_____ Develop a weekly study group to hear each other's essays and to discuss literature.

MAY First Week (THIS IS IT!)

_____ Complete Practice Test 2.

_____ Score yourself and analyze your errors.

_____ Refer to appropriate chapters to correct your weaknesses.

_____ Go to the movies. Call a friend.

_____ Get a good night's sleep. Fall asleep knowing you are well prepared.

GOOD LUCK ON THE TEST.

KEY IDEA

Make certain you become familiar with and make good use of AP Central's APCLASSROOM site at https://myap.collegeboard.org/login?.

STEP **2**

Determine Your Test Readiness

CHAPTER **3**   The Diagnostic/Master Exam

CHAPTER 3

The Diagnostic/Master Exam

IN THIS CHAPTER

Summary: Put yourself to the test with the diagnostic exam.

Key Ideas
- ✪ Peruse the multiple-choice section in Section I of the exam
- ✪ Familiarize yourself with the essays in Section II

A Walk Through the Diagnostic/Master Exam

"You know, from my experience with AP exams, I've learned never to assume anything."
—Jeremy G.
    AP student

This chapter presents our version of an Advanced Placement Literature and Composition exam which we use throughout this book to demonstrate processes, examples, terms, and so on. We call this the Diagnostic/Master exam. You will not be taking this exam at this point, but we would like you to "walk through" the exam with us now.

The first part of this 3-hour exam is always the multiple-choice section, which lasts 1 hour. It is related to both prose passages and poetry. The multiple-choice section of the Diagnostic/Master exam contains two prose passages from different time periods and of different styles. It also has two poems from different time periods and of different forms. The multiple-choice questions for each selection were developed to provide you with a wide range of question types and terminology that have been used in the actual AP Lit exams over the years.

To begin to know what the exam looks like, take some time to look through the multiple-choice section of the Diagnostic/Master exam. Do not try to answer the questions; just peruse the types of passages and questions.

- Take a turn through all of the pages of the test and familiarize yourself with the format.
- See where the longer and shorter readings are.
- See how many prose and poetry passages there are.

- Check the total number of questions and know what you are facing.
- Check out the essay prompts.

A Word About Our Sample Student Essays

We field-tested each of the essay questions in a variety of high schools, both public and private. We could have chosen to present essays that would have "knocked your socks off," but we chose to present samples that are truly representative of the essays usually written within the time constraints of the exam.

These essays are indicative of a wide range of styles and levels of acceptability. We want you to recognize that there is not one model to which all essays must conform.

"To Thine Own Self Be True" (Polonius—*Hamlet*)

"Be true to yourself" is always the best advice and is especially appropriate for a writer. Listen to your teacher's advice; listen to our advice; **listen to your own voice**. Yours is the voice we want to "hear" in your writing. Use natural vocabulary and present honest observations. It is wonderful to read professional criticism, but you cannot adopt someone else's ideas and remain true to your own thoughts. Trust your brain—if you've prepared well, you'll do well.

DIAGNOSTIC/MASTER EXAM

Advanced Placement Literature and Composition

Section I

Total time—1 hour

Carefully read the following passages and answer the questions that come after them.
Questions 1–10 are based on the next passage.

Now Goes Under . . .
by Edna St. Vincent Millay

Now goes under, and I watch it go under, the sun
    That will not rise again.
Today has seen the setting, in your eyes cold
    and senseless as the sea,
Of friendship better than bread, and of bright charity   5
That lifts a man a little above the beasts that run.

That this could be!
That I should live to see
Most vulgar Pride, that stale obstreperous clown,
So fitted out with purple robe and crown   10
To stand among his betters! Face to face
With outraged me in this once holy place,
Where Wisdom was a favoured guest and hunted
Truth was harboured out of danger,
He bulks enthroned, a lewd, and insupportable stranger!   15

I would have sworn, indeed I swore it:
The hills may shift, the waters may decline,
Winter may twist the stem from the twig that bore it,
But never your love from me, your hand from mine.

Now goes under the sun, and I watch it go under.   20
Farewell, sweet light, great wonder!
You, too, farewell—but fare not well enough to dream
You have done wisely to invite the night before the darkness came.

1. The poem is an example of a(n)
  A. sonnet
  B. lyric
  C. ode
  D. ballad
  E. dramatic monologue

2. The setting of the sun is a symbol for
  A. the beginning of winter
  B. encountering danger
  C. the end of a relationship
  D. facing death
  E. the onset of night

3. The second stanza is developed primarily by
   A. metaphor
   B. simile
   C. personification
   D. hyperbole
   E. allusion

4. "He" in line 15 refers to
   A. Wisdom
   B. Truth
   C. I
   D. Pride
   E. charity

5. According to the speaker, what separates man from beast?
   A. love
   B. friendship
   C. charity
   D. truth
   E. wisdom

6. For the speaker, the relationship has been all of the following *except*
   A. honest
   B. dangerous
   C. spiritual
   D. ephemeral
   E. nourishing

7. The reader can infer from the play on words in the last stanza that the speaker is
   A. dying
   B. frantic
   C. wistful
   D. bitter
   E. capricious

8. "This once holy place" (line 12) refers to
   A. the sunset
   B. the relationship
   C. the sea
   D. the circus
   E. the Church

9. The cause of the relationship's situation is
   A. a stranger coming between them
   B. the lover not taking the relationship seriously
   C. the lover feeling intellectually superior
   D. the lover's pride coming between them
   E. the lover being insensitive

10. The speaker acknowledges the finality of the relationship in line(s)
    A. 1–2
    B. 7
    C. 8
    D. 16
    E. 18–19

Questions 11–23 are based on the following passage from *The Heart of Darkness* by Joseph Conrad, 1899.

The sea-reach of the Thames stretched before us like the beginning of an
interminable waterway. The air was dark above Gravesend, and farther back still
seemed condensed into a mournful gloom, brooding motionless over the biggest and
the greatest town on earth.
   "I was thinking of very old times, when the Romans first came here, nineteen   5
hundred years ago—the other day . . . Light came out of this river since—you say knights?
Yes; but it is like a running blaze on a plain, like a flash of lightning in the clouds. We live
in the flicker—may it last as long as the old earth keeps rolling! But darkness was here
yesterday. Imagine the feelings of a commander of a fine—what d'ye call 'em?—trireme
in the Mediterranean, ordered suddenly to the north; run overland across the Gauls in a   10
hurry; put in charge of one of these craft the legionnaires—a wonderful lot of handy men
they must have been, too—used to build, apparently by the hundred, in a month or two, if
we may believe what we read. Imagine him here—the very end of the world, a sea the color
of lead, a sky the color of smoke, a kind of ship about as rigid as a concertina—and going
up this river with stores, or orders, or what you like. Sandbanks, marshes, forests, savages—   15
precious little to eat for a civilized man, nothing but Thames water to drink. No Falernian

wine here, no going ashore. Here and there a military camp lost in a wilderness, like a
needle in a bundle of hay—cold, fog, tempests, disease, exile, and death—death skulking
in the air, in the water, in the bush. They must have been dying like flies here. Oh yes—he
did it. Did it very well, too, no doubt, and without thinking much about it either, except   20
afterwards to brag of what he had gone through in his time, perhaps. They were men enough
to face darkness. And perhaps he was cheered by keeping his eye on a chance of promotion
to the fleet at Ravenna by and by, if he had good friends in Rome and survived the awful
climate. Or think of a decent young citizen in a toga—perhaps too much dice, you know—
coming out here in the train of some prefect, or tax-gatherer, or trader even, to mend his   25
fortunes. Land in a swamp, march through the woods, and in some inland post feel the
savagery, the utter savagery, had closed round him—all that mysterious life of the wilderness
that stirs in the forest, in the jungles, in the hearts of wild men. There's no initiation either
into such mysteries. He has to live in the midst of the incomprehensible, which is also
detestable. And it has a fascination, too, that goes to work upon him. The fascination of the   30
abomination—you know, imagine the growing regrets, the longing to escape, the powerless
disgust, the surrender, the hate."

He paused.

"Mind," he began again, lifting one arm from the elbow the palm of the hand
outwards, so that, with his legs folded before him, he had the pose of a Buddha preaching in   35
European clothes and without a lotus flower—"Mind, none of us would feel exactly like this.
What saves us is efficiency—the devotion to efficiency. But these chaps were not much
account, really. They were no colonists; their administration was merely a squeeze, and
nothing more, I suspect. They were conquerors, and for that you want only brute force—
nothing to boast of, when you have it, since your strength is just an accident arising from the   40
weakness of others. They grabbed what they could get for the sake of what was to be got. It
was just robbery with violence, aggravated murder on a great scale, and men going at it blind—
as is very proper for those who tackle a darkness. The conquest of the earth, which mostly
means taking it away from those who have a different complexion or slightly flatter noses
than ourselves, is not a pretty thing when you look at it too much. What redeems it is the idea   45
only. An idea at the back of it; not a sentimental pretense but an idea; and an unselfish belief
in the idea—something you can set up, and bow down before, and offer a sacrifice to . . ."

11. In the passage, *darkness* implies all of the
following *except*
A. the unknown
B. savagery
C. ignorance
D. death
E. exploration

12. The setting of the passage is
A. Africa
B. Ancient Rome
C. the Thames River
D. the Mediterranean
E. Italy

13. The tone of the passage is
A. condescending
B. indignant
C. scornful
D. pensive
E. laudatory

14. Later events may be foreshadowed by all of the
following phrases *except*
A. "Imagine the feelings of a commander . . ."
B. ". . . live in the midst of the
incomprehensible . . ."
C. ". . . in some inland post feel the
savagery . . ."
D. "They must have been dying like flies
here."
E. ". . . the very end of the world . . ."

15. The narrator draws a parallel between
    A. light and dark
    B. past and present
    C. life and death
    D. fascination and abomination
    E. decency and savagery

16. In this passage, "We live in the flicker . . ." (lines 7–8) may be interpreted to mean all of the following *except*
    A. In the history of the world, humanity's span on earth is brief.
    B. Future civilizations will learn from only a portion of the past.
    C. Periods of enlightenment and vision appear only briefly.
    D. The river has been the source of life throughout the ages.
    E. A moment of present-day insight about conquest.

17. One may conclude from the passage that the speaker
    A. admires adventurers
    B. longs to be a crusader
    C. is a former military officer
    D. recognizes and accepts the presence of evil in human experience
    E. is prejudiced

18. In the context of the passage, which of the following phrases presents a paradox?
    A. "The fascination of the abomination . . ."
    B. ". . . in the hearts of wild men"
    C. "There's no initiation . . . into such mysteries"
    D. ". . . a flash of lightning in the clouds"
    E. ". . . death skulking in the air . . ."

19. The lines "Imagine him here . . . concertina . . ." (lines 13–14) contain examples of
    A. hyperbole and personification
    B. irony and metaphor
    C. alliteration and personification
    D. parallel structure and simile
    E. allusion and simile

20. According to the speaker, the one trait which saves Europeans from savagery is
    A. sentiment
    B. a sense of mystery
    C. brute force
    D. religious zeal
    E. efficiency

21. According to the speaker, the only justification for conquest is
    A. the "weakness of others"
    B. it's being "proper for those who tackle a darkness . . ."
    C. their grabbing "what they could get for the sake of what was to be got"
    D. ". . . an unselfish belief in the idea . . ."
    E. "The fascination of the abomination"

22. In the statement by the speaker, "Mind, none of us would feel exactly like this" (line 36), "this" refers to
    A. ". . . a Buddha preaching in European clothes . . ." (lines 35–36)
    B. ". . . imagine the growing regrets . . . the hate." (lines 31–32)
    C. "What redeems it is the idea only." (lines 45–46)
    D. ". . . think of a decent young citizen in a toga . . ." (line 24)
    E. "I was thinking of very old times . . ." (line 5)

23. The speaker presents all of the following reasons for exploration and conquest *except*
    A. military expeditions
    B. ". . . a chance of promotion"
    C. ". . . to mend his fortunes . . ."
    D. religious commitment
    E. punishment for a crime

Questions 24–35 are based on the following poem by William Shakespeare.

> That time of year thou mayst in me behold
> When yellow leaves, or none, or few, do hang
> Upon those boughs which shake against the cold,
> Bare ruin'd choirs, where late the sweet birds sang.
> In me thou see'st the twilight of such day   5
> As after sunset fadeth in the west;
> Which by and by black night doth take away,
> Death's second self, that seals up all in rest.
> In me thou see'st the glowing of such fire,
> That on the ashes of his youth doth lie,   10
> As the deathbed whereon it must expire,
> Consum'd with that which it was nourish'd by.
> This thou perceiv'st, which makes thy love more strong,
> To love that well which thou must leave ere long.

24. "That time of year" (line 1) refers to
    A. youth
    B. old age
    C. childhood
    D. senility
    E. maturity

25. "Death's second self" (line 8) refers to
    A. "That time of year"
    B. "sunset fadeth"
    C. "the west"
    D. "ruin'd choirs"
    E. "black night"

26. Line 12 is an example of
    A. paradox
    B. caesura
    C. parable
    D. hyperbole
    E. metonymy

27. "Twilight of such day" (line 5) is supported by all of the following images *except*
    A. "sunset fadeth"
    B. "the glowing of such fire"
    C. "west"
    D. "Death's second self"
    E. "ashes of his youth"

28. "This thou perceiv'st" (line 13) refers to
    A. the beloved's deathbed
    B. the sorrow of unrequited love
    C. the passion of youth expiring
    D. the beloved's acknowledgment of the speaker's mortality
    E. the speaker sending the lover away

29. The poem is an example of a(n)
    A. elegy
    B. Spenserian sonnet
    C. Petrarchan sonnet
    D. Shakespearean sonnet
    E. sestina

30. The poem is primarily developed by means of
    A. metaphor
    B. argument
    C. synecdoche
    D. alternative choices
    E. contradiction

31. The irony of the poem is best expressed in line
    A. 5
    B. 7
    C. 10
    D. 11
    E. 12

32. "It" in line 12 can best be interpreted to mean
A. a funeral pyre
B. spent youth
C. the intensity of the speaker's love
D. the impending departure of his beloved
E. the immortality of the relationship

33. An apt title for the poem could be
A. Love Me or Leave Me
B. Death Be Not Proud
C. The End Justifies the Means
D. Love's Fall
E. Grow Old Along with Me

34. The tone of the poem can best be described as
A. contemplative
B. defiant
C. submissive
D. arbitrary
E. complaining

35. The speaker most likely is
A. jealous of the beloved's youth
B. pleased that the lover will leave
C. unable to keep up with the young lover
D. unwilling to face his own mortality
E. responsive to the beloved's constancy

Questions 36–47 are based on a careful reading of the following excerpt from the first chapter of the 2001 novel *White Teeth* by Zadie Smith that centers on two families who live in North London.

Archie's marriage felt like buying a pair of shoes, taking them home and finding they don't fit. For the sake of appearances, he put up with them. And then, all of a sudden and after thirty years, the shoes picked themselves up and walked out of the house. She left. Thirty years.

As far as he remembered, just like everybody else they began well. The first spring of 1946, he had stumbled out of the darkness of war and into a Florentine coffee house, where he was served by a waitress truly like the sun: Ophelia Diagilo, dressed all in yellow, spreading warmth and the promise of sex as she passed him a frothy cappuccino. They walked into it blinkered as horses. She was not to know that women never stayed as daylight in Archie's life; that somewhere in him he didn't like them, he didn't trust them, and he was able to love them only if they wore haloes. No one told Archie that lurking in the Diagilo family tree were two hysteric aunts, an uncle who talked to aubergines[1] and a cousin who wore his clothes back to front. So they got married and returned to England, where she realized very quickly her mistake, he drove her very quickly mad, and the halo was packed off to the attic to collect dust with the rest of the bric-a-brac[2] and broken kitchen appliances that Archie promised one day to repair. Amongst that bric-a-brac was a Hoover.

On Boxing Day[3] morning, six days before he parked outside Mo's halal[4] butchers, Archie had returned to their semi-detached in Hendon[5] in search of that Hoover. It was his fourth trip to the attic in so many days, ferrying out the odds and ends of a marriage to his new flat, and the Hoover was amongst the very last items he reclaimed—one of the most broken things, most ugly things, the things you demand out of sheer bloody-mindedness because you have lost the house. This is what divorce is: taking things you no longer want from people you no longer love.

"So you again," said the Spanish home-help at the door, Santa-Maria or Maria-Santa or something. "Meester Jones, what now? Kitchen sink, si?"

"Hoover," said Archie, grimly. "Vacuum."

She cut her eyes at him and spat on the doormat inches from his shoes. "Welcome, señor."

The place had become a haven for people who hated him. Apart from the home-help, he had to contend with Ophelia's extended Italian family, her mental-health nurse, the woman from the council,[6] and of course Ophelia herself, who was to be found in the kernel of this nuthouse, curled up in a fetal ball on the sofa, making lowing sounds into a bottle of Bailey's.[7] It took him an hour and a quarter just to get through enemy lines—and for what? A perverse Hoover, discarded months earlier because it was determined to perform the opposite of every vacuum's objective: spewing out dust instead of sucking it in.

5

10

15

20

25

30

"Meester Jones, why do you come here when it make you so unhappy? Be reasonable. What can you want with it?" The home-help was following him up the attic stairs, armed with some kind of cleaning fluid: "It's broken. You don't need this. See? See?" She plugged it into a socket and demonstrated the dead switch. Archie took the plug out and silently wound the cord round the Hoover. If it was broken, it was coming with him. All broken things were coming with him. He was going to fix every damn broken thing in this house, if only to show that he was good for something.

"You good for nothing!" Santa whoever chased him back down the stairs. "Your wife is ill in her head, and this is all you can do!"

Archie hugged the Hoover to his chest and took it into the crowded living room, where, under several pairs of reproachful eyes, he got out his toolbox and started work on it.

"Look at him," said one of the Italian grandmothers, the more glamorous one with the big scarves and fewer moles, "he take everything, capisce?[8] He take-a her mind, he take-a the blender, he take-a the old stereo—he take-a everything except the floorboards. It make-a you sick . . ."

The woman from the council, who even on dry days resembled a long-haired cat soaked to the skin, shook her skinny head in agreement. "It's disgusting, you don't have to tell me, it's disgusting . . . and naturally, we're the ones left to sort out the mess; it's muggins[9] here who has to—"

Which was overlapped by the nurse: "She can't stay here alone, can she . . . now he's buggered off, poor woman . . . she needs a proper home, she needs . . ."

I'm here, Archie felt like saying, I'm right here you know, I'm bloody right here. And it was my blender.

But he wasn't one for confrontation, Archie. He listened to them all for another fifteen minutes, mute as he tested the Hoover's suction against pieces of newspaper, until he was overcome by the sensation that Life was an enormous rucksack[10] so impossibly heavy that, even though it meant losing everything, it was infinitely easier to leave all baggage here on the roadside and walk on into the blackness. You don't need the blender, Archie-boy, you don't need the Hoover. This stuff's all dead weight. Just lay down the rucksack, Arch, and join the happy campers in the sky. Was that wrong? To Archie—ex-wife and ex-wife's relatives in one ear, spluttering vacuum in the other—it just seemed that The End was unavoidably nigh. Nothing personal to God or whatever. It just felt like the end of the world. And he was going to need more than poor whisky, novelty crackers and a paltry box of Quality Street[11]—all the strawberry ones already scoffed—to justify entering another annum.

Patiently he fixed the Hoover, and vacuumed the living room with a strange methodical finality, shoving the nozzle into the most difficult corners. Solemnly he flipped a coin (heads, life, tails, death) and felt nothing in particular when he found himself staring at the dancing lion.[12] Quietly he detached the Hoover tube, put it in a suitcase, and left the house for the last time.

---

[1]**aubergines:** eggplants

[2]**bric-a-brac:** odds and ends, objects of little value

[3]**Boxing Day:** The British celebration of the day after Christmas

[4]**halal:** food prepared according to Muslim law

[5]**Hendon:** a suburb of London

[6]**council:** a type of elected British advisory or legislative body

[7]**Bailey's:** a brand of whiskey

[8]**capisce:** Italian for *understand*

[9]**muggins:** a foolish, gullible person

[10]**rucksack:** backpack

[11]**Quality Street:** a brand of candy

[12]**dancing lion:** reverse side of a twenty-pence coin

36. The function of the first paragraph can best be described as
    A. a diatribe against marriage
    B. an introduction to the setting
    C. an introduction to the central plot
    D. an introduction to Archie's attitude toward his former wife and their marriage
    E. an introduction to Ophelia

37. After reading the second paragraph, one can infer all of the following *except*
    A. Archie and Ophelia's love was based on passion.
    B. Archie was self-motivated.
    C. Archie wanted to be able to place his wife on a pedestal.
    D. Ophelia and Ophelia were quick to make important decisions.
    E. Archie was unsure and suspicious of women.

38. The metaphor of the halo in the second paragraph serves mainly to emphasize
    A. the beauty and innocence of Ophelia
    B. the religion of both Ophelia and Archie
    C. the inevitability of future events
    D. the hastiness of Archie and Ophelia's marriage
    E. an unrealistic desire for the perfect love

39. In line 7, *it* is referring to
    A. pledge of love
    B. move to England
    C. marriage
    D. divorce
    E. sexual relationship

40. The response of "Santa-Maria or Maria-Santa" (23–26) to Archie's arrival can best be described as
    A. hostile and denigrating
    B. suspicious and cowering
    C. warm and welcoming
    D. condescending and dismissive
    E. curious and insecure

41. Paragraph 7, lines 27–33, progresses from a primarily third-person, objective narrator to
    A. stream-of-consciousness
    B. interior monologue
    C. first-person narrator
    D. third-person subjective
    E. third-person omniscient

42. Lines 39–40, reveal that Archie
    A. believes he is capable of fixing broken appliances
    B. wants to prove that he is not a failure
    C. feels he has been taken advantage of
    D. is basically selfish
    E. wants to show the help that he is in charge

43. For Archie, the Hoover vacuum symbolizes each of the following *except*
    A. ownership
    B. potential to redeem himself
    C. failure of his life so far
    D. his love for Ophelia
    E. control

44. As a way to characterize Archie's perceived burden, the author uses the image of
    A. pair of shoes (first paragraph)
    B. halo (second paragraph)
    C. Hoover vacuum (throughout passage)
    D. the blender (lines 47 and 56)
    E. rucksack (next-to-last paragraph)

45. The author uses dialect with the home-help's dialogue primarily
    A. to add a sense of realism to the narrative
    B. to indicate the class differences between Archie and the home-help
    C. to make a point about the working conditions of the working class
    D. to add a bit of humor to the passage
    E. to gain more sympathy for Archie

46. Archie's behavior in the last two paragraphs suggests he
   A. wants to move on
   B. believes it's possible to help Ophelia
   C. is beginning to feel hopeless
   D. wonders why he bothered fixing the Hoover
   E. wants to get back at the home-help and Ophelia's relatives

47. Which of the following best describes the effect of the last paragraph?
   A. hopeful
   B. looking for redemption
   C. impending doom
   D. loss of control
   E. anger at the world

Questions 48–55 are based on a careful reading of the 2002 poem "Litany" by Billy Collins.

Litany[1]

You are the bread and the knife,
The crystal goblet and the wine . . .
—Jacques Crickillon

You are the bread and the knife,
the crystal goblet and the wine.   5
You are the dew on the morning grass
and the burning wheel of the sun.
You are the white apron of the baker,
and the marsh birds suddenly in flight.

However, you are not the wind in the orchard,   10
the plums on the counter,
or the house of cards.
And you are certainly not the pine-scented air.
There is just no way that you are the pine-scented air.

It is possible that you are the fish under the bridge   15
maybe even the pigeon on the general's head,
but you are not even close
to being the field of cornflowers at dusk.

And a quick look in the mirror will show
that you are neither the boots in the corner   20
nor the boat asleep in its boathouse.
It might interest you to know,
speaking of the plentiful imagery of the world,
that I am the sound of rain on the roof.

I also happen to be the shooting star,   25
the evening paper blowing down an alley
and the basket of chestnuts on the kitchen table.

I am also the moon in the trees
and the blind woman's tea cup.

But don't worry, I'm not the bread and the knife.
You are still the bread and the knife.
You will always be the bread and the knife,
not to mention the crystal goblet and—somehow—the wine.

_____

[1]**litany**: (secondary meaning) a recital or a repetitive series of phrases with a type of call-and-response

48. This poem is an example of
  A. blank verse
  B. rhymed verse
  C. metered verse
  D. free verse
  E. rhymed, metered verse

49. The tone of the poem can best be described as
  A. formal and critical
  B. uncaring and suspicious
  C. informal and indifferent
  D. brusque and patronizing
  E. casual and playful

50. Line 9, "and the marsh birds suddenly in flight"
  A. hints at an element of uncertainty
  B. sums up the preceding five lines
  C. indicates the speaker's fear
  D. introduces a new setting
  E. suggests the speaker's fascination with nature

51. As the poem progresses, it becomes clear that this poem is
  A. an elegy for a deceased loved one
  B. a description of the depth of the speaker's love
  C. an ode to love
  D. an apology to the speaker's loved one
  E. a tribute to the speaker's beloved

52. The turning point in the poem occurs in stanza
  A. 1
  B. 2
  C. 5
  D. 6
  E. 7

53. All of the following literary devices are used in the poem *except*
  A. rhyme
  B. metaphor
  C. alliteration
  D. simile
  E. repetition

54. Elements of humor in the poem are created by using
  A. improbable circumstances
  B. counterbalance and exaggeration
  C. gentle criticism and apologies
  D. slapstick put-downs
  E. satirical comments

55. The repetition in the last four lines of the poem can best be interpreted to mean
  A. the speaker will always be the opposite of the beloved
  B. the beloved holds the key to the speaker's life and always will
  C. both the speaker and the beloved will remain in separate worlds
  D. the speaker will always accept the beloved's point of view
  E. the speaker cannot imagine living without the beloved

END OF SECTION I

The second part of the test is the 2-hour essay-writing section. You take this part of the exam after the break following your completion of the multiple-choice section. You will be required to write three different essays. In all likelihood, one of the questions will be based on a prose passage, one on a poem or two, and one will be what is called the free-response essay.

Do not write any essays at this time. Just take a careful look at each of the questions to get an idea of the types of writing assignments you are expected to be able to handle. Essay questions are called "prompts" by the AP.

Section II

Total time—2 hours

Question 1

(Suggested time 40 minutes. This question counts as one-third of the total score for Section II.)

In the following passage from the 1914 short story "The Dead," James Joyce presents an insight into the character of Gabriel. Carefully read the passage. Then, in a well-written essay analyze how Joyce uses literary strategies and techniques to reveal various aspects of Gabriel's complex character to the reader and to Gabriel himself.

In your response you should do the following:

- Respond to the prompt with a thesis that presents an assertion that requires defense and support.
- Select and use evidence to support your line of reasoning.
- Explain how the evidence supports your line of reasoning.
- Use appropriate grammar and punctuation in communicating your argument.

The Dead

She was fast asleep.

Gabriel, leaning on his elbow, looked for a few moments
unresentfully on her tangled hair and half-open mouth, listening to her
deep-drawn breath. So she had had that romance in her life: a man had
died for her sake. It hardly pained him now to think how poor a part   5
he, her husband, had played in her life. He watched her while she slept
as though he and she had never lived together as man and wife. His
curious eyes rested long upon her face and on her hair and, as he thought
of what she must have been then, in that time of her first girlish beauty,
a strange friendly pity for her entered his soul. He did not like to say   10
even to himself that her face was no longer beautiful but he knew that it
was no longer the face for which Michael Furey had braved death.

Perhaps she had not told him all the story. His eyes moved to the
chair over which she had thrown some of her clothes. A petticoat string
dangled to the floor. One boot stood upright, its limp upper fallen down: 15
the fellow of it lay upon its side. He wondered at his riot of emotions of
an hour before. From what had it proceeded? From his aunt's supper,
from his own foolish speech, from the wine and dancing, the merry-making
when saying good-night in the hall, the pleasure of the walk along the river
in the snow. Poor Aunt Julia! She, too, would soon be a shade with the   20

shade of Patrick Morkan and his horse. He had caught that haggard look upon her face for a moment when she was singing *Arrayed for the Bridal*. Soon, perhaps, he would be sitting in the same drawing-room dressed in black, his silk hat on his knees. The blinds would be drawn down and Aunt Kate would be sitting beside him, crying and blowing her nose and telling him how Julia had died. He would cast about in his mind for some words that might console her, and would find only lame and useless ones. Yes, yes: that would happen very soon. 25

Question 2

(Suggested time 40 minutes. This question counts as one-third of the total score for Section II.)

In "On the Subway," Sharon Olds brings two worlds into close proximity. Carefully read the poem. Then, in a well-written essay analyze how Olds uses poetic elements and techniques to develop the complex contrasts and insights presented in the poem.

In your response you should do the following:

- Respond to the prompt with a thesis that presents an assertion that requires defense and support.
- Select and use evidence to support your line of reasoning.
- Explain how the evidence supports your line of reasoning.
- Use appropriate grammar and punctuation in communicating your argument.

On the Subway
by Sharon Olds

The boy and I face each other
His feet are huge, in black sneakers
laced with white in a complex pattern like a
set of intentional scars. We are stuck on
opposite sides of the car, a couple of 5
molecules stuck in a rod of light
rapidly moving through darkness.
He has the casual cold look of a mugger,
alert under hooded lids. He is wearing
red, like the inside of the body 10
exposed. I am wearing dark fur, the
whole skin of an animal taken and
used. I look at his raw face,
he looks at my fur coat, and I don't
know if I am in his power— 15
he could take my coat so easily, my
briefcase, my life—
or if he is in my power, the way I am
living off his life, eating the steak
he does not eat, as if I am taking 20
the food from his mouth. And he is black
and I am white, and without meaning or
trying to I must profit from his darkness,
the way he absorbs the murderous beams of the

25

nation's heart, as black cotton
absorbs the heat of the sun and holds it. There is
no way to know how easy this
white skin makes my life, this
life he could take so easily and
break across his knee like a stick the way his
own back is being broken, the
rod of his soul that at birth was dark and
fluid and rich as the heart of a seedling
ready to thrust up into any available light

30

Question 3

(Suggested time 40 minutes. This question counts as one-third of the total score for Section II.)

Often in literature, a literal or figurative journey is a significant factor in the development of a character or the meaning of the work as a whole. Either from your own reading or from the list below, choose a work of fiction that illustrates this idea. Then, in a well-written essay analyze how the journey contributes to the character's complex development or the work's meaning as a whole. Do not merely summarize.

In your response you should do the following:

- Respond to the prompt with a thesis that presents an assertion that requires defense and support.
- Select and use evidence to support your line of reasoning.
- Explain how the evidence supports your line of reasoning.
- Use appropriate grammar and punctuation in communicating your argument.

As I Lay Dying	*Moby Dick*
Jane Eyre	*The Sun Also Rises*
The Odyssey	*The Grapes of Wrath*
Don Quixote	*The Stranger*
Candide	*Ulysses*
A Streetcar Named Desire	*Their Eyes Were Watching God*
A Passage to India	*Obasan*
Gulliver's Travels	*Twelfth Night*
No Exit	*The Namesake*
The Kite Runner	*The Color Purple*
Tom Jones	*The Bonesetter's Daughter*
Heart of Darkness	*Life of Pi*

END OF SECTION II

Afterword

So that's what the Advanced Placement Literature and Composition exam looks like. If you're being honest with yourself, you're probably feeling a bit overwhelmed at this point. Good! This is primarily why we are going to deconstruct this entire Diagnostic/Master exam for you and with you throughout this book. By the time you reach Practice Exams 1 and 2, you should be feeling much more confident and comfortable about doing well on the AP Literature exam.

As you progress through this book, you will:

- Take each section of the Diagnostic/Master exam.
- Read the explanations for the answers to the multiple-choice questions.
- Read sample student essays written in response to each of the three prompts.
- Read the rubrics and ratings of the student essays.
- Evaluate your own performance in light of this information.

STEP 3

Develop Strategies for Success

CHAPTER 4 >

Section I of the Exam:
The Multiple-Choice Questions

IN THIS CHAPTER

Summary: Become comfortable with the multiple-choice section of the exam. If you know what to expect, you can prepare.

Key Ideas

✪ Review the types of multiple-choice questions asked on the exam
✪ Learn strategies for approaching the multiple-choice questions
✪ Prepare yourself for the multiple-choice section of the exam
✪ Take the multiple-choice section of the exam
✪ Score yourself by checking the answer key and explanations for the multiple-choice section of the Diagnostic/Master exam

Introduction to the Multiple-Choice Section of the Exam

Multiple choice? Multiple guess? Multiple anxiety? The day after the exam, students often bemoan the difficulties and uncertainties of Section I of the AP Literature exam.

"It's unfair."

"It's crazy."

"Was that in English?"

"Did you get four Ds in a row for the second poem?"

"I just closed my eyes and pointed."

Is it really possible to avoid these and other exam woes? We hope that by following along with us in this chapter, you will begin to feel a bit more familiar with the world of multiple-choice questions and, thus, become a little more comfortable with the multiple-choice section of the exam.

What Is It About the Multiple-Choice Questions That Causes Such Anxiety?

Basically, a multiple-choice literature question demands that you concentrate on items that are incorrect before you can choose what is correct. We know, however, that complex literature has a richness that allows for ambiguity. When you are taking the exam, you are expected to match someone else's take on a work with the answers you choose. This is what often causes the student to feel intimidated. However, the test is designed to allow you to shine, *not* to be humiliated. To that end, you will not find "cutesy" questions, and the test writers will not play games with you. What they will do is present several valid options as a response to a challenging and appropriate question. These questions are designed to separate the perceptive and thoughtful reader from the superficial and impulsive one.

This said, it's wise to develop a strategy for success. Practice is the key to this success. You've been confronted with all types of multiple-choice questions during your career as a student. The test-taking skills you have learned in your social studies, math, and science classes may also apply to the AP Literature exam.

What Should I Expect in Section I Multiple Choice?

For this first section of the AP Literature exam, you are allotted 1 hour to answer 55 objective questions on four or five prose and poetry selections. The prose passage will comprise works of fiction or drama. The multiple-choice section will contain 4–5 texts with at least two prose passages and two poetry passages. Each text will have 8–13 questions. You can expect the poems to be complete and from different time periods and of different styles and forms with an emphasis on contemporary works and those of the twentieth century. In other words, you will not find two Shakespearean sonnets on the same exam.

These are *not* easy readings. They are representative of the college-level work you have been doing throughout the year. You will be expected to

- Follow sophisticated syntax
- Respond to diction
- Be comfortable with upper-level vocabulary
- Be familiar with literary terminology
- Make inferences
- Be sensitive to irony and tone
- Recognize components of style

With these skills in mind, the multiple-choice section will ask you to consider the following functions within each of the five texts:

- Character
- Setting
- Plot and structure
- Narrator or speaker
- Diction
- Imagery
- Symbols
- Comparison

You will also be asked to consider interpretations supported by the text.

Areas of Multiple-Choice Questions

Short Fiction: 42–49 percent of the questions
Poetry: 36–45 percent of the questions
Longer Works: 15–18 percent of the questions

The good news is that the selection is self-contained. This means that if it is about the Irish Potato Famine, you will not be at a disadvantage if you know nothing about it prior to the exam. Frequently there will be biblical references in a selection. This is especially true of works from an earlier time period. You are expected to be aware of basic allusions to biblical and mythological works often found in literature, but the passage will never require you to have any specific religious background.

Do not let the subject matter of a passage throw you. Strong analytical skills will work on any passage.

How Should I Begin to Work with Section I?

Take no more than a minute and thumb through the exam, looking for the following:

- The length of the selections
- The time periods or writing styles, if you can recognize them
- The number of questions asked
- A quick idea of the type of questions

This brief skimming of the test will put your mind into gear because you will be aware of what is expected of you.

How Should I Proceed Through This Section of the Exam?

"Creating my own multiple-choice questions was a terrific help to me when it came to doing close readings and correctly answering multiple-choice questions on the exam."
—Bill N.
    AP student

Timing is important. Always maintain an awareness of the time. Wear a watch. (Some students like to put it directly in front of them on the desk.) Remember, this will not be your first encounter with the multiple-choice section of the test. You've probably been practicing timed exams in class; in addition, this book provides you with three timed experiences. We're sure you will notice improvements as you progress through the timed practice activities.

Depending on the given selections, you may take less or more time on a particular passage, but you must know when to move on. The test *does not* become more difficult as it progresses. So, you will want to give yourself adequate opportunity to answer each set of questions.

Work at a pace of about one question per minute. Every question is worth the same number of points, so don't get bogged down on those that involve multiple tasks. Don't panic if a question is beyond you. Remember, it will probably be beyond a great number of other students as well. There has to be a bar that determines the 5's and 4's for this exam. Just do your best.

Reading the text carefully is a must. Begin at the beginning and work your way through. Do not waste time reading questions before you read the selection.

Most people read just with their eyes. We want you to slow down and read with your senses of sight, sound, and touch.

- Underline, circle, bracket, or highlight the text.
- Read closely, paying attention to punctuation and rhythms of the lines or sentences.
- Read as if you were reading the passage aloud to an audience, emphasizing meaning and intent.

- As corny as it may seem, hear those words in your head.
- This technique may seem childish, but it works. Using your finger as a pointer, underscore the line as you are reading it aloud in your head. This forces you to slow down and to really notice the text. This will be helpful when you have to refer to the passage.
- Use all the information given to you about the passage, such as title, author, date of publication, and footnotes.
- Be aware of foreshadowing.

- Be aware of thematic lines and be sensitive to details that will obviously be material for multiple-choice questions.
- When reading poetry, pay particular attention to enjambment and end-stopped lines because they carry meaning.
- With poetry, it's often helpful to paraphrase a stanza, especially if the order of the lines has been inverted.

> You can practice these techniques any time. Take any work and read it aloud. Time yourself. A good rate is about 1½ minutes per page.

Types of Multiple-Choice Questions

Multiple-choice questions are not written randomly. There are certain formats you will encounter. The answers to the following questions should clarify some of the patterns.

Is the Structure the Same for All of the Multiple-Choice Questions?

No. Here are several basic patterns that the AP test makers often employ:

1. **The straightforward question,** such as:
   - The poem is an example of a
     C. lyric
   - The word "smooth" refers to
     B. his skin

2. **The question that refers you to specific lines and asks you to draw a conclusion or to interpret.**
   - Lines 52–57 serve to
     A. reinforce the author's thesis

3. **The "all . . . except" question** requires extra time because it demands that you consider every possibility.
   - The AP Literature exam is all of the following *except*:
     A. It is given in May of each year.
     B. It is open to high school seniors.
     C. It is published in the *New York Times*.
     D. It is used as a qualifier for college credit.
     E. It is a 3-hour test.

Note: There are fewer and fewer of this type of question on the exam.

4. **The question that asks you to make an inference or to abstract a concept that is not directly stated in the passage.**
   - In the poem "My Last Duchess," the reader can infer that the speaker is
     E. arrogant

The infamous Roman Numeral question has been eliminated from the exam.

What Kinds of Questions Should I Expect on the Exam?

The 55 multiple-choice questions center around:

- the function of character, setting, plot, structure, narrator/speaker, diction, imagery, symbols, comparison;
- the interpretation of a text.

The test makers want to assess your understanding of the meaning of the selection as well as your ability to draw inferences and perceive implications based on it. They also want to know whether you understand *how* a writer develops his or her ideas.

One way of thinking about these multiple-choice questions is to categorize them as factual, technical, analytical, or inferential. Remember that this is merely a way of approaching a multiple-choice question, but it can prove to be helpful in both reading the question and determining the best answer. The two tables that follow illustrate the types of key words and phrases in these four categories that you can expect to find in questions for both the prose and the poetry selections.

Note: Do not memorize these tables. Also, do not panic if a word or phrase is unfamiliar to you. You may or may not encounter any or all of these words or phrases on any given exam. You can, however, count on meeting up with many of these in the practice exams in this book.

Prose: Key Words and Phrases Found in Multiple-Choice Questions

FACTUAL	TECHNICAL	ANALYTICAL	INFERENTIAL
words refer to	sentence structure	rhetorical strategy	effect of diction
allusions	style	shift in development	tone
antecedents	grammatical purpose	rhetorical stance	inferences
pronoun referents	dominant technique	style	effect of last paragraph
genre	imagery	metaphor	effect on reader
setting	point of view	contrast	narrator's attitude
	organization of passage	comparison	image suggests
	narrative progress of passage	cause/effect	effect of detail
	conflict	argument	author implies
	irony	description	author most concerned with
	function of	narration	
		specific-general	symbol
		how something is characterized	
		imagery	
		passage is primarily concerned with	
		function of	

Poetry: Key Words and Phrases Found in Multiple-Choice Questions

FACTUAL	TECHNICAL	ANALYTICAL	INFERENTIAL
all except	imagery	character portrayal	mood
definition	literary devices	imagery	attitude of
thesis	paradox	literary devices	poet's attitude
sequence of events	organizational pattern	paradox	purpose of
the object of ___ is ___	syntax	purpose of	tone of the poem
allusion	metrics	rhetorical shifts	theme of the poem
the subject of dramatic situation	parallel structure	ironies presented	reader may infer
	rhetorical shifts	least important	best interpreted as
paraphrasing	ironies presented	most important	effect of diction
subject	function of diction		speaker implies
references	dramatic moment		___ is associated with ___
	meaning conveyed by		context
			symbol

A word about jargon. Jargon refers to words that are unique to a specific subject. A common language is important for communication, and there must be agreement on the basic meanings of terms. Even though it is important to know the universal language of a subject, it is also important that you *not* limit the scope of your thinking to a brief definition. All the terms used in the tables are interwoven in literature. They are categorized only for easy reference. They also work in many other contexts. *In other words, think beyond the box.*

Scoring the Multiple-Choice Section

How Does the Scoring of the Multiple-Choice Section Work?

The College Board has implemented a new scoring process for the multiple-choice section of the AP English Literature and Composition exam. No longer are points deducted for incorrect responses, so there is no longer a penalty for guessing incorrectly. Therefore, it is to your advantage to answer ALL of the multiple-choice questions. Your chances of guessing the correct answer improve if you skillfully apply the process of elimination to narrow the choices.

Multiple-choice scores are based solely on the number of questions answered correctly. If you answered 36 questions correctly, then your raw score is 36. This raw score, which is 45 percent of the total, is combined with that of the essay section to make up a composite score. This is then manipulated to form a scale on which the final AP grade is based.

Strategies for Answering the Multiple-Choice Questions

You've been answering multiple-choice questions most of your academic life, and you've probably figured out ways to deal with them. However, there may be some points you have not considered that will be helpful for this particular exam.

General Guidelines

- Work in order. This is a good approach for several reasons:
  - It's clear.
  - You will not lose your place on the scan sheet.
  - There may be a logic to working sequentially that will help you answer previous questions. But, this is your call. If you are more comfortable moving around the exam, do so.
- Write on the exam booklet. Mark it up. Make it yours. Interact with the test.
- Do not spend too much time on any one question.
- Focus on your strengths. If you are more comfortable working with poetry, answer the poetry questions first.
- Don't be misled by the length or appearance of a selection. There is no correlation between length or appearance and the difficulty of the questions.
- Don't fight the question or the passage. You may know other information about the subject of the text or a question. It's irrelevant. Work within the given context.
- Consider all the choices in a given question. This will keep you from jumping to a false conclusion. It helps you to slow down and to really look at each possibility. You may find that your first choice is not the best or most appropriate one.
- Maintain an open mind as you answer subsequent questions in a series. Sometimes the answer to a later question will contradict your answer to a previous one. Reconsider both answers. Also, the phrasing of a question may point to an answer in a previous question.
- Remember that all parts of an answer must be correct.
- When in doubt, go to the text.

Specific Techniques

- **Process of elimination:** This is your primary tool, except for direct knowledge of the answer.
  1. Read the five choices.
  2. If no choice immediately strikes you as correct, you can
     - Eliminate those choices that are obviously wrong
     - Eliminate those choices that are too narrow or too broad
     - Eliminate illogical choices
     - Eliminate answers that are synonymous
     - Eliminate answers that cancel each other out

3. If two answers are close, do one *or* the other of the following:
   - Find the one that is general enough to cover all aspects of the question
   - Find the one that is limited enough to be the detail the question is looking for

- **Substitution/fill in the blank**
  1. Rephrase the question, leaving a blank where the answer should go.

  2. Use each of the choices to fill in the blank until you find the one that is the best fit.

- **Using context**
  1. Consider the context when the question directs you to specific lines, words, or phrases.

  2. Locate the given word, phrase, sentence, or poetic line and read the sentence or line before and after the section of the text to which the question refers. Often this provides the information or clues you need to make your choice.

- **Anticipation:** As you read the passage for the first time, mark any details and ideas that you would ask a question about. You may be able to anticipate the test makers this way.
- **Intuition or the educated guess:** You have a wealth of skills and knowledge in your literary subconscious. A question or a choice may trigger a "remembrance of things past." This can be the basis for your educated guess. Have the confidence to use the educated guess as a valid technique. Trust your own resources.

Survival Plan

If time is running out and you haven't finished the final selection:

1. Scan the remaining questions and look for:
   - The shortest questions
   - The questions that direct you to a specific line.

2. Look for specific detail/definition questions.

3. Look for self-contained questions. For example: "The sea slid silently from the shore" is an example of C. alliteration. You do not have to go to the passage to answer this question.

If I Don't Know an Answer, Should I Guess?

You can't be seriously hurt by making *educated guesses* based on a careful reading of the selection. Be smart. Understand that you need to come to this exam well prepared. You must have a foundation of knowledge and skills. You cannot guess through the entire exam and expect to do well.

This is not Lotto. This book is **not** about how to "beat the exam." We want to maximize the skills you already have. There is an inherent integrity in this exam and your participation in it. With this in mind, when there is no other direction open to you, it is perfectly fine to make an educated guess.

Is There Anything Special I Should Know About Preparing for the Prose Multiple-Choice Questions?

After you have finished with the Diagnostic/Master exam, you will be familiar with the format and types of questions asked on the AP Lit exam. However, just practicing answering multiple-choice questions on specific works will not give you a complete understanding of this questioning process. We suggest the following to help you hone your skills with answering prose multiple-choice questions:

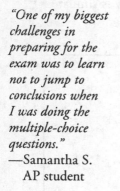

- Choose a challenging passage from a full-length prose work.
- Read the selection a couple of times and create several multiple-choice questions about specific sections of the selection.
- Make certain the section is self-contained and complex.
- Choose a dialogue, monologue, introductory setting, set description, stage directions, philosophical passage, significant event, or moment of conflict.
- Create a variety of question types based on the previous chart.
- Refer to the prose table given earlier in this chapter for suggested language and type.
- Administer your mini-quiz to a classmate, study group, or class.
- Evaluate your results.
- Repeat this process through several different full-length works during your preparation for the exam. The works can certainly come from those you are studying in class.

"One of my biggest challenges in preparing for the exam was to learn not to jump to conclusions when I was doing the multiple-choice questions."
—Samantha S.
 AP student

Here's what should happen as a result of your using this process:

- Your expectation level for the selections in the actual test will be more realistic.
- You will become familiar with the language of multiple-choice questions.
- Your understanding of the process of choosing answers will be heightened.
- Questions you write that you find less than satisfactory will trigger your analytical skills as you attempt to figure out "what went wrong."
- Terminology will become more accurate.
- *Bonus:* If you continue to do this work throughout your preparation for the AP exam, you will have created a mental storehouse of literary information. So when you are presented with a prose or free-response essay in Section II, you will have an extra resource at your disposal.

Your Turn

To Do:

1. Circle/highlight/underline the words and/or phrases that appear to be important for the meaning of the excerpt.

2. Carefully consider each of the given sample questions.

3. Construct your own question that is an example of the specific type.

from Mark Twain's *Huckleberry Finn*

Sometimes we'd have the whole river all to ourselves for the longest time. Yonder was the banks and the islands, across the water; and maybe a spark—which was a candle in a cabin window—and sometimes on the water you could see a spark or two—on a raft or a scow, you know; and maybe you could hear a fiddle or a song coming over from one of them crafts. It's lovely to live on a raft. We had the sky, up there, all speckled with stars, and we used to lay on our backs and look up at

5

them, and discuss about whether they was made, or only just happened—Jim he allowed they was made, but I allowed they happened; I judged it would have took too long to make so many. Jim said the moon could a laid them; well, that looked kind of reasonable, so I didn't say nothing against it, because I've seen a frog lay most as many, so of course it could be done. We used to watch the stars that fell, too, and see them streak down. Jim allowed they'd got spoiled and was hove out of the nest.

10

Title: *Huckleberry Finn*
Author: Mark Twain
Type of passage: Narrative description

Sample <u>Factual</u> Question: In lines 10–11, "I've seen a frog lay most as many" refers to

<u>Answer:</u> stars

<u>Rationale:</u> The implied comparison has Huck inferring that the number of stars in the sky is similar to the number of eggs a frog lays.

Your <u>Factual</u> Question:

<u>Answer:</u>   <u>Rationale:</u>

Sample <u>Technical</u> Question: A primary function of the sentence "It's lovely to live on a raft" is

<u>Answer:</u> to contrast with the lyrical description in the passage

<u>Rationale:</u> The straightforward break in the middle of the passage emphasizes the key point of the description.

Your <u>Technical</u> Question:

<u>Answer:</u>   <u>Rationale:</u>

Sample <u>Analytical</u> Question: The primary purpose of using dialect is most likely to

<u>Answer:</u> reinforce the innocence and natural state of Huck and Jim

<u>Rationale:</u> The regional dialect illustrates the lack of the stereotypical education and background of the period.

Your <u>Analytical</u> Question:

<u>Answer:</u>

<u>Rationale:</u>

Sample <u>Inferential</u> Question: The tone of the passage can best be described as

<u>Answer:</u> nostalgic and philosophical

<u>Rationale:</u> The diction supports their reverie and their curiosity about their place in the universe.

Your <u>Inferential</u> Question:

<u>Answer:</u>

<u>Rationale:</u>

Is There Anything Special I Should Do to Prepare for the Poetry Questions?

The points made about prose hold true for the poetry multiple-choice questions as well. But there are a few specific pointers that may prove helpful:

- Choose thoughtful and interesting poems of some length. (See our suggested reading list.)
- Read the poems several times. Practice reading the poems aloud.
- The greatest benefit will be that as you read any poem, you will automatically begin to respond to areas of the poem that would lend themselves to a multiple-choice question.

- Here is a list of representative poets you may want to read.

  - Shakespeare
  - John Donne
  - Philip Larkin
  - Emily Dickinson
  - Sylvia Plath
  - Dylan Thomas
  - May Swenson
  - Theodore Roethke
  - Sharon Olds
  - Billy Collins
  - Pablo Neruda

  - Richard Wilbur
  - Adrienne Rich
  - Edmund Spenser
  - W. H. Auden
  - W. B. Yeats
  - Gwendolyn Brooks
  - Elizabeth Bishop
  - Langston Hughes
  - Galway Kinnell
  - Marianne Moore
  - May Sarton

> You might want to utilize this process throughout the year with major works studied in and out of class and keep track of your progress. See the Bibliography of this book.

Your Turn

To Do:

1. Circle/highlight/underline the words and/or phrases that appear to be important for the meaning of the poem.

2. Carefully consider each of the given sample questions.

3. Construct your own question that is an example of the specific type.

It Sifts from Leaden Sieves
By Emily Dickinson

It sifts from leaden sieves,
It powders all the wood,
It fills with alabaster wool
The wrinkles of the road.

It makes an even face   5
Of mountain and of plain, –
Unbroken forehead from the east
Unto the east again.

It reaches to the fence,
It wraps it, rail by rail,   10
Till it is lost in fleeces,
It flings a crystal veil

On stump and stack and stem, –
The summer's empty room,
Acres of seams where harvests were,   15
Recordless, but for them.

It ruffles wrists of posts,
As ankles of a queen, –
Then stills its artisans like ghosts,
Denying they have been.   20

Title: "It Sifts from Leaden Sieves"
Poet: Emily Dickinson

Sample Factual Question: The subject of the poem's dramatic situation is

Answer: the falling snow   Rationale: The images all support the snow
                                                metaphor.

Your Factual Question:

Answer: Rationale:

Sample Technical Question: The primary literary device used in the poem is

Answer: metaphor   Rationale: Metaphor is used in every stanza.

Your Technical Question:

Answer: Rationale:

Sample <u>Analytical</u> Question: Paradox is most readily seen in

<u>Answer</u>: the softness imagery vs. the last two lines of the poem

<u>Rationale</u>: There is a shift from description to the effect of the cold in the last two lines.

Your <u>Analytical</u> Question:

<u>Answer</u>:

<u>Rationale</u>:

Sample <u>Inferential</u> Question: Based on the poem, the reader could infer that

<u>Answer</u>: the power of nature is all-encompassing

<u>Rationale</u>: Nothing in the poem is excluded from the power of the snow.

Your <u>Inferential</u> Question:

<u>Answer</u>:

<u>Rationale</u>:

The Time Is at Hand

It is now time to try the Diagnostic/Master exam, Section I. Do this section in *one* sitting. Time yourself! Be honest with yourself when you score your answers.

Note: If the 1 hour passes before you finish all the questions, stop where you are and score what you have done up to this point. Afterwards, answer the remaining questions, but do not count the answers as part of your score.

When you have completed all the multiple-choice questions in this Diagnostic/Master exam, carefully read the explanations of the answers. Spend time here and assess which types of questions give you trouble. Use this book to learn from your mistakes.

ANSWER SHEET FOR DIAGNOSTIC
MULTIPLE-CHOICE QUESTIONS

1. _____   15. _____   29. _____   43. _____

2. _____   16. _____   30. _____   44. _____

3. _____   17. _____   31. _____   45. _____

4. _____   18. _____   32. _____   46. _____

5. _____   19. _____   33. _____   47. _____

6. _____   20. _____   34. _____   48. _____

7. _____   21. _____   35. _____   49. _____

8. _____   22. _____   36. _____   50. _____

9. _____   23. _____   37. _____   51. _____

10. _____   24. _____   38. _____   52. _____

11. _____   25. _____   39. _____   53. _____

12. _____   26. _____   40. _____   54. _____

13. _____   27. _____   41. _____   55. _____

14. _____   28. _____   42. _____

I _____ did _____ did not finish all the questions in the allotted 1 hour.

I had _____ correct answers. I had _____ incorrect answers. I left _____ questions blank.

I have carefully reviewed the explanations of the answers, and I think I need to work on the following types of questions:

THE MULTIPLE-CHOICE SECTION OF
THE DIAGNOSTIC/MASTER EXAM

The multiple-choice section of the Diagnostic/Master exam follows. You have seen the questions in the "walk through" in Chapter 3.

Advanced Placement Literature and Composition

Section 1

Total time—1 hour

Carefully read the following passages and answer the accompanying questions. Questions 1–10 are based on the following poem.

Now Goes Under . . .
by Edna St. Vincent Millay

Now goes under, and I watch it go under, the sun
    That will not rise again.
Today has seen the setting, in your eyes cold
    and senseless as the sea,
Of friendship better than bread, and of bright charity   5
That lifts a man a little above the beasts that run.

That this could be!
That I should live to see
Most vulgar Pride, that stale obstreperous clown,
So fitted out with purple robe and crown   10
To stand among his betters! Face to face
With outraged me in this once holy place,
Where Wisdom was a favoured guest and hunted
Truth was harboured out of danger,
He bulks enthroned, a lewd, and insupportable stranger!   15

I would have sworn, indeed I swore it:
The hills may shift, the waters may decline,
Winter may twist the stem from the twig that bore it,
But never your love from me, your hand from mine.

Now goes under the sun, and I watch it go under.   20
Farewell, sweet light, great wonder!
You, too, farewell—but fare not well enough to dream
You have done wisely to invite the night before the darkness came.

1. The poem is an example of a(n)
   A. sonnet
   B. lyric
   C. ode
   D. ballad
   E. dramatic monologue

2. The setting of the sun is a symbol for
   A. the beginning of winter
   B. encountering danger
   C. the end of a relationship
   D. facing death
   E. the onset of night

3. The second stanza is developed primarily by
   A. metaphor
   B. simile
   C. personification
   D. hyperbole
   E. allusion

4. "He" in line 15 refers to
   A. Wisdom
   B. Truth
   C. I
   D. Pride
   E. charity

5. According to the speaker, what separates man from beast?
   A. love
   B. friendship
   C. charity
   D. truth
   E. wisdom

6. For the speaker, the relationship has been all of the following *except*
   A. honest
   B. dangerous
   C. spiritual
   D. ephemeral
   E. nourishing

7. The reader can infer from the play on words in the last stanza that the speaker is
   A. dying
   B. frantic
   C. wistful
   D. bitter
   E. capricious

8. "This once holy place" (line 12) refers to
   A. the sunset
   B. the relationship
   C. the sea
   D. the circus
   E. the Church

9. The cause of the relationship's situation is
   A. a stranger coming between them
   B. the lover not taking the relationship seriously
   C. the lover feeling intellectually superior
   D. the lover's pride coming between them
   E. the lover being insensitive

10. The speaker acknowledges the finality of the relationship in line(s)
    A. 1–2
    B. 7
    C. 8
    D. 16
    E. 18–19

Questions 11–23 are based on the following passage from *The Heart of Darkness* by Joseph Conrad, 1899.

The sea-reach of the Thames stretched before us like the beginning of an
interminable waterway. The air was dark above Gravesend, and farther back still
seemed condensed into a mournful gloom, brooding motionless over the biggest and
the greatest town on earth.
   "I was thinking of very old times, when the Romans first came here, nineteen   5
hundred years ago—the other day . . . Light came out of this river since—you say knights?
Yes; but it is like a running blaze on a plain, like a flash of lightning in the clouds. We live
in the flicker—may it last as long as the old earth keeps rolling! But darkness was here
yesterday. Imagine the feelings of a commander of a fine—what d'ye call 'em?—trireme
in the Mediterranean, ordered suddenly to the north; run overland across the Gauls in a   10

hurry; put in charge of one of these craft the legionnaires—a wonderful lot of handy men they must have been, too—used to build, apparently by the hundred, in a month or two, if we may believe what we read. Imagine him here—the very end of the world, a sea the color of lead, a sky the color of smoke, a kind of ship about as rigid as a concertina—and going up this river with stores, or orders, or what you like. Sandbanks, marshes, forests, savages— precious little to eat for a civilized man, nothing but Thames water to drink. No Falernian wine here, no going ashore. Here and there a military camp lost in a wilderness, like a needle in a bundle of hay—cold, fog, tempests, disease, exile, and death—death skulking in the air, in the water, in the bush. They must have been dying like flies here. Oh yes—he did it. Did it very well, too, no doubt, and without thinking much about it either, except afterwards to brag of what he had gone through in his time, perhaps. They were men enough to face darkness. And perhaps he was cheered by keeping his eye on a chance of promotion to the fleet at Ravenna by and by, if he had good friends in Rome and survived the awful climate. Or think of a decent young citizen in a toga—perhaps too much dice, you know— coming out here in the train of some prefect, or tax-gatherer, or trader even, to mend his fortunes. Land in a swamp, march through the woods, and in some inland post feel the savagery, the utter savagery, had closed round him—all that mysterious life of the wilderness that stirs in the forest, in the jungles, in the hearts of wild men. There's no initiation either into such mysteries. He has to live in the midst of the incomprehensible, which is also detestable. And it has a fascination, too, that goes to work upon him. The fascination of the abomination—you know, imagine the growing regrets, the longing to escape, the powerless disgust, the surrender, the hate."

He paused.

"Mind," he began again, lifting one arm from the elbow, the palm of the hand outwards, so that, with his legs folded before him, he had the pose of a Buddha preaching in European clothes and without a lotus flower—"Mind, none of us would feel exactly like this. What saves us is efficiency—the devotion to efficiency. But these chaps were not much account, really. They were no colonists; their administration was merely a squeeze, and nothing more, I suspect. They were conquerors, and for that you want only brute force— nothing to boast of, when you have it, since your strength is just an accident arising from the weakness of others. They grabbed what they could get for the sake of what was to be got. It was just robbery with violence, aggravated murder on a great scale, and men going at it blind— as is very proper for those who tackle a darkness. The conquest of the earth, which mostly means taking it away from those who have a different complexion or slightly flatter noses than ourselves, is not a pretty thing when you look at it too much. What redeems it is the idea only. An idea at the back of it; not a sentimental pretense but an idea; and an unselfish belief in the idea—something you can set up, and bow down before, and offer a sacrifice to . . . "

15

20

25

30

35

40

45

11. In the passage, *darkness* implies all of the following *except*
A. the unknown
B. savagery
C. ignorance
D. death
E. exploration

12. The setting of the passage is
A. Africa
B. Ancient Rome
C. the Thames River
D. the Mediterranean
E. Italy

13. The tone of the passage is
   A. condescending
   B. indignant
   C. scornful
   D. pensive
   E. laudatory

14. Later events may be foreshadowed by all of the following phrases *except*
   A. "Imagine the feelings of a commander . . ."
   B. " . . . live in the midst of the incomprehensible . . ."
   C. " . . . in some inland post feel the savagery . . ."
   D. "They must have been dying like flies here."
   E. " . . . the very end of the world . . ."

15. The narrator draws a parallel between
   A. light and dark
   B. past and present
   C. life and death
   D. fascination and abomination
   E. decency and savagery

16. In this passage, "We live in the flicker..." (lines 7–8) may be interpreted to mean *all* of the following *except*
   A. In the history of the world, humanity's span on earth is brief.
   B. Future civilizations will learn from only a portion of the past.
   C. Periods of enlightenment and vision appear only briefly.
   D. The river has been the source of life throughout the ages.
   E. A moment of present-day insight about conquest.

17. One may conclude from the passage that the speaker
   A. admires adventurers
   B. longs to be a crusader
   C. is a former military officer
   D. recognizes and accepts the presence of evil in human experience
   E. is prejudiced

18. In the context of the passage, which of the following phrases presents a paradox?
   A. "The fascination of the abomination . . ."
   B. " . . . in the hearts of wild men"
   C. "There's no initiation . . . into such mysteries"
   D. " . . . a flash of lightning in the clouds"
   E. " . . . death skulking in the air . . ."

19. The lines "Imagine him here . . . concertina . . ." (lines 13–14) contain examples of
   A. hyperbole and personification
   B. irony and metaphor
   C. alliteration and personification
   D. parallel structure and simile
   E. allusion and simile

20. According to the speaker, the one trait which saves Europeans from savagery is
   A. sentiment
   B. a sense of mystery
   C. brute force
   D. religious zeal
   E. efficiency

21. According to the speaker, the only justification for conquest is
   A. the "weakness of others"
   B. it's being "proper for those who tackle a darkness . . ."
   C. their grabbing "what they could get for the sake of what was to be got"
   D. " . . . an unselfish belief in the idea . . ."
   E. "The fascination of the abomination . . ."

22. In the statement by the speaker, "Mind, none of us would feel exactly like this" (line 36), "this" refers to
   A. " . . . a Buddha preaching in European clothes . . ." (lines 35–36)
   B. " . . . imagine the growing regrets . . . the hate." (lines 31–32)
   C. "What redeems it is the idea only." (lines 45–46)
   D. " . . . think of a decent young citizen in a toga . . ." (line 24)
   E. "I was thinking of very old times . . ." (line 5)

23. The speaker presents all of the following
reasons for exploration and conquest *except*
  A. military expeditions
  B. " . . . a chance of promotion"
  C. " . . . to mend his fortunes"
  D. religious commitment
  E. punishment for a crime

Questions 24–35 are based on the following poem by William Shakespeare.

> That time of year thou mayst in me behold
> When yellow leaves, or none, or few, do hang
> Upon those boughs which shake against the cold,
> Bare ruin'd choirs, where late the sweet birds sang.
> In me thou see'st the twilight of such day   5
> As after sunset fadeth in the west;
> Which by and by black night doth take away,
> Death's second self, that seals up all in rest.
> In me thou see'st the glowing of such fire,
> That on the ashes of his youth doth lie,   10
> As the deathbed whereon it must expire,
> Consum'd with that which it was nourish'd by.
> This thou perceiv'st, which makes thy love more strong,
> To love that well which thou must leave ere long.

24. "That time of year" (line 1) refers to
  A. youth
  B. old age
  C. childhood
  D. senility
  E. maturity

25. "Death's second self" (line 8) refers to
  A. "That time of year"
  B. "sunset fadeth"
  C. "the west"
  D. "ruin'd choirs"
  E. "black night"

26. Line 12 is an example of
  A. paradox
  B. caesura
  C. parable
  D. hyperbole
  E. metonymy

27. "Twilight of such day" (line 5) is supported by
all of the following images *except*
  A. "sunset fadeth"
  B. "the glowing of such fire"
  C. "west"
  D. "Death's second self"
  E. "ashes of his youth"

28. "This thou perceiv'st" (line 13) refers to
  A. the beloved's deathbed
  B. the sorrow of unrequited love
  C. the passion of youth expiring
  D. the beloved's acknowledgment of the
      speaker's mortality
  E. the speaker sending the lover away

29. The poem is an example of a(n)
  A. elegy
  B. Spenserian sonnet
  C. Petrarchan sonnet
  D. Shakespearean sonnet
  E. sestina

30. The poem is primarily developed by
   A. metaphor
   B. argument
   C. synecdoche
   D. alternative choices
   E. contradiction

31. The irony of the poem is best expressed in line
   A. 5
   B. 7
   C. 10
   D. 11
   E. 14

32. "It" in line 12 can best be interpreted to mean
   A. a funeral pyre
   B. spent youth
   C. the intensity of the speaker's love
   D. the impending departure of his beloved
   E. the immortality of the relationship

33. An apt title for the poem could be
   A. Love Me or Leave Me
   B. Death Be Not Proud
   C. The End Justifies the Means
   D. Love's Fall
   E. Grow Old Along with Me

34. The tone of the poem can best be described as
   A. contemplative
   B. defiant
   C. submissive
   D. arbitrary
   E. complaining

35. The speaker most likely is
   A. jealous of the beloved's youth
   B. pleased that the lover will leave
   C. unable to keep up with the young lover
   D. unwilling to face his own mortality
   E. responsive to the beloved's constancy

Questions 36–47 are based on a careful reading of the following excerpt from the first chapter of the 2001 novel *White Teeth* by Zadie Smith that centers on two families who live in North London.

Archie's marriage felt like buying a pair of shoes, taking them home and finding they don't fit. For the sake of appearances, he put up with them. And then, all of a sudden and after thirty years, the shoes picked themselves up and walked out of the house. She left. Thirty years.

As far as he remembered, just like everybody else they began well. The first spring of 1946, he had stumbled out of the darkness of war and into a Florentine coffee house, where he was served by a waitress truly like the sun: Ophelia Diagilo, dressed all in yellow, spreading warmth and the promise of sex as she passed him a frothy cappuccino. They walked into it blinkered as horses. She was not to know that women never stayed as daylight in Archie's life; that somewhere in him he didn't like them, he didn't trust them, and he was able to love them only if they wore haloes. No one told Archie that lurking in the Diagilo family tree were two hysteric aunts, an uncle who talked to aubergines[1] and a cousin who wore his clothes back to front. So they got married and returned to England, where she realized very quickly her mistake, he drove her very quickly mad, and the halo was packed off to the attic to collect dust with the rest of the bric-a-brac[2] and broken kitchen appliances that Archie promised one day to repair. Amongst that bric-a-brac was a Hoover.

On Boxing Day[3] morning, six days before he parked outside Mo's halal[4] butchers, Archie had returned to their semi-detached in Hendon[5] in search of that Hoover. It was his fourth trip to the attic in so many days, ferrying out the odds and ends of a marriage to his new flat, and the Hoover was amongst the very last items he reclaimed—one of the most broken things, most ugly things, the things you demand out of sheer bloody-mindedness because you have lost the house. This is what divorce is: taking things you no longer want from people you no longer love.

"So you again," said the Spanish home-help at the door, Santa-Maria or Maria-Santa or something. "Meester Jones, what now? Kitchen sink, si?"

"Hoover," said Archie, grimly. "Vacuum."

5

10

15

20

25

She cut her eyes at him and spat on the doormat inches from his shoes. "Welcome, señor."

The place had become a haven for people who hated him. Apart from the home-help, he had to contend with Ophelia's extended Italian family, her mental-health nurse, the woman from the council,[6] and of course Ophelia herself, who was to be found in the kernel of this nuthouse, curled up in a fetal ball on the sofa, making lowing sounds into a bottle of Bailey's.[7] It took him an hour and a quarter just to get through enemy lines—and for what? A perverse Hoover, discarded months earlier because it was determined to perform the opposite of every vacuum's objective: spewing out dust instead of sucking it in.

"Meester Jones, why do you come here when it make you so unhappy? Be reasonable. What can you want with it?" The home-help was following him up the attic stairs, armed with some kind of cleaning fluid: "It's broken. You don't need this. See? See?" She plugged it into a socket and demonstrated the dead switch. Archie took the plug out and silently wound the cord round the Hoover. If it was broken, it was coming with him. All broken things were coming with him. He was going to fix every damn broken thing in this house, if only to show that he was good for something.

"You good for nothing!" Santa whoever chased him back down the stairs. "Your wife is ill in her head, and this is all you can do!"

Archie hugged the Hoover to his chest and took it into the crowded living room, where, under several pairs of reproachful eyes, he got out his toolbox and started work on it.

"Look at him," said one of the Italian grandmothers, the more glamorous one with the big scarves and fewer moles, "he take everything, capisce?[8] He take-a her mind, he take-a the blender, he take-a the old stereo—he take-a everything except the floorboards. It make-a you sick . . ."

The woman from the council, who even on dry days resembled a long-haired cat soaked to the skin, shook her skinny head in agreement. "It's disgusting, you don't have to tell me, it's disgusting . . . and naturally, we're the ones left to sort out the mess; it's muggins[9] here who has to—"

Which was overlapped by the nurse: "She can't stay here alone, can she . . . now he's buggered off, poor woman . . . she needs a proper home, she needs . . ."

I'm here, Archie felt like saying. I'm right here you know, I'm bloody right here. And it was my blender.

But he wasn't one for confrontation, Archie. He listened to them all for another fifteen minutes, mute as he tested the Hoover's suction against pieces of newspaper, until he was overcome by the sensation that Life was an enormous rucksack[10] so impossibly heavy that, even though it meant losing everything, it was infinitely easier to leave all baggage here on the roadside and walk on into the blackness. You don't need the blender, Archie-boy, you don't need the Hoover. This stuff's all dead weight. Just lay down the rucksack, Arch, and join the happy campers in the sky. Was that wrong? To Archie—ex-wife and ex-wife's relatives in one ear, spluttering vacuum in the other—it just seemed that The End was unavoidably nigh. Nothing personal to God or whatever. It just felt like the end of the world. And he was going to need more than poor whisky, novelty crackers and a paltry box of Quality Street[11]—all the strawberry ones already scoffed—to justify entering another annum.

Patiently he fixed the Hoover, and vacuumed the living room with a strange methodical finality, shoving the nozzle into the most difficult corners. Solemnly he flipped a coin (heads, life, tails, death) and felt nothing in particular when he found himself staring at the dancing lion.[12] Quietly he detached the Hoover tube, put it in a suitcase, and left the house for the last time.

---

[1]**aubergines:** eggplants

[2]**bric-a-brac:** odds and ends, objects of little value

[3]**Boxing Day:** The British celebration of the day after Christmas

[4]**halal:** food prepared according to Muslim law
[5]**Hendon:** a suburb of London
[6]**council:** a type of elected British advisory or legislative body
[7]**Bailey's:** a brand of whiskey
[8]**capisce:** Italian for *understand*
[9]**muggins:** a foolish, gullible person
[10]**rucksack:** backpack
[11]**Quality Street:** a brand of candy
[12]**dancing lion:** reverse side of a twenty-pence coin

36. The function of the first paragraph can best be described as
    A. a diatribe against marriage
    B. an introduction to the setting
    C. an introduction to the central plot
    D. an introduction to Archie's attitude toward his former wife and their marriage
    E. an introduction to Ophelia

37. After reading the second paragraph, one can infer all of the following *except*
    A. Archie and Ophelia's love was based on passion.
    B. Archie was self-motivated.
    C. Archie wanted to be able to place his wife on a pedestal.
    D. Ophelia and Ophelia were quick to make important decisions.
    E. Archie was unsure and suspicious of women.

38. The metaphor of the halo in the second paragraph serves mainly to emphasize
    A. the beauty and innocence of Ophelia
    B. the religion of both Ophelia and Archie
    C. the inevitability of future events
    D. the hastiness of Archie and Ophelia's marriage
    E. an unrealistic desire for the perfect love

39. In line 7, *it* is referring to
    A. pledge of love
    B. move to England
    C. marriage
    D. divorce
    E. sexual relationship

40. The response of "Santa-Maria or Maria-Santa" (23–26) to Archie's arrival can best be described as
    A. hostile and denigrating
    B. suspicious and cowering
    C. warm and welcoming
    D. condescending and dismissive
    E. curious and insecure

41. Paragraph 7, lines 27–33, progresses from a primarily third-person, objective narrator to
    A. stream-of-consciousness
    B. interior monologue
    C. first-person narrator
    D. third-person subjective
    E. third-person omniscient

42. Lines 39–40, reveal that Archie
    A. believes he is capable of fixing broken appliances
    B. wants to prove that he is not a failure
    C. feels he has been taken advantage of
    D. is basically selfish
    E. wants to show the help that he is in charge

43. For Archie, the Hoover vacuum symbolizes each of the following *except*
    A. ownership
    B. potential to redeem himself
    C. failure of his life so far
    D. his love for Ophelia
    E. control

44. As a way to characterize Archie's perceived burden, the author uses the image of
    A. pair of shoes (first paragraph)
    B. halo (second paragraph)
    C. Hoover vacuum (throughout passage)
    D. the blender (lines 47 and 56)
    E. rucksack (next-to-last paragraph)

45. The author uses dialect with the home-help's dialogue primarily
  A. to add a sense of realism to the narrative
  B. to indicate the class differences between Archie and the home-help
  C. to make a point about the working conditions of the working class
  D. to add a bit of humor to the passage
  E. to gain more sympathy for Archie

46. Archie's behavior in the last two paragraphs suggests he
  A. wants to move on
  B. believes it's possible to help Ophelia
  C. is beginning to feel hopeless
  D. wonders why he bothered fixing the Hoover
  E. wants to get back at the home-help and Ophelia's relatives

47. Which of the following best describes the effect of the last paragraph?
  A. hopeful
  B. looking for redemption
  C. impending doom
  D. loss of control
  E. anger at the world

Questions 48–55 are based on a careful reading of the 2002 poem "Litany" by Billy Collins.

Litany[1]

You are the bread and the knife,
The crystal goblet and the wine . . .
—Jacques Crickillon

You are the bread and the knife,
the crystal goblet and the wine.
You are the dew on the morning grass   5
and the burning wheel of the sun.
You are the white apron of the baker,
and the marsh birds suddenly in flight.

However, you are not the wind in the orchard,   10
the plums on the counter,
or the house of cards.
And you are certainly not the pine-scented air.
There is just no way that you are the pine-scented air.

It is possible that you are the fish under the bridge   15
maybe even the pigeon on the general's head,
but you are not even close
to being the field of cornflowers at dusk.

And a quick look in the mirror will show
that you are neither the boots in the corner   20
nor the boat asleep in its boathouse.

It might interest you to know,
speaking of the plentiful imagery of the world,
that I am the sound of rain on the roof.

I also happen to be the shooting star,   25
the evening paper blowing down an alley
and the basket of chestnuts on the kitchen table.

I am also the moon in the trees
and the blind woman's tea cup.
But don't worry, I'm not the bread and the knife.   30
You are still the bread and the knife.
You will always be the bread and the knife,
not to mention the crystal goblet and—somehow—the wine.

---

¹**litany**: (secondary meaning) a recital or a repetitive series of phrases with a type of call-and-response

48. This poem is an example of
A. blank verse
B. rhymed verse
C. metered verse
D. free verse
E. rhymed, metered verse

49. The tone of the poem can best be described as
A. formal and critical
B. uncaring and suspicious
C. informal and indifferent
D. brusque and patronizing
E. casual and playful

50. Line 9, "and the marsh birds suddenly in flight"
A. hints at an element of uncertainty
B. sums up the preceding five lines
C. indicates the speaker's fear
D. introduces a new setting
E. suggests the speaker's fascination with nature

51. As the poem progresses, it becomes clear that this poem is
A. an elegy for a deceased loved one
B. a description of the depth of the speaker's love
C. an ode to love
D. an apology to the speaker's loved one
E. a tribute to the speaker's beloved

52. The turning point in the poem occurs in stanza
A. 1
B. 2
C. 5
D. 6
E. 7

53. All of the following literary devices are used in the poem *except*
A. rhyme
B. metaphor
C. alliteration
D. simile
E. repetition

54. Elements of humor in the poem are created by using
A. improbable circumstances
B. counterbalance and exaggeration
C. gentle criticism and apologies
D. slapstick put-downs
E. satirical comments

55. The repetition in the last four lines of the poem
can best be interpreted to mean
  A. the speaker will always be the opposite of
     the beloved
  B. the beloved holds the key to the speaker's
     life and always will
  C. both the speaker and the beloved will
     remain in separate worlds
  D. the speaker will always accept the beloved's
     point of view
  E. the speaker cannot imagine living without
     the beloved

STOP.

THIS IS THE END OF THE MULTIPLE-CHOICE SECTION OF THE DIAGNOSTIC/MASTER EXAM

ANSWERS TO MULTIPLE-CHOICE QUESTIONS

Answer Key

1. B	20. E	39. C
2. C	21. D	40. A
3. C	22. B	41. D
4. D	23. E	42. 3
5. C	24. B	43. D
6. B	25. E	44. E
7. D	26. A	45. A
8. B	27. B	46. C
9. D	28. D	47. C
10. A	29. D	48. D
11. E	30. A	49. E
12. C	31. E	50. A
13. D	32. C	51. E
14. A	33. D	52. C
15. B	34. A	53. D
16. B	35. E	54. B
17. D	36. D	55. B
18. A	37. B	
19. D	38. E	

Answers and Explanations

Now Goes Under . . .
by Edna St. Vincent Millay

1. **B.** This question requires the student to know the characteristics of various poetic forms. (See Chapter 9.) Using the process of elimination, the correct answer B is readily confirmed. Lyric poetry is emotional and personal.

2. **C.** Although the setting sun is often associated with winter, death, and darkness, these answers are not symbolic of the literal topic of the poem—the end of the love relationship.

3. **C.** The poet uses personification in lines 9–15: "vulgar Pride," "Where Wisdom was a favoured guest," "hunted Truth" as characters to develop the conflicts apparent in the poem. [TIP: Capitalization of nouns often indicates personification.]

4. **D.** This is an antecedent question. The student must retrace the reference "He" back to its origins to locate the correct answer. Try asking "who is enthroned, lewd and unsupportable?" Since truth, charity, and wisdom are described positively, only *vulgar* pride qualifies as the answer.

5. **C.** This question requires you to find the antecedent. Ask yourself, "Who or what lifts man?" The answer, *charity*, should be obvious.

6. **B.** Sometimes you can find information from a previous question. In question 2, "danger" was eliminated as a choice; therefore, it probably wouldn't be suitable for this question either. Try finding proof of the others. Truth = honest; holy = spiritual; bread = nourishment. Therefore, *dangerous* has to be the answer.

7. **D.** This is a tone question based on a repetitive contradictory phrase. She does *not* wish him well; therefore, she is bitter and resigned. There is nothing playful, wistful, or frantic in the conclusion.

8. **B.** This is a relationship question. You should realize this by the intensity of the opposing lewd force, pride, which destroyed the sanctity of the love. (If you see this, you could validate your answer to question 9.)

9. **D.** The cause is developed in the longest stanza, lines 7–15. Find the proof for your answer in lines 7–12.

10. **A.** Interestingly enough, the speaker reveals the conclusion in the first two lines of the poem. "The sun that will not rise again" establishes the totality of the circumstances.

Heart of Darkness
by Joseph Conrad

11. **E.** Here's an easy question to start you off. For years you heard your English teachers and your classmates discussing all the elements that could be associated with *darkness*. All the choices given in this question would qualify except for *exploration*.

12. **C.** Line 1 gives you the answer. The Thames is the river that runs through the heart of London.

13. **D.** A careful reading of the passage will introduce you to a speaker who is *thinking* about the past, *thinking* about exploration and conquest, and *thinking* about the conqueror and the conquered.

14. **A.** Here, the speaker is asking his listeners to picture the past. Therefore, it is *not* pointing to the future. The feelings of a commander have nothing to do with a future event; whereas each of the other choices hints at a future concept.

15. **B.** The second paragraph is about ancient Rome and its conquests. The third paragraph has the speaker considering "us" and what saves "us." This is past and present.

16. **B.** The first ten lines support inclusion of A. Choice B is NOT part of the speaker's conversation. Choice C is supported in the second paragraph. Choice D may be found in lines 5–8. Lines 36–47 support Choice E.

17. **D.** Lines 26–30 and 39–45 indicate the speaker's attitude toward the human condition. There is no evidence in the passage to support any of the other choices.

18. **A.** The question assumes you know the definition of *paradox*. Therefore, you should

be able to see that to be fascinated by that which is repulsive, awful, and horrible is a paradox.

19. D. "A sea," "a sky," "a kind," "or orders," "or what" are examples of parallel structure. The simile is "ship about as rigid as a concertina."

20. E. This is a straightforward, factual question. The answer is found in line 37.

21. D. In lines 45–47 the speaker is philosophizing about what it is that "redeems" the "conquest of the earth." It is the *idea*.

22. B. This question asks you to locate the antecedent of "this." You could use the substitution method here. Just replace "this" with the word or phrase. Or, you could look carefully at the text itself. The omniscient narrator is describing the speaker as a Buddha. Lines 45–46 come after "this." D and E are not real possibilities. Also, they are too far away from the pronoun.

23. E. A careful reading of the passage allows you to find references to A and D and to locate the quoted phrases in B and C. What you will *not* find are any references to "punishment for a crime."

Sonnet 73
by William Shakespeare

24. B. The difficulty with this question lies in the similarity between B and E. However, it should be apparent from the numerous references to death and the contrast to youth that the poet is speaking of a literal time period in life and not of a state of emotional development.

25. E. Use the process of substitution and work backward in the poem to find the antecedent. Recognize the appositive phrase, which is set off by commas, to spot the previous image—"black night." Another trick is to recast the line into a directly stated sentence instead of the poetic inversion. Asking "who or what is Death's second self" will help you locate the subject of the line.

26. A. Once again you are being tested on terminology and your ability to recognize an example. Deconstruct the line and find its

essence; here it is obvious that "consumed" and "nourished" are contradictory.

27. B. Even without returning to the poem, you should notice that A, C, D, and E suggest death or diminishment. The only image of intensity and life appears in choice B.

28. D. The keys to this question can be found in lines 10–12 and line 14, which restate the irony of the beloved's devotion and the speaker's mortality. A good technique is to always check the previous and subsequent lines in order to clarify your answer. Also, careful reading would eliminate A and B. Passion is not mentioned in the poem.

29. D. For the prepared student, this question is a giveaway. Definitions of these terms in Chapter 9 clarify the differences among the types of sonnets. The rhyme scheme should lead you to choose D.

30. A. The sonnet depends on several extended comparisons with nature—the seasons, day and night, and fire. Although there may be a contradiction in the final three lines, the primary means of development is metaphor. (See Chapter 8 for examples of synecdoche.)

31. E. Since contradiction and paradox are techniques that create irony, you should be able to see that choice E restates the essential opposing forces in the sonnet.

32. C. You must reread and interpret the entire third quatrain to clearly figure out this question. You need to decode the metaphor and realize that fires must be fed and that they expire when they exhaust the source of fuel.

33. D. Even though E is a lovely thought, the speaker never expresses the desire to have the beloved age along with him. This answer depends on the pun in the title of choice D—fall. Here it may refer to the season of age as well as to the decline of the speaker and the relationship. No other choice is supported in the sonnet.

34. A. At first glance, one might think the speaker is submissive to the greater force of death; however, at no time does he acquiesce to the demands of mortality. The speaker thinks about and reflects on his circumstances.

35. E. You should notice that three of the five choices are negative. If you have read carefully, you will be aware that the poem is laudatory and positive with regard to the depth of the beloved's love. And, at no time is the speaker looking forward to his lover's departure.

White Teeth
by Zadie Smith

36. D. A diatribe is a bitter, verbal attack. Even though the first paragraph is negative, it does not meet the criteria for a diatribe. Without specific details of time or place, this paragraph could be anywhere. There is no real indication of a conflict brewing between characters that will be developed, and Ophelia is introduced in the second paragraph. The best answer is D, supported with details like "don't fit," "put up with this," "for the sake of appearance."

37. B. The second paragraph presents Archie as a character who goes along to get along without too much introspection. This, together with the chaotic attic and the Hoover that Archie had promised to fix and never did, lead to the inference stated in choice B.

38. E. A halo is a universal symbol of saintliness, holiness. Wanting his women and the resulting love to wear halos is indicative of his desire for perfection in his women.

39. C. Without the first paragraph as a lead-in, choice E could be viable. However, given the entire first paragraph and the first part of the second, marriage is the best choice.

40. A. What the home-helper says, how she says it, and what she does ("cut her eyes at him," "spat on the doormat next his shoes,") support the choice of hostility and belittling. The other choices do not have any support in this passage.

41. D. Third-person subjective has a narrator speaking through the viewpoint of a specific character at a specific time and place so that the reader can experience the thoughts of that character. In paragraph seven, the narrator moves from a reportorial overview of the general ambiance of the house to what are obviously Archie's personal thoughts.

42. B. Choice B is almost a paraphrasing of the last sentence. Choices A, C, and E are all the cause of his desire to fix the Hoover. Choice D is not supported in the text.

43. D. It is the world inside this house that is pushing Archie to try to prove his worth, to prove he can do things. At this point in the narrative, Ophelia is not an active player.

44. E. Archie is carrying a heavy load of life's baggage. This is emphasized in line 59 with the metaphor "…Life was an enormous rucksack."

45. A. Since the attitude of the home-helper would be the same with or without her dialect, it can best be seen as a way to inject a bit of realism into both the characterization and the situation.

46. C. "Losing everything," "walk into blackness," "I felt like the end of the world," "This stuff's all dead weight," "feel nothing in particular": These phrases and sentences, plus others, build a picture of a character who is less and less able to deal with his life. The last two paragraphs are about ONLY Archie and his personal situation. None of the other choices are supported in this set of paragraphs.

47. C. The flipping of the coin with one side being life and the other death is not hopeful, nor does it indicate loss of control, anger, or redemption. What it does signify is Archie's willingness to leave his living or dying up to a flip of a coin and his nonchalant acceptance of its outcome.

Litany
by Billy Collins

48. D. Rhymed iambic pentameter, a pattern of specific rhyme, and specific meter are NOT part of the construction of this poem. Because of this, the poem is classified as free verse.

49. E. The ordinary language, the contrasts, the everyday details, and the personal comments best leads the reader to conclude that the tone is casual and playful. Remember that BOTH descriptors have to be applicable to the text.

50. A. "Suddenly" indicates surprise among the marsh in early morning. This surprise forces the birds to flee. This suggests a sense of uncertainty. None of the other choices will allow for this sudden flight to the birds.

51. E. As the title of the poem suggests, this is a listing of the qualities the speaker primarily attributes to the beloved. It is not a poem mourning a death, nor a description of the beloved's appearance, nor a song or apology to the beloved.

52. C. In the first line of the fifth stanza, the speaker switches from addressing *you* to speaking about *I*. Here the focus switches from the beloved to the speaker.

53. D. Metaphors based on "You are . . ." and "I am . . ." are found throughout the poem. "You are" is repeated frequently. Alliteration is found in lines 24 and 25. Rhyme is used with "show" and "know." Simile is the only listed literary device not found in this poem.

54. B. The speaker introduces counterbalance in the second stanza when he stops repeating "you are" with "However," together with "It might interest you to know" in the fifth stanza. This, combined with switching between addressing both the negative and the positive aspects of the beloved and the speaker as well as the creation of several rather absurd comparisons, provide the components of the poem's humor.

55. B. The first three lines of the last stanza imply that the speaker accepts the beloved, "But" he will still have his own take on life. The last two lines with "You will always" implies the speaker and the beloved will be forever connected. This negates choices A, C, D and E.

CHAPTER 5

The Prose Passage Essay

IN THIS CHAPTER

Summary: Complete explanation of the prose passage essay and its purpose as it is presented on the AP English Literature exam

Key Ideas

✪ Learn the types of prose passage prompts you might encounter on the AP English Literature exam
✪ Learn about the rubrics and rating of the AP English Literature prose passage essay
✪ Learn the basics of reading and notating a given passage
✪ Learn the basics of constructing your response to the prompt
✪ Examine the student models that respond to the diagnostic exam's prose passage essay prompt
✪ Learn how the rubrics were used to rate the student sample essays

Introduction to the Prose Passage Essay

This section of the exam gives you an opportunity to read and analyze a prose piece of literature. This is your chance to become personally involved in the text and to demonstrate your literary skills.

The free-response prose fiction essay will present a prose fiction passage of approximately 500 to 700 words. You will be expected to:

- Respond to the prompt with a thesis that presents an assertion that requires defense and support
- Select and use evidence to support your line of reasoning

- Explain how the evidence supports your line of reasoning
- Use appropriate grammar and punctuation in communicating your argument

The wording of the prose fiction prompt will be consistent. Only the title of the text and information about it will differ. For example: "The following excerpt is from [text and author, date of publication]. In this passage, [comment on what is being addressed in the passage]. Read the passage carefully. Then, in a well-written essay, analyze how [author] uses literary elements and techniques to [convey/portray/develop a thematic, topical, or structural aspect of the passage that is complex and specific to the passage provided]." (*AP English Literature and Composition Course and Exam Description*, The College Board, 2020, p. 139.)

What Is an AP Literature Prose Passage?

Generally, it is a one-page excerpt from a work of fiction. More often than not, the selection will be from a novel or short story. Be aware that the exam may also present an excerpt from a drama.

What Is the Purpose in Writing an Essay About a Prose Piece?

First, the people at the College Board want to determine your facility in reading and interpreting a sustained piece of literature. It requires you to understand the text and to analyze those techniques and devices the author uses to achieve his or her purpose.

Second, the AP exam is designed to allow you to demonstrate your ease and fluency with terminology, interpretation, and criticism. Also, the level of your writing should be a direct reflection of your critical thinking.

Third, the AP exam determines your ability to make connections between analysis and interpretation. For example, when you find a metaphor, you should identify and connect it to the author's intended purpose or meaning. You should not just list items as you locate them. You must connect them to your interpretation.

> **TIP** Before beginning to work with an actual prose passage, read the review of processes and terms in the Comprehensive Review section of this book. You should also have completed some of the activities in that section.

Types of Prose Passage Essay Questions

Let's look at a few prose passage questions that have been asked on the AP Literature exam in the past:

- Analyze narrative and literary techniques and other resources of language used for characterization.
- How does a narrator reveal character? (i.e., tone, diction, syntax, point of view)
- How does the author reveal a character's predicament? (i.e., diction, imagery, point of view)
- Explain the effect of the passage on the reader.
- Compare/contrast two passages concerning diction and details for the effect on the reader.
- How does the passage provide characterization and evaluation of one character over another? (i.e., diction, syntax, imagery, tone)
- What is the attitude of the speaker toward a particular subject?

- Analyze the effect of revision when given both the original and the revised version of a text.
- Analyze style and tone and how they are used to explore the author's attitudes toward his or her subject.
- How is the reader prepared for the conclusion of the piece?

You should be prepared to write an essay based on any of these prompts. Practice. Practice. Practice anticipating questions. Keep a running list of the kinds of questions your teacher asks.

Don't be thrown by the complexity of a passage. Remember, *you* choose the references you wish to incorporate into your essay. So, even if you haven't understood everything, you are still able to write an intelligent essay—*as long as you address the prompt* and refer to the parts of the passage you do understand.

Watch out for overconfidence when you see what you believe to be an easy question with an easy passage. You are going to have to work extra hard to find the nuances in the text that will allow you to write a mature essay.

Rating the Prose Passage Essay

You will be relieved to know that the rating of your essay is *not* based on whether or not the reader likes you or agrees with your point of view.

How Do the Test Readers Evaluate My Essay?

It's important to understand just what it is that goes into rating your essay. This is called a *rubric*, but don't let that word frighten you. A rubric is a word that simply refers to the rating standards that are set and used by the people who read the essays. These standards are fairly consistent, no matter what the prompt might be. The primary change is in the citing of the specifics in a particular prompt.

Let us assure you that, as experienced readers of the AP English exams, we know that the readers are trained to reward those things you do well in addressing the question. They are *not* looking to punish you. They are aware of the time constraints, and they read your essay just as your own instructor would read the first draft of an essay you wrote on a 40-minute exam. These readers look forward to an interesting, insightful, and well-constructed essay.

So, let's take a look at the following rubrics:

Prose Passage Essay Rubric

- 1 point for thesis/claim/introduction that is appropriate to the prompt
- 4 points for evidence/support of the thesis/claim
  - Clear and appropriate references to the text
  - Clear presentation of how the references relate to the thesis
- 1 point for complexity of the commentary and syntax

Remember, the essay is really a first draft. The test readers know this and approach each essay with this in mind.

AP Literature Prose Analysis Essay Scoring Guide

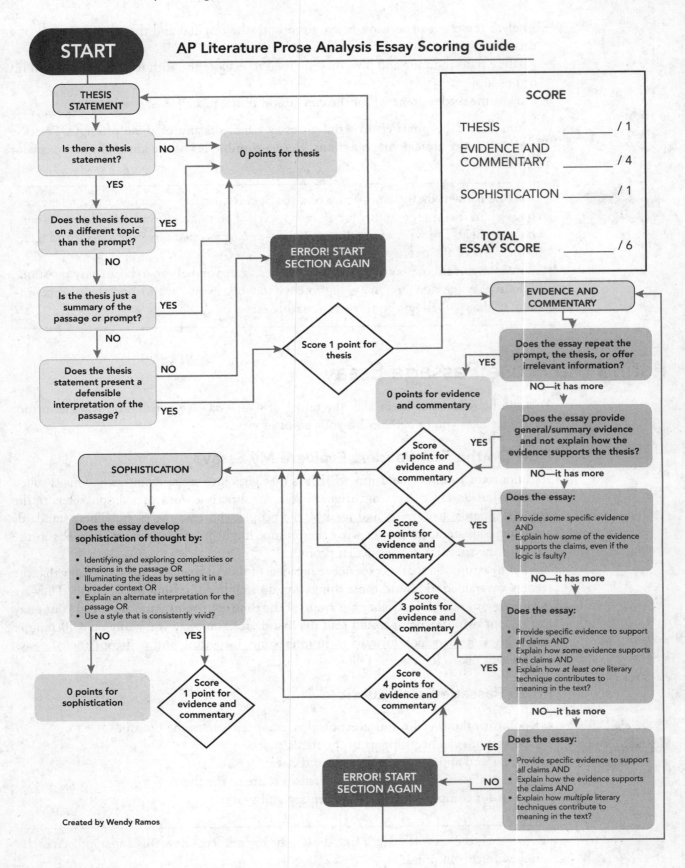

START

THESIS STATEMENT

Is there a thesis statement? — NO → 0 points for thesis

YES ↓

Does the thesis focus on a different topic than the prompt? — YES → ERROR! START SECTION AGAIN

NO ↓

Is the thesis just a summary of the passage or prompt? — YES → ERROR! START SECTION AGAIN

NO ↓

Does the thesis statement present a defensible interpretation of the passage? — NO → 0 points for thesis

YES → Score 1 point for thesis

SCORE

THESIS _____ / 1

EVIDENCE AND COMMENTARY _____ / 4

SOPHISTICATION _____ / 1

TOTAL ESSAY SCORE _____ / 6

EVIDENCE AND COMMENTARY

Does the essay repeat the prompt, the thesis, or offer irrelevant information? — YES → 0 points for evidence and commentary

NO—it has more ↓

Does the essay provide general/summary evidence and not explain how the evidence supports the thesis? — YES → Score 1 point for evidence and commentary

NO—it has more ↓

Does the essay:
- Provide *some* specific evidence AND
- Explain how *some* of the evidence supports the claims, even if the logic is faulty?

YES → Score 2 points for evidence and commentary

NO—it has more ↓

Does the essay:
- Provide specific evidence to support *all* claims AND
- Explain how *some* evidence supports the claims AND
- Explain how *at least one* literary technique contributes to meaning in the text?

YES → Score 3 points for evidence and commentary

NO—it has more ↓

Does the essay:
- Provide specific evidence to support *all* claims AND
- Explain how the evidence supports the claims AND
- Explain how *multiple* literary techniques contribute to meaning in the text?

YES → Score 4 points for evidence and commentary

NO → ERROR! START SECTION AGAIN

SOPHISTICATION

Does the essay develop sophistication of thought by:
- Identifying and exploring complexities or tensions in the passage OR
- Illuminating the ideas by setting it in a broader context OR
- Explain an alternate interpretation for the passage OR
- Use a style that is consistently vivid?

NO → 0 points for sophistication

YES → Score 1 point for evidence and commentary

Created by Wendy Ramos

Timing the Essay

Timing is crucial. With that in mind, here's a workable strategy:

- 1–3 minutes reading and "working the prompt."
- 5 minutes reading and making marginal notes about the passage. Try to isolate 2 quotations that strike you. This may give you your opening and closing.
- 5–10 minutes preparing to write. (Choose one or two of the following methods that you feel comfortable with.)
  - Underlining, bracketing, circling
  - Marginal notations
  - Charts or key word/one word/line number outlining
- 20–25 minutes to write your essay, based on your preparation.
- 3 minutes for proofreading.

Using a highlighter is not allowed during the exam. However, it is a strong tool for practice in critical reading.

Note: Throughout this book, the term **highlight** will also refer to underlining, circling, or bracketing.

> In the margin, note what time you should be finished with each essay. For example, the test starts at 1 P.M. You write 1:40 in the margin. Time to move on.

Working the Prompt

You can't write clearly unless you know *Why* you are writing and *What's Expected* of you. When you "Work the Prompt," you are maximizing both of these areas.

How Should I Go About Reading the Prose Prompt?

To bring the answer home to you, we will deconstruct a prompt for you now. (This is the same question that is in the Diagnostic/Master exam.) Plan to spend 1–3 minutes carefully reading the question. This will give you time to really digest what the question is asking you to do.

Here's the prompt:

In the following passage from his 1914 short story "The Dead," James Joyce presents an insight into the character of Gabriel. Read the passage carefully. Then, in a well-written essay analyze how Joyce uses literary strategies and techniques to reveal various aspects of Gabriel's complex character to the reader and to Gabriel himself.

Here are three reasons why you should do a 1–3-minute careful analysis of the prompt.

1. Once you know what is expected, you will read in a more directed manner.

2. Once you internalize the question, you will be sensitive to those details that will apply.

3. Once you know all the facets that need to be addressed, you will be able to write a complete essay demonstrating adherence to the topic.

> Topic adherence, which means sticking to the question, is key to achieving a high score.

Do this now. Underline, circle, or bracket the essential terms and elements in the prompt. Time yourself. How long did it take you? _____ Don't worry if it took you longer than 1–3 minutes in this first attempt. You will be practicing this technique throughout this review, and it will become almost second nature to you.

Compare our working of the prompt with yours.

In the following passage from his 1914 <u>short story</u> "<u>The Dead</u>," James Joyce presents an <u>insight</u> into the <u>character of Gabriel</u>. Read the passage carefully. Then, in a well-written essay <u>analyze</u> how Joyce uses <u>literary strategies and techniques</u> to reveal various <u>aspects of Gabriel's complex character</u> to the reader and to Gabriel himself.

In this prompt, anything else you may have highlighted is extraneous.

When the question uses the expression "such as," you are *not* required to use only those ideas presented; you are free to use your own selection of techniques and devices. Notice that the prompt requires more than one technique. One will not be enough. You *must* use more than one. If you fail to use more than one technique, no matter how well you present your answer, your essay will be incomplete.

Reading and Notating the Prose Passage

Depending on your style and comfort level, choose one of these approaches to your reading:

1. A. Read quickly to get the gist of the passage.
   B. Reread, using the visual and marginal notes approach.
2. A. Read slowly, using highlighting and making marginal notes.
   B. Reread to confirm that you understand the full impact of the passage.

Note: In both approaches, you *must* highlight and make marginal notes. There is no way to avoid this. Ignore what you don't immediately understand. It may become clear to you after you finish reading the passage. Practice. Practice. Concentrate on those parts of the passage that apply to what you highlighted in the prompt.

There are many ways to read and interpret any given passage. You have to choose which one to use and which specifics to include for support. Don't be rattled if there is leftover material.

We've reproduced the passage for you below so that you can practice both the reading and the process of deconstructing the text. Use highlighting, arrows, circles, underlining, notes, numbers, and whatever you need to make the connections clear to you.

Do this now. Spend 8–10 minutes working the material. *Do not skip this step.* It is time well spent and is a key to the high-score essay.

The Dead

She was fast asleep.

Gabriel, leaning on his elbow, looked for a few moments
unresentfully on her tangled hair and half-open mouth, listening to her
deep-drawn breath. So she had had that romance in her life: a man had
died for her sake. It hardly pained him now to think how poor a part   5
he, her husband, had played in her life. He watched her while she slept
as though he and she had never lived together as man and wife. His
curious eyes rested long upon her face and on her hair and, as he thought
of what she must have been then, in that time of her first girlish beauty,
a strange friendly pity for her entered his soul. He did not like to say   10
even to himself that her face was no longer beautiful but he knew that it
was no longer the face for which Michael Furey had braved death.

Perhaps she had not told him all the story. His eyes moved to the
chair over which she had thrown some of her clothes. A petticoat string
dangled to the floor. One boot stood upright, its limp upper fallen down: 15
the fellow of it lay upon its side. He wondered at his riot of emotions of
an hour before. From what had it proceeded? From his aunt's supper,
from his own foolish speech, from the wine and dancing, the merry-making
when saying good-night in the hall, the pleasure of the walk along the river
in the snow. Poor Aunt Julia! She, too, would soon be a shade with the   20
shade of Patrick Morkan and his horse. He had caught that haggard look
upon her face for a moment when she was singing *Arrayed for the Bridal*.
Soon, perhaps, he would be sitting in the same drawing-room dressed in
black, his silk hat on his knees. The blinds would be drawn down and
Aunt Kate would be sitting beside him, crying and blowing her nose and   25
telling him how Julia had died. He would cast about in his mind for some
words that might console her, and would find only lame and useless ones.
Yes, yes: that would happen very soon.

Now, compare your reading notes with what we've done below. Yours may vary from
ours, but the results of your note-taking should be similar in scope.

The Dead

who?

alike?

Bible? She was fast asleep. ← short sentence

angel? — Gabriel, leaning on his elbow, looked for a few moments   *time*

death?   *he hears*

time — unresentfully on her tangled hair and half-open mouth, listening to her

last? — deep-drawn breath. So she had had that romance in her life: a man had   *not him*

died for her sake. It hardly pained him now to think how poor a part   *he thinks*

detached? — he, her husband, had played in her life. He watched her while she slept   *he sees*

death — as though he and she had never lived together as man and wife. His   *death-like?*

time — curious eyes rested long upon her face and on her hair and, as he thought

of what she must have been then, in that time of her first girlish beauty,   *time—again*

he's kind? — a strange friendly pity for her entered his soul. He did not like to say — *back to death*
even to himself that her face was no longer beautiful but he knew that it — *time*
weak
coward? was no longer the face for which Michael Furey had braved death. — *fury?*
self-image   *time*   Perhaps she had not told him all the story. His eyes moved to the — *not a coward*

chair over which she had thrown some of her clothes. A petticoat string

dangled to the floor. One boot stood upright, its limp upper fallen down: — *weak?*
lack of
the fellow of it lay upon its side. He wondered at his riot of emotions of — *control?*
time — an hour before. From what had it proceeded? From his aunt's supper, — *afraid to let go?*
self-image
death? from his own foolish speech, from the wine and dancing, the merry-making

when saying good-night in the hall, the pleasure of the walk along the river

cold death? in the snow. Poor Aunt Julia! She, too, would soon be a shade with the — *time*
ghost?
cold shade of Patrick Morkan and his horse. He had caught that haggard look — *cold*
time upon her face for a moment when she was singing *Arrayed for the Bridal*.
time Soon, perhaps, he would be sitting in the same drawing-room dressed in — *mourning*
death — black, his silk hat on his knees. The blinds would be drawn down and — *closed off*
mourning
Aunt Kate would be sitting beside him, crying and blowing her nose and
death — telling him how Julia had died. He would cast about in his mind for some — *self-image*
weak? *detached*
uncertain? words that might console her, and would find only lame and useless ones.
Yes, yes: that would happen very soon.——— *time* — *weakness*

After you have marked the passage, review the prompt. You are asked to look for ways Joyce reveals Gabriel's character. When you consult your notes, certain categories will begin to pop out at you. These can be the basis for the development of the body of your essay. For example, we saw details and images that support the concepts of:

- Death
- Passivity
- Time
- Detachment
- Insecurity

In addition, stylistically, we noticed the use of short sentences.

Here's how one category developed using the notations made on the passage. Notice that we have ignored notes that did not apply to the prompt.

Concept: Time

Words/Phrases from the Text:

"a few moments"   "no longer the face"
"had had that romance"   "an hour before"
"he thought of what she must   "soon be a shade"
  have been then"   "for a moment"
"girlish beauty"   "soon"
"no longer beautiful"   "that would happen very soon"

Conclusion: Gabriel moves from the distant past to the near future. He becomes aware of the change in the marital relationship with his wife and with his own passage.

Your Turn

Now you choose a concept you are able to explore and defend that reveals Gabriel's character.

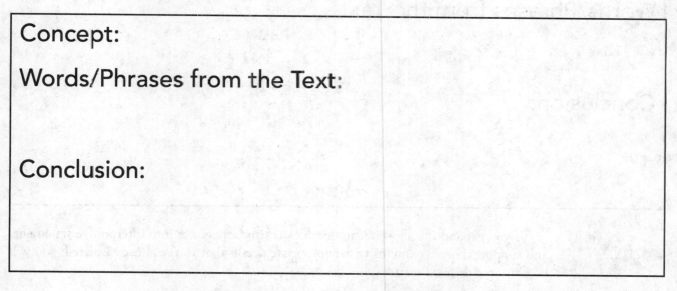

Concept:

Words/Phrases from the Text:

Conclusion:

In response to the prompt, we have decided that the techniques/devices we will analyze are:

- Imagery
- Diction
- Style
- Motif

Here's one technique/device and how it is developed in the passage. Again, notice that we use our margin notes to trace this development.

Technique/Device: Imagery

Words/Phrases from the Text:

the title "The Dead"   Gabriel's very name
"entered his soul"   "braved death"
"fallen down"   "good-night"
"in the snow"   "would soon be a shade"
"dressed in black"   "the blinds would be drawn"
"crying and blowing her nose"

Conclusion: These images foreshadow and emphasize that there is a coldness and a loss in relationships and self-image.

Your Turn

Now you choose the technique/device you are able to explore and defend that reveals Gabriel's character.

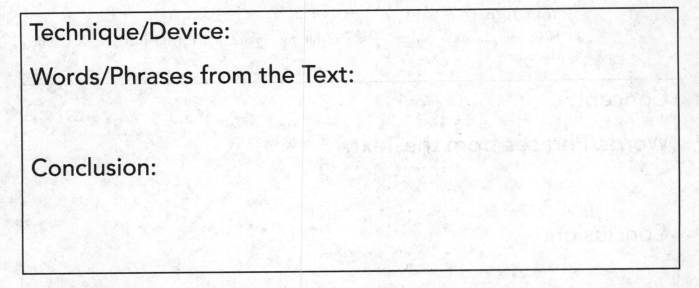

Technique/Device:

Words/Phrases from the Text:

Conclusion:

KEY IDEA

If you expand the above techniques/devices and categories into interpretive statements and support those statements with appropriate details that you've already isolated, you will be writing a detailed essay.

Writing the Opening Paragraph

Your opening statement is the one that sets the tone of your essay and possibly raises the expectations of the reader. Spend time on your first paragraph to maximize your score.

Make certain that your topic is very clear. This reinforces the idea that you fully understand what is expected of you and what you will communicate to the reader. Generally, identify both the text and its author in this first paragraph.

A suggested approach is to relate a direct quotation from the passage to the topic.

TIP

Consider the "philosophy of firsts." It is a crucial strategy to spend focused time on the first part of the question and on the first paragraph of the essay because:

1. It establishes the direction and tone of your essay.

2. It gives you the guidelines for what to develop in your essay.

3. It connects you to the reader.

Remember our philosophy: **In the Beginning:** if you focus on the beginning, the rest will fall into place. A wonderful thing happens after much practice, highlighting, and note-taking. Your mind starts to focus automatically. Trust us on this. It is the winning edge that can take an average essay and raise it to a higher level.

Do this now. Take 5 minutes to write your opening paragraph for "The Dead" prompt. Write quickly, referring to your notes.

Let's check what you've written:

Highlight these points to see if you've done them. You may be surprised at what is actually there.

• Have you included author and title? _____ Yes _____ No

• Have you addressed the character of Gabriel? _____ Yes _____ No

- Have you specifically mentioned the techniques you will refer to in your essay?

_____ Yes _____ No

Here are four sample opening paragraphs that address all of the criteria:

A

In "The Dead" by James Joyce, the character Gabriel is revealed through diction, point of view, and imagery as he watches his wife sleep.

B

Poor Gabriel! Who would have thought he knew so little about himself and his life. And yet, in "The Dead," James Joyce, through diction, point of view, and imagery, makes it clear to the reader and to Gabriel that there is much to reveal about his character.

C

"Yes, yes: that would happen very soon." And, yes, very soon the reader of the excerpt from Joyce's "The Dead" gets to know the character of Gabriel. Through diction, point of view, and imagery, we are introduced to Gabriel and what he thinks of himself.

D

"The Dead." How apt a title. James Joyce turns his reader into a fly on the wall as Gabriel is about to realize the many losses in his life. Death pervades the passage, from his sleeping wife to his dying aunt.

Each of these opening paragraphs is an acceptable beginning to an AP Literature exam essay. Note what each of these paragraphs accomplishes:

- Each has identified the title and author.
- Each has stated which techniques/devices will be used.
- Each has stated the purpose of analyzing these techniques/devices.

Now, note what is different about each opening paragraph:

- Sample **A** restates the question without anything extra. It is to the point, so much so that it does nothing more than repeat the question. It's correct, but it does not really pique the reader's interest. (Use this type of opening if you feel unsure of or uncomfortable with the prompt.)
- Sample **B** reveals the writer's attitude toward the subject. The writer has already determined that Gabriel is flawed and indicates an understanding of how Gabriel's character is revealed in the passage.
- Sample **C**, with its direct quotation, places the reader immediately into the passage. The reader quickly begins to hear the writer's voice through his or her choice of words (diction).
- Sample **D**, at first glance, reveals a mature, confident writer who is not afraid to _imply_ the prompt's criteria.

Note: There are many other types of opening paragraphs that could do the job as well. The paragraphs above are just a few samples.

Into which of the above samples would you classify your opening paragraph?

Writing the Body

When you write the body of your essay, take only 20–25 minutes. Time yourself and try your best to finish within that time frame.

Since this is practice, don't panic if you can't complete the essay within the allotted time. You will become more and more comfortable with the tasks presented to you as you gain experience with this type of question.

What Should I Include in the Body of the Prose Passage Essay?

1. Obviously, this is where you present your interpretation and the points you wish to make that are related to the prompt.

2. Use specific references and details from the passage.
   - Don't always paraphrase the original; refer directly to it.
   - Place quotation marks around those words and phrases that you extract from the passage.

3. Use "connective tissue" in your essay to establish adherence to the question.
   - Use the repetition of key ideas from your opening paragraph.
   - Try using "echo words" (i.e., synonyms, such as death/loss/passing or character/ persona/personality).
   - Create transitions from one paragraph to the next.

To understand the process, carefully read the following sample paragraphs. Each develops one of the categories and techniques/devices asked for in the prompt. Notice the specific references and the "connective tissue." Also, notice that details that do not apply to the prompt have been ignored.

A
This paragraph develops **imagery**.

Joyce creates imagery to lead his reader to sense the cloud of death that pervades Gabriel's world. From its very title "The Dead," the reader is prepared for loss. Just what has Gabriel lost: his wife, his confidence, his job, a friend, a relative, what? As his "wife slept," Gabriel sees her "half-open mouth" and "listens" to her "deep-drawn breath." The reader almost senses this to be a death watch. The images about the room reinforce this sense of doom. One boot is "limp" and the other is "upon its side." Picturing the future, Gabriel sees a "drawing-room dressed in black" with blinds "drawn down" and his Aunt Kate "crying" and "telling him how Julia had died." And to underscore his own feelings of internal lifelessness, he can only find "lame and useless" words of comfort.

B
This paragraph develops the **motif of time**.

Time is a constant from the beginning to the end of the passage. In the first paragraph, Gabriel is in the present while thinking of the past. He is an observer, watching his wife as he, himself, is observed by the narrator, and as we, as readers, observe the entire scene. Time moves the reader and Gabriel through the experience. Immediately, we spend a "few moments" with Gabriel as he goes back and forth in time assessing his relationship with his wife. He recognizes she "had had romance in her life." But, "it hardly pains him now." He thinks of what she had been "then" in her "girlish" beauty, which may indicate his own aging. His "strange friendly pity," because she is "no longer beautiful," may be self-pity, as well. In the next paragraph, we are with Gabriel as he reflects on his emotional "riot" only an hour before. However, he jumps to the future because he can't sustain self-examination. He chooses to allow himself to jump to this future and a new subject—Aunt Julia's death. In this future, he continues to see only his inability and incompetence. For Gabriel, all this will happen "very soon."

C

This passage develops **diction**.

Gabriel appears to be a man who is on the outside of his life. Joyce's diction reveals his passive nature. Gabriel "looked on" and "watched" his wife sleeping. He spent time "listening to her breath" and was "hardly pained by his role in her life." His eyes "rest" on her, and he "thinks of the past." All of Gabriel's actions are as weak as a "limp" and "fallen down" boot, "inert in the face of life." He is in direct contrast to Michael Furey, who has "braved death." And he knows this about himself. The narrator's diction reveals that Gabriel "did not like to say even to himself," implying that he is too weak to face the truth.

Later in the text, Gabriel's word choice further indicates his insecurity. He is troubled by his "riot of emotions," his "foolish speech." It is obvious that Gabriel will not take such risks again.

D

This passage develops **style**.

Joyce's very straightforward writing style supports the conclusions he wishes the reader to draw about the character of Gabriel. Most sentences are in the subject/verb, simple sentence form, reflecting the plain, uncomplicated character of Gabriel.

Joyce employs a third person narrator to further reinforce Gabriel's detachment from his own circumstances. We watch him observing his own life with little or no connection on his part. He wonders at his "riot of emotions." All this is presented without Joyce using obvious poetic devices. This punctuates the lack of "romance" in Gabriel's life when compared with that of Michael Furey.

> Start a study group. Approach an essay as a team. After you've deconstructed the prompt, have each person write a paragraph on a separate area of the question. Then come together and discuss what was written. You'll be amazed at how much fun this is because the work will carry you away. This is a chance to explore exciting ideas.
>
> Again, sharing your writing with members of your class or study group will allow you to gain experience and find a comfort zone with requirements and possibilities.

We urge you to spend more time developing the body paragraphs than worrying about a concluding paragraph, especially one that begins with "In conclusion," or "In summary." In such a brief essay, the reader will have no problem remembering what you have already stated. It is not necessary to repeat yourself in a summary-type final paragraph.

If you want to make a final statement, try to link your ideas to a particularly effective line or image from the passage.

Note: Look at the last line of Sample **B** on motif. For Gabriel, all this will happen "very soon." This final sentence would be fine as the conclusion to the essay. A conclusion does not have to be a paragraph. It can be the writer's final remark or observation presented in a sentence or two.

Do this now. Write the body of your essay. Time yourself. Allow 15–20 minutes to complete this task.

Sample Student Essays

Following are two actual student essays followed by a rubric and comments on each. Read both of the samples in sequence to clarify the differences between "high" and "mid-range" essays.

Student Essay A

A picture is worth a thousand words, but James Joyce manages to paint a pretty vivid one in only two short paragraphs. Joyce offers tremendous insight into the character of Gabriel in the short story "The Dead." He captures the essence of a scene laden with death and laced with tones of despair and hopelessness. By employing third person narration alternating with a stream of consciousness, Joyce demonstrates his abilities to delve deep into Gabriel's mind, illustrating this somewhat detached disposition and low self-image.

The passage takes us through Gabriel's reflections upon past, present, and future events while his inner character unfolds. Joyce's careful use of diction suggests that Gabriel has emotionally closed himself off to the world as he tries to cope with some aforementioned incident. He was "hardly pained" to think about a situation which caused a "riot of emotions" just a little earlier on that evening. Here, Joyce is emphasizing Gabriel's way of coping with an unfavorable event by blocking it out. He continues to "unresentfully" reflect upon what had occurred, closing himself off from any pain he obviously experienced a short while ago.

With the powerful omniscience of a third-person narrator, Joyce is able to describe the workings of Gabriel's inner consciousness without writing from the first-person point of view. Gabriel further detaches himself as he thinks about his wife. He watches her from the point of view of an outsider, as if they were never married. The mere fact that Gabriel is able to do this suggests that he and his wife do not have a truly loving relationship. This assertion is underscored by the "friendly" pity Gabriel feels for his wife, emphasizing the lack of true love in their relationship. Gabriel later questions his wife's honesty, further emphasizing a troubled relationship. The reader may be inclined to infer that Gabriel is completely devoid of compassion; however, this idea is refuted. Gabriel proceeds to express an element of sorrow when he thinks back to his wife's youth and beauty.

The evening's events had evidently triggered some type of emotional outburst which Gabriel cannot stop thinking about. His mental state is paralleled by the chaotic state of disorder in the room he is in. With a masterful control of language and syntax, Joyce describes in short, choppy sentences the array of clothing strewn around the room. This is followed by one of the longest sentences in the passage. Joyce reveals this series of events all at once, paralleling Gabriel's release of a multitude of emotions at once.

Joyce weaves a motif of darkness and death into the story. His aunt's "haggard" appearance ironically catches Gabriel's attention during the recitation of <u>Arrayed for the Bridal</u>, a seemingly happy song. This image of happiness and

marriage is further contrasted with images of the woman's funeral and a detailed
description of how Gabriel will mourn for her. Joyce also takes time to underscore
Gabriel's low self-esteem, in that he will only think of "lame and useless" words at a
time when comforting tones are necessary. He is essentially describing himself,   40
since it has been established that he failed as a husband and that he is emotionally
distraught even though he blocks out the pain he feels. "The blinds would be drawn
down," Gabriel says, as he describes both the room at his aunt's funeral and his
mental state of affairs.

    The true originator of "stream-of-consciousness" techniques, Joyce delves   45
deep into Gabriel's mind, describing his wide range of emotions and state of mind.
His powerful diction reveals a great deal about Gabriel's character while his implied
insights penetrate into the reader's mind, reinforcing the abstract meanings behind
the actions and events that transpire throughout the course of his story.

Student Essay B

    In the excerpt from the short story "The Dead" from Dubliners by James
Joyce, the author describes some personality traits of the character Gabriel as he
sits watching a sleeping woman. The point of view from which this excerpt is
expressed helps the reader to get to know Gabriel because the narrator is omniscient
and knows how Gabriel perceives things and what he is thinking. With the use of   5
many literary devices such as imagery, diction, and syntax, the reader is able to see
that Gabriel is an observant and a reflective person, but he is also detached.

    Gabriel comes across as observant, because throughout the entire passage he
is observing a woman, his wife, sleeping. He scans the room looking over
everything and taking note of everything. An example of this is looking at "her   10
tangled hair and half-open mouth, listening to her deep-drawn breath." The author
uses the technique of syntax ("deep-drawn breath" and "half-open mouth") in the
above quotation to show us exactly what Gabriel is seeing. Gabriel notices many
details, and they are described so that the reader can clearly formulate a picture of
what he is gazing at. This imagery can be seen in lines such as the one where the   15
woman's boots are being described. "One boot stood upright, its limp upper fallen
down: the fellow of it lay upon the side." The diction used such as "limp" and
"upright," are concrete words that create clear pictures. Another reason that Gabriel
comes across as observant is because he catches and notices little things. For
example, he "caught" the "haggard look" on his Aunt Julia's face.   20

    Resulting from the fact that Gabriel is observant, he is also reflective. He
thinks over past events that had happened and wonders what caused them and why
he did what he did. In the first paragraph he reflects on his wife's "fading beauty,"
what she used to look like, and the story of the death of Michael Furey. He realizes
that it is a possibility that she had not told him the entire story concerning the boy's   25
death. He further reflects when he is thinking about his emotional outburst. He
asks himself many questions including "From what had it proceeded?"

    A feeling of detachment is also present. The way he looks at his wife "as
though he and she had never lived together as man and wife" shows that he is
viewing his own life from an objective standpoint. He is able to look at his own life   30
as though it wasn't his. The sentence that reads "it hardly pained him now to think
how poor a part he, her husband, had played in her life," further exemplifies this feeling
of detachment. Feelings that he used to feel no longer even touched him. He was able
to recognize them, yet remain separate. In the second paragraph Gabriel continues

to come across as remote. He is able to picture and describe in great detail the death and funeral of his Aunt Julia. He narrates the future drastic event in a matter-of-fact way. Gabriel goes so far as to describe what he will be thinking at the time of his Aunt Julia's death which is "he would cast about in his mind for some words that might console her (his Aunt Kate), and would find only lame and useless ones." This statement finalizes the idea that Gabriel is a person who is, at least to some degree, detached from his own life.

Even though the passage is fairly short, the author is able to impart a fair amount of information concerning the character Gabriel. It becomes apparent that he possesses the qualities of observance, reflection, and detachment. These qualities are all interconnected because of the fact that he is observant leading to his ability to reflect on his actions and actions of others. This in turn leads to his detachment, because when he reflects on his life he does it from the standpoint of a third-person narrator. The author's use of literary techniques helps to convey these personality traits of Gabriel to a reader.

Let's take a look at a set of rubrics for this prose passage essay. (If you want to see actual AP rubrics as used in a recent AP Lit. exam, log on to the College Board website: www.collegeboard.org/ap). As you probably know, essays are rated on a 6–1 scale, with 6 the highest and 1 the lowest. Since we are not there with you to personally rate your essay and to respond to your style and approach, we are going to list the criteria for high-, middle-, and low-range papers. These criteria are based on our experience with rubrics and reading AP Literature essays.

A HIGH-range essay can be a 6 or a 5. MIDDLE refers to essays in the 4–3 range. And the LOW-scoring essays are rated 2–1.

After reading the following rubrics, evaluate the two essays that you have just read.

Rating the Student Essays

High-Range Essay (5, 6)
- The thesis statement presents a defensible assertion related to the prompt.
- The thesis clearly presents a possible interpretation and indicates how the support will be developed (line of reasoning).
- Distinguishes between what Gabriel acknowledges about himself and what the reader comes to know about him.
- Explores the complexity of Gabriel's character.
- Identifies and analyzes Joyce's literary techniques, such as imagery, diction, point of view, motif, and style.
- Cites specific references to the passage.
- Illustrates and supports the points being made.
- The line of reasoning is clear, well-organized, and coherent.
- Relates points made to a broader context.
- Reflects the ability to manipulate language at an advanced level.
- Contains only minor errors or flaws, if any.

Middle-Range Essay (3, 4)

- Refers accurately to the prompt.
- Refers accurately to the literary devices used by Joyce.
- Provides a less thorough analysis of Gabriel's character than the higher-rated paper.
- Is less adept at linking techniques to the purpose of the passage and a broader context.
- Demonstrates writing that is adequate to convey the writer's intent.
- May not be sensitive to the implications about Gabriel's character.

Low-Range Essay (1, 2)

- Does not respond adequately to the prompt.
- Demonstrates insufficient and/or inaccurate understanding of the passage.
- Does not link literary devices to Gabriel's character.
- Underdevelops and/or inaccurately analyzes literary techniques.
- Fails to demonstrate an understanding of Gabriel's character.
- Demonstrates weak control of the elements of diction, syntax, and organization.

How would you rate these student essays?

Now, compare your evaluation of the two student essays with ours.

Note: With specific reference to the 6-point rubric, we will use the following abbreviations to indicate into which column the comment would fall: **T** = **thesis,** **E** = **evidence,** **C** = **complexity,** **S** = **sophistication**.

Student Essay A

This is a high-range paper for the following reasons:

- Thesis presents a defensible assertion that is clearly related to the prompt and indicates a probable line of reasoning. **T**
- Indicates perceptive, subtle analysis (line 8). **E/C**
- Maintains excellent topic adherence (lines 9, 17, 28, 39). **E**
- Uses good "connective tissue" (repetition of key words). **S**
- Chooses good specific references (lines 11, 12, 21, 35). **E**
- Knows how to distinguish between the author and the narrator. **C**
- Understands point of view well. **E**
- Makes suggestions and inferences (lines 7, 20). **C/S**
- Demonstrates good critical thinking. **S**
- Is perceptive about syntax and the style of the author (lines 27–33). **S**
- Links techniques with character (line 34). **C**
- Demonstrates mature language manipulation (line 34). **S**
- Understands function of diction and motif (lines 40–44). **S**

It's best to omit extraneous judgmental words from your essay (line 45).

This is obviously a mature, critical reader and writer. Using subtle inferences and implications, the writer demonstrates an understanding of the character of Gabriel both as Joyce presents him and as Gabriel views himself. There is nothing extraneous or repetitious in this essay. Each point leads directly and compellingly to the next aspect of Gabriel's character.

Student Essay B

This is a middle-range essay for the following reasons:

- Sets up an introduction that indicates the line of reasoning, but it neglects to clearly set up the required discussion of how Gabriel views himself. T
- Immediately establishes that the essay will address Gabriel's character as drawn by the narrator and seen by the reader. T
- Addresses three aspects of Gabriel's character without fully developing the analysis of literary techniques. E
- Adheres to the essay's topic. E
- Uses "connective tissue" (lines 21, 28). E
- Uses "echo words" (lines 8, 9, 10). E
- Uses citations from the passages. E
- Isolates some details to illustrate Gabriel's character (lines 31–32, 39). C
- Lacks development of literary technique in paragraph 4. E/C
- Displays faulty diction and syntax. S
- Does not develop an important part of the prompt—how Gabriel views himself. E/C
- Incorporates faulty logic at times (lines 44–49). C

This essay is a solid, middle-range paper. The writer has a facility with literary analysis. Even though there are flashes of real insight, they are not sustained throughout the essay. There is a strong opening paragraph that makes it clear to the reader what the topic of the paper is. The writer obviously grasps Gabriel's character and the needed details to support the character analysis. But the weakness in this paper is the writer's incomplete development of the relationship of literary techniques to character analysis.

Note: Both essays have concluding paragraphs that are repetitive and largely unnecessary. It is best to avoid this type of ending.

Your Turn

How about sharing these samples with members of your class or study group and discussing possible responses?

Try a little reverse psychology. Now that you are thoroughly familiar with this passage, construct two or three alternative prompts. (Walk a little in the examiner's shoes.) This will help you gain insight into the process of test-making. Create two questions of your own. (See the Types of Prose Passage Essay Questions section of this chapter for ideas.)

1ˢᵗ alternative prompt for "The Dead"

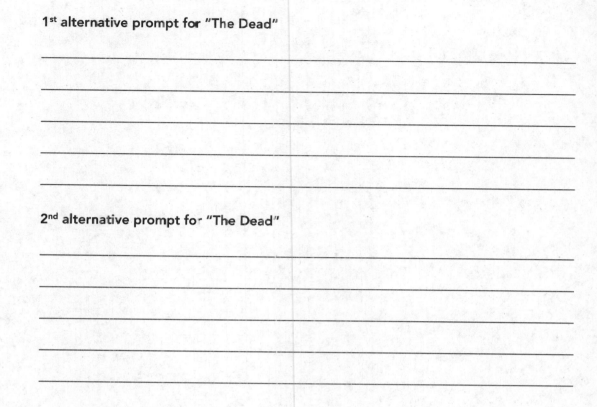

2ⁿᵈ alternative prompt for "The Dead"

Rapid Review

After you've absorbed the ideas in this chapter, the following points will provide you with a quick refresher when needed:

- Familiarize yourself with the types of prose questions (prompts).
- Highlight the prompt and understand all the required tasks.
- Time your essay carefully.
- Spend sufficient time "working the passage" before you begin writing.
- Mark up the passage.
- Create a strong opening paragraph.
- Refer often to the passage
- Use concrete details and quotes to support your ideas.
- Always stay on topic.
- Avoid plot summary.
- Include transitions and echo words.
- Check the models and rubrics for guidance for self-evaluation.
- Practice—vary the question and your approach.
- Share ideas with others.

CHAPTER 6

The Poetry Essay

IN THIS CHAPTER

Summary: Examination of the poetry essay and its purpose as it is presented in the AP English Literature exam

KEY IDEA

Key Ideas

✪ Learn the types of poetry prompts you might encounter in the AP English Literature exam
✪ Learn the basics of reading and notating a given poem
✪ Learn the basics of constructing your response to the poetry prompt
✪ Learn about the rubrics and rating of the AP poetry essays
✪ Examine model student essays
✪ Learn how rubrics were used to rate student essays

Introduction to the Poetry Essay

It's obvious to any reader that poetry is different from prose. And, writing about each is different also. This chapter will guide you through the expectations and processes associated with the AP Poetry section.

The free-response poetry essay will present a complete poem or a passage from a poem of approximately 100 to 300 words. According to The College Board, you will be expected to:

• respond to the prompt with a thesis that presents a defensible interpretation
• select and use evidence to support your line of reasoning
• explain how the evidence supports your line of reasoning
• use appropriate syntax and diction in communicating your argument

The following is the format for the poetry prompt:

"In the following poem [or excerpt from poem] by [author, date of publication], the speaker [comment on what is being addressed in the poem]. Read the poem carefully. Then, in a well-written essay, analyze how [author] uses [poetic or literary] elements and techniques to [convey/portray/develop a thematic, topical, or structural aspect of the poem that is complex and specific to the passage of the poem provided]." (*AP English Literature and Composition Course and Exam Description*, The College Board, 2020, p. 138.)

What Is the Purpose of the Poetry Essay?

The College Board wants to determine your facility in reading and interpreting a sustained piece of literature. You are required to understand the text and to analyze those techniques and devices the poet uses to achieve his or her purpose.

The AP Lit exam is designed to allow you to demonstrate your ease and fluency with terminology, interpretation, and analysis. The level of your writing should be a direct reflection of your critical thinking.

The AP Lit exam is looking for connections between analysis and interpretation. For example, when you find a metaphor, you should identify it and connect it to the poet's intended purpose or meaning. You shouldn't just list items as you locate them. You must connect them to your interpretation.

> Before beginning to work with an actual poem, read the review of processes and terms in the Comprehensive Review section of this book. Make certain to complete some of the activities in that section.

Types of Prompts Used for the Poetry Essay

Not every poetry essay prompt is the same. Familiarizing yourself with the various types is critical. This familiarity will both increase your confidence and provide you with a format for poetry analysis.

What Will the Poetry Prompt Ask Me to Do?

Let's look at several typical tasks that have been used for the poetry essay in the AP Literature exam in the past:

- How does the language of the poem reflect the speaker's perceptions, and how does that language determine the reader's perception?
- How does the poet reveal character? (i.e., diction, sound devices, imagery, allusion)
- Discuss how poetic elements, such as language, structure, imagery, and point of view, convey meaning in a poem.
- Relate the imagery, form, or theme of a particular section of a poem to another part of that same poem. Discuss changing attitude or perception of speaker or reader.
- Analyze a poem's extended metaphor and how it reveals the poet's or speaker's attitude.
- Discuss the way of life revealed in a poem. Refer to such poetic elements as tone, imagery, symbol, and verse form.
- Discuss the poet's changing reaction to the subject developed in the poem.
- Discuss how the form of the poem affects its meaning.
- NOTE: There will be NO "paired poem prompts" on the exam.

You should be prepared to write an essay based on any of these prompts. Apply these questions to poems you read throughout the year. Practice anticipating questions. Keep a running list of the kinds of questions your teacher asks. Practice. Practice.

Timing and Planning the Poetry Essay

Successful writing is directly related to both thought and structure, and you will need to consider the following concepts related to pre-writing.

How Should I Plan to Spend My Time Writing the Poetry Essay?

Remember, timing is crucial. With this in mind, here's a workable strategy:

- 1–3 minutes reading and "working the prompt."
- 5 minutes reading and making marginal notes about the poem. Try to isolate two references that strike you. This may give you your opening and closing.
- 5–10 minutes preparing to write. (Choose one or two of the following methods that you feel comfortable with.)
  - Highlighting, underlining, circling, bracketing
  - Marginal mapping (see Chapter 5 for samples)
  - Key word/one word/line number outlining
  - Numerical clustering
- 20–25 minutes to write your essay, based on your preparation.
- 3 minutes for proofreading.

Working the Prompt

It is important to understand that the quality of your essay greatly depends upon your correctly addressing the prompt.

How Should I Go About Reading the Poetry Prompt?

As we did in the prose section, we will deconstruct a poetry essay prompt for you now. (This is the same question that is in the Diagnostic/Master exam earlier in this book.)

You should plan to spend 1–3 minutes carefully reading the question. This will give you time to really digest what the question is asking you to do.

Here's the prompt:

In her 1987 poem "On the Subway," Sharon Olds brings two worlds into close proximity. Read the poem carefully. Then, in a well-written essay analyze how Olds uses poetic elements and techniques to develop the complex contrasts and insights the speaker comes to as a result of the experience.

In the margin, note what time you should be finished with this essay. For example, the test starts at 1 P.M. You write 1:40 in the margin. Time to move on.

Here are three reasons why you should do a 1–3-minute careful analysis of the prompt:

1. Once you know what is expected, you will read in a more directed manner.
2. Once you internalize the question, you will be sensitive to the details that will apply as you read the poem.
3. Once you know all the facets that need to be addressed, you will be able to write a complete essay that demonstrates adherence to the topic.

Do this now. Highlight, circle, or underline the essential terms and elements in the prompt. Time yourself. How long did it take you?

Compare our highlighting of the prompt with yours.

In her 1987 poem "<u>On the Subway</u>," <u>Sharon Olds</u> brings <u>two worlds into close proximity</u>. Read the poem carefully. Then, in a well-written essay analyze how Olds uses <u>poetic elements and techniques</u> to develop the <u>complex contrasts and insights</u> the speaker comes to as a result of the experience.

In this prompt, anything else you may have highlighted is extraneous.

You are free to use your own selection of techniques and devices. Notice that the prompt requires more than one technique. One will not be enough. You must use more than one. If you fail to use more than one technique, no matter how well you present your answer, your essay will be incomplete.

Reading and Notating the Poetry Selection

Finally, read the poem. Depending on your style and comfort level, choose one of these approaches to your reading:

1. A. Read quickly to get the gist of the poem.
    B. Reread, using the highlighting and marginal notes approach.

2. A. Read slowly, as if speaking aloud. Let the structure of the poem help you with meaning. (See the terms *enjambment* and *caesura* in the Glossary at the back of this book.)
    B. Reread to confirm that you understand the full impact of the poem. Do your highlighting and make marginal notes.

Note: In both approaches, you *must* highlight and make marginal notes. There is no way to avoid this. Ignore what you don't immediately understand. It may become clear to you after reading the poem. Practice. Practice. Concentrate on those parts of the poem that apply to what you highlighted in the prompt.

There are many ways to read and interpret any poetry. You have to choose your own approach and which specifics to include for support. *Don't be rattled if there is leftover material.*

We've reproduced the poem for you below so that you can practice both the reading and the process of deconstructing the text. Use highlighting, arrows, circles, underlining, notes, numbers, and whatever you need to make the connections clear to you.

Do this now. Spend 8–10 minutes working the material. *Do not skip this step*. It is time well spent and is a key to the high-score essay.

On the Subway
by Sharon Olds

The boy and I face each other
His feet are huge, in black sneakers
laced with white in a complex pattern like a
set of intentional scars. We are stuck on

opposite sides of the car, a couple of   5
molecules stuck in a rod of light
rapidly moving through darkness.
He has the casual cold look of a mugger,
alert under hooded lids. He is wearing
red, like the inside of the body   10
exposed. I am wearing dark fur, the
whole skin of an animal taken and
used. I look at his raw face,
he looks at my fur coat, and I don't
know if I am in his power—   15
he could take my coat so easily, my
briefcase, my life—
or if he is in my power, the way I am
living off his life, eating the steak
he does not eat, as if I am taking   20
the food from his mouth. And he is black
and I am white, and without meaning or
trying to I must profit from his darkness,
the way he absorbs the murderous beams of the
nation's heart, as black cotton   25
absorbs the heat of the sun and holds it. There is
no way to know how easy this
white skin makes my life, this
life he could take so easily and
break across his knee like a stick the way his   30
own back is being broken, the
rod of his soul that at birth was dark and
fluid and rich as the heart of a seedling
ready to thrust up into any available light

KEY IDEA

Now compare your reading notes with what we've done below. Yours may vary from ours, but the results of your note-taking should be similar in scope.

On the Subway
by Sharon Olds

first part = narrator as observer

first person

oppositions

The <u>boy and I</u> face each other

<u>His feet are huge</u>, in <u>black sneakers</u>

<u>laced with white</u> in a <u>complex pattern like a</u> — *dark*

light — <u>set of intentional scars</u>. We are <u>stuck</u> on — *no control*

violence? — <u>opposite sides</u> of the car, a couple of   5

opposite sides of the "tracks" — molecules stuck in a <u>rod of light</u>

rapidly moving <u>through darkness</u>. — *light and dark metaphor*

metaphor — He has the casual cold look of a <u>mugger</u>. — *narrator's fear*

simile — alert under <u>hooded lids</u>. <u>He</u> is wearing

<u>red, like the inside of the body</u> — *surgical, clinical, autopsy*   10

exposed. I am wearing <u>dark fur</u>, the — *hunting and skinning*

whole <u>skin of an animal taken and</u>

<u>used</u>. I look at his <u>raw face</u>, — *violence*

he looks at <u>my fur coat</u>, and <u>I don't</u>

<u>know if I am in his power</u>—   *fear of possible violence*   15

he could take my coat so easily, my

briefcase, my life—

break!!! could narrator be the aggressor? looks for deeper implications — or if he is in my power, the way I am

<u>living off his life, eating the steak</u>

he does not eat, as if I am taking   *animal imagery—again hunting and skinning*   20

<u>the food from his mouth</u>. And <u>he is black</u>

narrator as philosopher? — and <u>I am white</u>, and <u>without meaning</u> or — *light and dark imagery*

trying to <u>I must profit from his darkness</u>,

the way <u>he absorbs the murderous beams of the</u> — *judgmental*

light and dark — nation's heart, as black cotton — *simile*   25

<u>absorbs the heat of the sun and holds it</u>. There is

light and dark — no way to know <u>how easy this</u>

<u>white skin makes my life</u>, this — *guilt!*

life he could take so easily and

reference to slavery? — <u>break across his knee like a stick the way his</u> — *simile*   30

<u>own back is being broken</u>, the

<u>rod of his soul</u> that at birth <u>was dark and</u>

reference to discrimination? — <u>fluid and rich as the heart of a seedling</u> — *simile*

<u>ready to thrust up into any available light</u> — *light and dark*

After you have marked the poem, review the prompt. When you look at your notes, certain categories will begin to pop out at you. These can be the basis for the development of the body of your essay. For example:

- Light and dark imagery
- Speaker's insights
- Contrast in status
- Metaphors
- Animal imagery
- Implied violence
- Shift in middle of poem
- Similes

Here's how we saw one category develop in the poem. Notice that we have ignored notes that did not apply to the prompt.

Category: Light and dark imagery

Examples:

"black sneakers"   "laced with white"   "rod of light"
"moving through darkness"   "profit from his darkness"   "he is black"
"and I am white"   "heat of the sun"   "murderous beams"
"black cotton"   "thrust up into any   "dark and fluid"
"how easy this white skin   available light"
    makes my life"

Comment: The use of black and white imagery emphasizes the opposite ends of the spectrum represented by the speaker and the boy.

Your Turn

Now you choose a category that seems to pop out at you and trace its use through the poem.

Category:

Examples:

Comment:

We chose to examine poetic devices used in "On the Subway."

Category: Poetic devices

Examples:

Simile	lines 3–4	"complex … scars"
Metaphor	lines 4–6	"We are … molecules"
Simile	lines 9–11	"He is wearing … exposed"
Simile	lines 24–26	"he absorbs … holds it"
Simile	lines 29–30	"he could … stick"
Simile	line 32	"rod of his soul"
Simile	lines 32–34	"rod of his soul … light"

Comment: By definition, similes and metaphors are comparisons. The poet uses these comparisons to develop and flesh out the juxtaposition of the life and situation of the speaker and the boy.

Your Turn

Refer to this chapter's earlier section about the types of poetry prompts to expect on the exam. Construct two alternative prompts for Sharon Olds's "On the Subway."

1ˢᵗ Alternative prompt:

2ⁿᵈ Alternative prompt:

Notice that we have ignored notes that did not apply to the prompt.

Now choose the techniques that develop the contrasting portraits and reveal the narrator's perceptions.

In response to the prompt, we have decided that the techniques/devices we will analyze are:

- Imagery
- Poetic devices
- Organization

If you expand the above techniques/devices and the above categories into interpretive statements and support those statements with appropriate details that you've already isolated, you will be writing a defenced essay.

Writing the Opening Paragraph

Your opening statement is the one that sets the tone of your essay and possibly raises the expectations of the reader. Spend time on your first paragraph to maximize your score.

Make certain that your topic is very clear. This reinforces the idea that you fully understand what is expected of you and what you will communicate to the reader. Generally, identify both the text and the poet in this first paragraph.

Do this now. Take 5 minutes to write your opening paragraph for the prompt. Write quickly, referring to your notes.

Let's check what you've written.

Highlight these points to see if you've done them. You may be surprised at what is actually there.

- Have you included the poet and the title?
- Have you addressed the portraits, contrasts, and insights?
- Have you specifically mentioned the techniques you will refer to in your essay?

Here are three sample opening paragraphs that address each of the above criteria.

A

Sharon Olds in the poem, "On the Subway," presents a brief encounter between two people of different races which leads to several insights of one participant. This is accomplished through Olds's use of poetic devices, imagery, and imagination.

B

The observer and the observed. One has control over the other. In her poem, "On the Subway," Sharon Olds asks her readers to enter the mind of a white woman who observes a young, black man as they travel together, neither knowing the other. Using poetic devices, imagery, and organization, Olds takes the reader on a ride through the contrasts and images that spark the imagination of the white onlooker.

C

"And he is black and I am white" establishes the basic contrast and conflict in Sharon Olds's poem, "On the Subway." Through imagery, organization, and poetic devices, Olds creates two contrasting portraits. The narrator's confrontation becomes the reader's also as she reveals her troubling fears and insights through her images and comments concerning her encounter with the black youth.

These three introductory paragraphs identify the poet and the title and clearly indicate an understanding of the prompt. Now, let's note what is different about each.

Sample **A** is a straightforward, unadorned restatement of the prompt. It is correct, yet lacks a writer's voice. (If you are unsure of how to proceed, this is the type of opening you may want to consider.) This type of opening paragraph will at least allow you to get into the essay with as little complexity as possible.

Sample **B** immediately reveals the writer's confidence and mature writing style. The prompt is addressed in a provocative and interesting manner, letting the reader know the tone of the essay.

Sample **C** incorporates a direct quotation from the poem which indicates the writer is comfortable with citation. The writer also links the reader with the poem and feels confident that his or her judgments about the encounter are supportable.

Note: There are many other types of opening paragraphs that could do the job as well. The paragraphs above are just a few samples.

Does your opening paragraph resemble any of these samples?

_____Yes_____No

Writing the Body of the Poetry Essay

When you write the body of your essay, take only 15–20 minutes. Time yourself and try your best to finish within that time frame.

Since this is practice, don't panic if you can't complete the essay within the allotted time. You will become more and more comfortable with the tasks presented to you as you gain experience with this type of question.

What Should I Include in the Body of the Poetry Essay?

1. Obviously, this is where you present your interpretation and the points you wish to make that are related to the prompt.

2. Use specific references and details from the poem.
   • Refer directly to the original. Don't always paraphrase.
   • Place quotation marks around those words and phrases that you extract from the poem.

3. Use "connective tissue" in your essay to establish adherence to the question.
   • Use the repetition of key ideas from your opening paragraph.
   • Try using "echo words" (i.e., synonyms such as *insight* can be inference/observation/perception; *fear* can be apprehension/insecurity).
   • Create transitions from one paragraph to the next.

To understand the process, carefully read the following sample paragraphs. Each develops one of the categories and techniques/devices asked for in the prompt. Notice the specific references and the "connective tissue." Also, notice that details that do not apply to the prompt have been ignored.

A

This paragraph develops **poetic devices**.

"Black sneakers laced with white in a complex pattern like a set of intentional scars" is the jarring simile Olds uses to establish the relationship between the woman and the "boy" on the subway. Immediately, the poetic device implies the bondage and pain of the oppressed minority and the deliberate complexity of race relations. This idea of interwoven lives is further developed by the metaphor that links both as "molecules stuck in a rod of light." The youth, however, is compared to a reptile with "hooded lids," and all the fear and repulsion associated with this creature is transferred to the boy who is hiding his true intentions with such a look. The woman follows her fearful insights with still another extreme simile—worrying about "this life he could take so easily and break across his knee like a stick." Still, she proves the complexity of her thoughts by creating a sympathetic metaphor to ponder "the rod of his soul—the heart of a seedling" yearning to grow into the light.

B

This paragraph develops **imagery**.

The images in the poem are predominantly drawn from the contrast between light and dark. "Black sneakers," "white laces," "rod of light rapidly moving through darkness" are all images that immediately establish the contrast that is at the heart of the meaning of the poem. This juxtaposition becomes reality in lines 21–22 when we learn that "he is black and I am white." The problem is how the "white" profits from his "darkness." [line 23] What should be light, "the beams of the nation's heart," is murderous, and he "as black cotton," absorbs this heat. This angry contrast leads the speaker to her insight about her life in lines 26–28. Empathizing with the black youth, the narrator moves beyond her prejudices and finds promise in the last three lines which see the dark being born into the light.

C

This paragraph develops **organization**.

The organization of "On the Subway" is rather linear. Olds's narrator proceeds from a frightened observer to a philosophical questioner to finally a mature, sympathetic forecaster of the promise of the young, black man. The first thirteen lines provide the interior monologue of a woman who sits across from a young, black male and looks him over from head to toe. In line 10 she begins to move deeply into the hidden person across from her, with this "introspection" ending in lines 14–16 with her questioning who actually has power over whom. Line 18 presents a true shift from personal observation to an almost societal conscience which is sympathetic to the plight of all blacks in America as seen in lines 21–26. Bringing the reader back to the opening section of the poem, the speaker intimates at the promise of the young man with "the rod of his soul . . . rich as the heart of a seedling/ready to thrust up into any available light." [lines 32–34]

> Refer to our list of recommended poets at the back of this book. Look for poems similar in length and complexity to those we've provided and apply a variety of prompts. You can try these alone, with a study group, or with your class.

Note: Look at the last sentence of Sample B on imagery: "Empathizing with the black youth, the narrator moves beyond her prejudices and finds promise in the last three lines which see the dark being born into the light."

This final sentence would be fine as the conclusion to the essay. A conclusion does not have to be a paragraph. It can be the writer's final remark, observation, or reference and may be only a sentence or two.

Do this now. Write the body of your essay. Time yourself. Allow 15–20 minutes to complete this task.

Sample Student Essays

Following are two actual student essays followed by a rubric and comments on each.

Student Essay A

The three sections of "On the Subway" by Sharon Olds express the complicated relationship between Caucasians and African-Americans. In the first section the author presents an exposition that contrasts a white person with a black (lines 1–13). In the second, the speaker begins to develop the apparent disparities so that inter-relationships emerge (lines 13–20). In the third, the narrator gains insight into how this scene is representative of American culture at large (lines 20–34). 5

The imagery Olds uses in the first section emphasizes the difference between the white woman who is the narrator and the observer and the black boy, who is the observed, as they ride the subway. The shoes he is wearing are black "laced with white" (line 3). The speaker describes the white zigzags as "intentional scars" 10 (line 4). The scars allude to the discrimination against the black man by white society. The adjective "intentional" denotes that whites purposely harm blacks. The image contrasts whites with blacks: whites are powerful; blacks are subservient. Similarly, the two characters are described as being "stuck on opposite sides" of the subway car; they are separated permanently from each other (lines 4–5). The description of the 15 clothing is a third contrasting element. Here, the black man is "exposed," while the speaker is covered in fur (line 11). This image reinforces the opposition between the white woman and the black boy.

The second section sees a shift in tone. Where the first section is composed of finite physical descriptions, the second is more philosophical and indicates the 20 speaker's apprehension. She is uncertain and writes that "I don't/know if I am in his power . . . or if he is in my power" (lines 14–15, 18). Such a statement is important because it illustrates that the boundaries between whites and blacks are not as clearcut as they may seem. Perhaps the speaker begins to realize that the image of the subservient black and the powerful white presented in the first section of the poem 25 is incorrect. The repetition of the word "Life" is another way the interconnection between the two characters is developed. The narrator cannot decide whether her wealth usurps the power of the black man or whether his potential aggression usurps her power (lines 17, 19).

The tone, again, shifts in the third segment. Here, it is clear that the speaker is trying to gain an understanding of the relationship between the white world and that of the black boy. At first, she realizes that they are different because "he is black and I am white" (lines 21–22). The image of the "black cotton" alludes to slavery, once again referring to the scars, or distinctions, imposed by the white society. Yet, at the end of this section, the differences between the two people are strangely reconciled. This is accomplished using the technique of repetition. Instead of repeating a word as in the second section, an image is repeated. Lines 29–31 state that the black man could hurt the white woman; he could "break [her] across his knee . . . the way his own back is being broken." In other words, both whites and blacks can hurt; both races can be injured by either repression or aggression, and so they are connected through their pain and unrealized dreams.

Student Essay B

In the poem "On the Subway" by Sharon Olds, she contrasts the worlds of an affluent white person and a poor black person. The two people have many opposing characteristics, and the author uses literary techniques such as tone, poetic devices, and imagery to portray these differences. The narrator is the white woman, and she realizes how people get "stuck" in places of society based on their skin color. The word "stuck" is repeated twice to stress this idea.

The major difference between the two people is obviously their skin color. This one difference causes many aspects of each person's life to be unlike the other's. The white woman is above the black man in the eyes of much of society. The narrator states that "without meaning or trying to I must profit from his darkness." This is basically saying that the black man is living in a white man's world, where his skin color alone has given him a predisposition in the eyes of many. This idea is further supported when the speaker thinks "There is no way to know how easy this white skin makes my life." Olds uses the following simile to show the black man's situation: ". . . he absorbs the murderous beams of the nation's heart, as black cotton absorbs the heat of the sun and holds it."

Another contrast that is in the poem is the rawness of the black man versus the sheltered and refined look of the white woman. Olds uses a simile to describe the red that the black youth is wearing: "Like the inside of the body exposed." The white woman is the outside of the animal wearing a fur coat. The black man is the inside of the body, the true animal, while the white woman is not; she is simply wearing the outer covering of an animal.

As a result of this experience, the narrator realizes that there is a balance of power and control between her and the young man. She realizes that at times, and in certain situations, she rules, while in others the black man does. Her life, her "easier" life, can be taken away by the black youth. Who has the power on the train? The big, strong, raw black man or the weaker, but richer, white woman? Society has given the white woman a false sense of superiority and security. She is protected by wealth, her job, and her possessions, but when alone on the subway with this black man, she feels fear. She is confronted by her own vulnerability. The black youth who is being broken by society can break the white woman who is society.

Overall, this poem effectively contrasts the two people and exposes a fallacy of society. The black man must live in eternal darkness because he is never allowed to "thrust up into any available light."

Rating the Student Essays

Let's take a look at a set of rubrics for the poetry essay.

- 1 point for thesis/claim/introduction that is appropriate to the prompt
  - The thesis clearly presents a possible interpretation and indicates how the support will be developed.
- 4 points for evidence/support of the thesis/claim
  - Clear and appropriate references to the text
  - Clear presentation of how the references relate to the thesis
- 1 point for complexity of the commentary and syntax

> *Note:* The essay is really a first draft. The readers know this and approach each essay with this in mind.

Note: With specific reference to the 6-point rubric, we will use the following abbreviations to indicate into which column the comment would fall: **T = thesis, E = evidence, C = complexity, S = sophistication**.

Student Essay A

This is a high-range essay (5, 6) for the following reasons:

- A sophisticated, indirect indication of the task of the prompt and line of reasoning. T
- Tightly constructed and thorough discussion of the contrasts and opposition in the poem. E/C
- Effective analysis of imagery (lines 1–13, 15–17). E/C
- Effective and coherent analysis of tone. E
- Understanding of the subtleties of tone (lines 19–21). C
- Strong support for assertions and interpretations (lines 22–29). C
- Effective analysis of literary techniques (lines 11, 33–34, 36–38). E
- Mature syntax, diction, and organization. S

This high-ranking essay is subtle, concise, and on target. There is nothing that takes away from the writer's focus. Each paragraph grows out of the previous one, and the reader always knows where the author is taking him or her.

Student Essay B

This is a middle-range essay (3, 4) for the following reasons:

- Clearly identifies the task, the poem, and the poet. T
- States the techniques that will be discussed in the essay and indicates a line of reasoning. T
- Lacks a transition to the body of the essay (lines 6–7). S
- Provides an adequate discussion of the insights of the speaker (lines 23–25). C
- Cites appropriate specifics to support the thesis of the essay (lines 14–16). E
- Uses standard style, diction, and structure, but does not reflect a sophisticated or mature writer. S
- Attempts a universal statement within a rather repetitive and summary-like conclusion (lines 32–34). S

"Even though I hate doing it, my writing really improves when I spend the time revising what I've written."
—Mike T.
  AP student

How about sharing these samples with members of your class or study group and discussing possible responses?

While adhering to the prompt, this mid-range essay is an adequate first draft. It shows promise but comes dangerously close to paraphrasing lines. The analysis is basic and obvious, depending on only one device, that of simile. The writer hints at the subtleties but misses the opportunity to respond to further complexities inherent in the poem.

Note: Both essays have concluding paragraphs that are repetitive and mostly unnecessary. It is best to avoid this type of ending.

Rapid Review

Need a Quick Review? Spend a minute or two reading through...that'll do.

- Review terms and techniques.
- Become familiar with types of poetry questions (prompts).
- Highlight the prompt to make certain you are aware of required tasks.
- Time your essay carefully.
- Read the poem a couple of times.
- Spend sufficient time "working the poem" before writing.
- Mark up the poem.
- Create a strong opening paragraph, including prompt information.
- Refer often to the poem for concrete details and quotes to support your ideas.
- Always stay on topic.
- Avoid simply paraphrasing.
- Include transitions and echo words.
- Practice—vary the prompt and your response.
- Consult the models and rubrics for self-evaluation.
- Share ideas with others.

CHAPTER 7

The Free-Response Essay/Literary Argument

IN THIS CHAPTER

Summary: Examination of the free-response essay and its purpose as it is presented in the AP English Literature exam

Key Ideas

- Learn the types of free-response prompts you might encounter in the AP English Literature exam
- Practice various ways of organizing the information based on your chosen literary work
- Learn the basics of constructing your response to the free-response prompt
- Learn about the rubrics and rating of the AP free-response essays
- Examine model student essays
- Learn how rubrics were used to rate student essays
- Learn how the synthesis essay differs from the argumentative and analysis essays
- Learn the process of dealing with many texts

Introduction to the Free-Response Essay/Literary Argument

Nothing in life is free, but this essay does indicate that the end is near. So, hang in there. This chapter will provide the information and the practice you need to "knock their socks off."

You will be given a literary idea or comment. This idea will be followed by a list of 30 to 40 texts deemed to have literary merit. You will then:

- Select one of these works or a work of literary merit from your own reading
- Analyze how your literary work relates to the prompt and to the work as a whole
- Select and discuss appropriate evidence to support your thesis
- Employ appropriate diction and syntax

The wording of the free-response prompt will be consistent. Only the statement of the idea/concept and the list of literary works will differ.

For example: "Either from your own reading or from the list below, choose a work of fiction in which [some aspect of the lead is addressed]. Then, in a well-written essay, analyze how [that same aspect of the lead] contributes to an interpretation of the work as a whole. Do not merely summarize the plot." (*AP English Literature and Composition Course and Exam Description*, The College Board, 2020, p. 139.)

What Is a Free-Response Essay?

The free-response essay is based on a provocative question that highlights specific insights applicable to a broad range of literary texts. The question provides for varied personal interpretations and multiple approaches. It allows students to truly create the specific substance of their own essay.

What Is the Purpose of the Free-Response Essay?

The College Board wants to assess your ability to discuss a work of literature in a particular context. The illustrations you include in your essay will demonstrate your insights and critical thinking as well as your writing ability.

What Makes This Essay "Free"?

Although the question is the same for all students, you have total freedom to choose the piece of literature to which you will refer. Once chosen, you have total freedom to select the specifics that will support your thesis. Unlike the other two essays, which have rubrics based on certain concrete interpretations and directions of the text, your free-response essay will be uniquely your own.

If This Is Total Freedom of Expression, How Can I Ever Get Less Than a 6?

The test reader is expecting an essay that demonstrates a mature understanding and defense of the prompt. Your paper must be specific and well organized. It must also adhere to the topic. You will lose major credit for providing only plot summary. Your illustrations should be cogent and insightful rather than obvious or superficial. For a high score, you must bring something specific and relevant to the conversation that is logically related to the thesis.

What Are the Pitfalls of the Free-Response Essay?

It is our experience that the free-response question is a double-edged sword. Students can suffer from overconfidence because of the open nature of this essay. They depend on memory rather than on preparation and often go for the most obvious illustrations. They tend to ramble on in vague and unsupported generalities, and they frequently provide incorrect information. *The failure to plan and limit can undermine this essay.*

Students often have trouble choosing the appropriate work and lose valuable time pondering a variety of choices. It is important to be decisive and confident in your presentation.

What Kinds of Works May I Refer to in This Essay?

Generally, you are asked to choose a full-length work, almost always a novel or play. However, if the prompt says "choose a work," you may use a poem, short story, novella, or work of nonfiction. *Note:* You may *never* use a film.

Note: The list of suggested texts for FRQ3 will have 36–42 works on it, NONE of which will be works in translation or ancient texts (e.g., *The Odyssey*, *The Iliad*). Students will be allowed to write about works in translation (e.g., *Crime and Punishment*, *Madame Bovary*), but translated works will not be listed in the prompt.

- What constitutes "literary merit" will no longer be an issue. Works of literature characterized by "complexity" will be acceptable choices.
- Literary nonfiction (e.g., *The Bell Jar*, *In Cold Blood*, *Night*) will be acceptable choices.

Must I Use the List of Works Provided at the Bottom of the Prompt?

<u>Absolutely not!</u> Since this is a free-response essay, the choice of a literary work is up to you. You should choose a work that is appropriate to the prompt, one that is appropriate to AP students, and one that is comfortable for you.

Must I Use Works Read This Year?

No, but why would you choose any work that could be a faded memory or unsuitable for AP-level analysis? We always recommend using works that you studied in class and have read and discussed throughout the year. One exception occurs when you have written a lengthy literary research paper or a sustained critical analysis. In this situation, you may have real in-depth familiarity with a work that you could adapt to a free-response question. By all means, go for it!

How Do I Prepare for the Free-Response Essay?

You need to tell yourself in September or October that you will be taking the exam next May. This will emphasize the point that throughout the year you will have to keep some type of record of the works you have read and some specific points you want to make about each of them. (In Chapter 8, we introduce several techniques and processes that will enable you to keep these records.)

By the time of the exam in May, you need to be thoroughly conversant with at least three to five full-length works from different genres, eras, and literary movements.

You also need to practice. Practice writing questions, practice choosing appropriate works, and practice writing responses to questions. Practice!

What Criteria Do the AP Readers Use to Rate a Free-Response Essay?

The readers are looking for literary insights and awareness of character, comprehension of theme, and the ability to transfer specific ideas and details to a universal concept. In addition, the readers are hoping to see a writer who reveals and understands the relationships among form, content, style, and structure and their effects on the meaning of the work. The essay should indicate the writer's ability to choose appropriate illustrations from a full-length work and to connect them in a thoughtful way. The sophisticated writer will refer to plot but will not summarize. As always, the reader is looking for a well-organized essay written in a mature voice.

According to The College Board, the scoring of a student's free-response will be based on how well the student:

- Responds to the prompt with a thesis that presents a defensible interpretation
- Provides evidence to support your line of reasoning
- Explains how the evidence supports your line of reasoning
- Uses appropriate grammar and punctuation in communicating your argument

What Happens If I Use a Work That the Reader Doesn't Know?

This should not be a major concern to you. Throughout the year, your AP instructor has provided you with appropriate literary experiences suitable for addressing this prompt. In addition, be assured that any work we mention in this book will be appropriate. Be sure to consult our suggested reading list to increase your range of choices. Any other works by the same author would probably be on an appropriate AP level. For the most part, the AP prefers works from the literary canon because they exhibit breadth and complexity for literary scholarship. Don't fight these requirements. <u>You do yourself a disservice when you insist on trying to outwit or beat the system.</u>

Having said all this, if by chance you do choose an obscure work and present it well, the reader will respond accordingly.

Types of Free-Response Prompts

Here are some topics that could be the basis for a free-response prompt. We also include some suggested works for these.

- The journey as a major force in a work. (*Gulliver's Travels, As I Lay Dying, The Stranger, The Kite Runner,* etc.)
- What happens to a dream deferred? (*Hedda Gabler, Desire Under the Elms, Their Eyes Were Watching God,* etc.)
- Transformation (literal and/or figurative). (*Dr. Jekyll and Mr. Hyde, Black Like Me, Metamorphosis,* etc.)
- Descent into madness/hell. (*Medea, Heart of Darkness, Secret Sharer,* etc.)
- An ironic reversal in a character's beliefs or actions. (*Heart of Darkness, The Stranger, Oedipus,* etc.)
- Perception and reality—"What is, is not." (*Life of Pi, Hamlet, Who's Afraid of Virginia Woolf?, The Things They Carried,* etc.)
- A child becomes a force to reveal _____ . (*Jane Eyre, Huckleberry Finn, Lord of the Flies,* etc.)
- Ceremony or ritual plays an important role. (*The Stranger, Lord of the Flies, The Sun Also Rises, The Handmaid's Tale,* etc.)
- The role of the fool, comic character, or wise servant who reveals _____ . (*King Lear, The Importance of Being Earnest, Tartuffe,* etc.)

Note: Fill in works you would use to respond to the above prompts.

_____

_____

_____

_____

"*I really like hearing and reading how the other students do the same questions. It helps me evaluate my own ideas and essays.*"
—Adam S.
  AP student

Here's another set of possible free-response prompts for development:

- How an opening scene or chapter establishes the character, conflict, or theme of a major literary work.
- How a minor character is used to develop a major character.
- How violence relates to character or theme.
- How time is a major factor.
- The ways in which an author changes the reader's attitude(s) toward a subject.
- The use of contrasting settings.
- Parent/child or sibling relationships and their significance.
- The analysis of a villain with regard to the meaning of the work.
- The use of an unrealistic character or element and its effect on the work.
- The relevance of a nonmodern work to the present day.
- The conflict between passion and responsibility.
- The conflict between character and society.

Note: To our knowledge, a free-response question has never been repeated. Therefore, we suggest:

1. Use the prompts cited earlier when you discuss works you read or when you write about those works throughout the year.

2. Generate a list of topics that would also be suitable for free-response prompts. Discuss, outline, or prepare sample essays utilizing these questions.

Anticipating prompts and responses is a productive way to prepare for this exam.

General Rubrics for the Free-Response Essay

Let's take a look at a set of rubrics for the free-response essay.

- 1 point for thesis/claim/introduction that is appropriate to the prompt
  - The thesis clearly cites a major work related to the prompt and indicates how the support will be developed.
- 4 points for evidence/support of the thesis/claim
  - Clear and appropriate references to the text
  - Clear presentation of how the references relate to the thesis
- 1 point for complexity of the commentary and syntax

Timing and Planning the Free-Response Essay

This essay is the real challenge of the exam. Keep in mind that with the other two essay questions, half the job was done for you; the material was limited and provided for you. But now you are faced with the blank page that you must fill. Therefore, you must plan this essay carefully and completely. With this in mind, here's a workable strategy:

- 1–3 minutes working the prompt. (At this point, you might even chart the prompt.)
- 3–5 minutes choosing your work. (You should mentally run through two or three works that might be appropriate.) This is a crucial step for laying the foundation for your essay.

- 5–10 minutes for brainstorming, charting, mapping, outlining, and so on the specifics you plan to use in your essay. (Remember, a vague, general, unsupported essay will cost you points.)
- 20–25 minutes to write your essay based on your preparation.
- 3 minutes for proofreading.

Working the Prompt from the Diagnostic/Master Exam

Before you read the prompt, immediately cover the list of suggested works. There are several good reasons for this:

- It requires time to read the list.
- Chances are you will have read very few works on the list. If you are like many students, this could make you feel insecure and rattle your confidence.
- If you are familiar with a work or two, you may be predisposed to use the work to answer the question even if it is not necessarily your best choice. You may find yourself considering a work that you would not have considered if it were not listed, and you may find yourself taking precious time to fit that choice unsuccessfully to the prompt.

Here is the PROMPT:

Often in literature, a literal or figurative journey is a significant factor in the development of a character or the meaning of the work.

Either from your own reading or from the list below, choose a work of fiction that presents the effect(s) of a literal or figurative journey on a character or on the meaning of the entire work. Then, in a well-written essay how the journey affects the character or the meaning of the work as a whole.

As I Lay Dying	*Beloved*
The Handmaid's Tale	*Heart of Darkness*
The Odyssey	*Moby Dick*
Brave New World	*The Sun Also Rises*
To the Lighthouse	*The Grapes of Wrath*
A Streetcar Named Desire	*The Poisonwood Bible*
A Passage to India	*Their Eyes Were Watching God*
Gulliver's Travels	*The Bonesetter's Daughter*
Jasmine	*Twelfth Night*
The Kite Runner	*The Brief Wondrous Life of Oscar Wao*

Notating the Prompt

We recommend that you chart or map the prompt. This is a simple visualization of your task. Before you look at our samples, you might want to try charting or mapping the prompt on your own.

Following is a sample chart:

Jane Eyre

	JOURNEY	EFFECT ON CHARACTER	EFFECT ON THEME
LITERAL			
FIGURATIVE			

Here is a sample map:

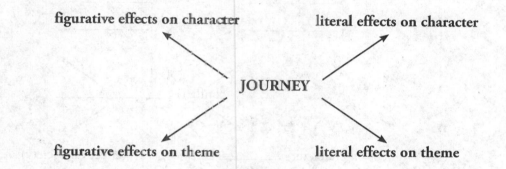

Following is a sample topic outline:

Journey

- Literal effect
  - character
  - theme
- Figurative effect
  - character
  - theme

Your Turn

Carefully read and highlight the following prompt.

Frequently, the tension in a literary work is created by the conflict between a character and society. Choose a full-length literary work and discuss the nature of the conflict, its effect on the character, on society, and on the resulting thematic implications.

A. **Construct a chart** that addresses the requirements of the prompt.

Title of literary work:

	NATURE OF CONFLICT	EFFECT OF CONFLICT
ON CHARACTER		
ON SOCIETY		
ON THEMATIC IMPLICATIONS		

B. Using the same literary work you chose for the chart, **create a map**.

(character) _____   (society) _____   (thematic) _____

_____   _____   _____

_____   _____   _____

(conflict) _____

(effect on character) _____   (effect on society) _____

_____   _____

_____   _____

C. With the same literary work and prompt in mind, **construct an outline**.

Conflict

Nature of conflict
– On character:
– On society:

Effect of conflict
– On character:
– On society:

Thematic implications
– On character:
– On society:

When you provide the specifics, either mentally or by writing them down, you will ensure that you have addressed all parts of the prompt. This also will provide the basic structure of your essay.

Note: Although it may feel awkward and contrived at first, if you actually practice this technique, it will become automatic and help you to immediately get into the writing of your essay.

KEY IDEA

Now that you are familiar with the prompt, take a few moments to think about works that might be appropriate for this question. One or two will immediately pop into your mind. Mentally examine them for scenes or details that you might be able to use. *If you can't think of specifics, abandon this choice.*

If you wish, now take a look at the list of suggested works, because:

- You may find your choice there, and you will feel very validated.
- You may see a different work by the same author, which may also boost your confidence.
- You might see another work or author you recognize you had not considered that could possibly spark a better response to the prompt.

This process should only take a minute or so.

Do this now. Spend 8–10 minutes working your choice to fit the requirements of the prompt. For example, prior to the exam, you will have prepared a cross section of works from various genres, time periods, and literary movements. Since these are works with depth, you will be able to take your basic scene or references and modify them to suit the task of the given prompt.

Using *Hamlet* as an example, let's assume you reviewed the graveyard scene prior to the exam. This scene would be appropriate to illustrate your thoughts on such varied prompts as:

- The use of humor—the gravedigger.
- The role of a minor character—Horatio.
- The concept of death as the great leveler—motif.
- Use of ritual—funeral.
- The impact of a character *not* seen in the work—Yorick.
- The use of coincidence or irony in the work—Ophelia's grave.
- The use of setting to develop theme or character—"To be or not to be."

You get the point. Obviously, you could not answer a question about the effectiveness of a work's conclusion by using this scene, which is exactly why you prepare *several* different literary examples.

We know that Shakespeare is so universal that any work could be used to answer almost any free-response question. Therefore, we urge you to prepare at least one Shakespearean play as a "safe" work.

There is another reason to spend several minutes planning your essay. Frequently, your first responses and examples are the obvious and common ones. This is not to say that you could not write an adequate essay using these. But, if they came to you this quickly, they probably also came to many thousands of other students taking the exam. It is usually more challenging and rewarding to find a unique focus for your essay. For example: choosing the gravedigger's scene in *Hamlet* rather than the "To be or not to be" scene may reveal a more creative thinker.

Sometimes, as you are planning, you realize that your work will answer only part of the prompt and that it would be better to switch to another work. If you have prepared well prior to the test, you will be able to do this without taking up much time. Sometimes it's better to abandon your initial choice in favor of the second and more productive one. This is why you have not yet begun to write.

Developing the Opening Paragraph

Now you are ready to write. Remember, your opening paragraph is the one that raises the expectations of the reader and sets the tone of your essay. Spend time on your first paragraph to maximize your score.

Make certain that your topic is very clear to the reader. This reinforces the idea that you fully understand what is expected of you and what you will communicate to the reader. Generally, identify both the text and the author in this first paragraph.

Do this now. Take 5 minutes and write your opening paragraph for this prompt. Write quickly, referring to your notes.

Let's check what you've written:

Actually highlight these to see if you've done it. You may be surprised at what is actually there.

- Have you included the author and title?
- Have you addressed the literal and figurative journeys?
- Have you addressed characterization and theme?

Here are three sample opening paragraphs that address each of the above criteria.

A

"There was no possibility of taking a walk that day" says young Jane in Chapter One of Charlotte Brontë's novel, *Jane Eyre*. Little did she know that her very existence would evolve from her personal odyssey as she journeyed from Gateshead to Lowood to Thornfield and beyond; from child to adolescent to woman. This literal and figurative journey enables Brontë to develop both the character and the theme of her work.

B

Up the hill, down the street, across the road from cafe to cafe, the characters in Ernest Hemingway's novel, *The Sun Also Rises*, wander interminably. Hemingway employs this aimless journey to reveal the lost nature of his characters and his theme of the search for meaning and direction in their post–World War I existence.

C

In *Heart of Darkness* by Joseph Conrad, a literal journey from England to Africa becomes a nightmare of realization and epiphany for the main character, Marlowe. Conrad develops his themes through Marlowe's observations and experiences on his figurative journey from innocence to corruption, idealism to cynicism, and optimism to despair.

Note: These three introductory paragraphs identify the author and the title and clearly indicate an understanding of the prompt. Let's note what is different about each.

Sample **A** begins with an appropriate, direct quotation. It clearly delineates the two types of journeys and their relationship to the character. The writer indicates an understanding of the difference between literal and figurative interpretation.

Sample **B** has a clear writer's voice. The writer is not afraid to be judgmental. The tone of the essay is apparent and sustained.

Sample **C** alludes to the content of the body of the essay and touches on vague generalities. However, the maturity of the vocabulary and thought indicate the writer's understanding of Conrad's complex themes and their relationship to the prompt.

Note: There are many other types of opening paragraphs that could also do the job. The paragraphs above are just a few samples. Does your opening paragraph resemble any of these samples? When you write the body of your essay, take only 15–20 minutes. Time yourself and try your best to finish within that time frame.

Developing the Body of the Essay

Time to pump some mental iron and to firm up and tone those flabby ideas and turn them into examples of intellectual fitness.

What Should I Include in the Body of the Free-Response Essay?

1. Obviously, this is where you present your interpretation and the points you wish to make that are related to the prompt.

2. Use specific references and details from the chosen work.
   • Incorporate direct quotations when possible.
   • Place quotation marks around those words or phrases taken directly from the work.

3. Use connective tissue in your essay to establish adherence to the question.
   • Use the repetition of key ideas in the prompt and in your opening paragraph.
   • Try using "echo words" (i.e., synonyms such as journey/wanderings/travels or figurative/symbolic/metaphoric).
   • Use transitions from one paragraph to the next.

To understand the process, carefully read the following sample paragraphs. Each illustrates an aspect of the prompt. Notice the specific references and the connective tissue.

A

At Gateshead, despite its material comforts, Jane was an orphaned outcast who felt "like a discord." She was, like Cinderella, abused by her cousins and aunt and nurtured only by Bessie, a servant. Jane's immaturity and rebellious nature cause her to be jealous and vengeful which culminates in a violent confrontation with her repulsive cousin, John. Her subsequent eviction from Gateshead forces her to embark on a journey that will affect her forever. The stark privations of Lowood humble Jane and open her to the true riches of friendship with Helen Burns. It is here she learns the academic, religious, and social skills that will enable her to move on to her destiny at Thornfield.

B

Throughout the novel Jake escorts the reader on the journeys that become the only purpose the group exhibits. The trip to San Fermin for the fiesta is also a journey to hell, away from civilization and morality. The fiesta "explodes" and for seven days any behavior is acceptable, for there is no accountability during this time. No one "pays the bill," yet. Brett is worshiped as a pagan idol; garlic is strung around her neck, and men drink to her powers. She is compared to Circe, and, indeed, she turns her companions into swine as they fight over her. This trip to the fiesta reinforces the lack of spirituality and direction that is a theme of the novel.

C

Referring to the map of the Congo, Marlowe states that "the snake had charmed me." This primal description prepares us for the inevitable journey up the river that will change the very core of his character. The snake implies temptation, and Marlowe is seduced by the mysteries of Africa and his desire to meet Kurtz in the interior. He is too naive and pure to anticipate the abominations that await him at the inner station. Like a descent into hell, the journey progresses. The encounters with Fresleven, the workers without rivets, the pilgrims shooting into the jungle, all foreshadow Marlowe's changing understanding of the absurdity of life and the flawed nature of man. Only when he is totally aware of "the horror, the horror" can he journey back to "another dark place of the universe," London, to see the Intended and to corrupt his own values for her sake.

Let's examine these three body paragraphs.

Sample **A** is about *Jane Eyre*. It addresses one aspect of the prompt—Jane's character at the beginning of the journey—and continues with the first major change in her life. The writer demonstrates familiarity with the novel through concrete details and quotations. Theme is implied and leads the reader to anticipate further development in the rest of the body of the essay.

Sample **B** refers to *The Sun Also Rises*. This paragraph uses a single incident to develop the discussion of the journey as it affects character and theme. The writer includes very specific details of the San Fermin fiesta to support comments about Brett and Jake. The integration of these details is presented in a cohesive, mature style.

Sample **C** delves into *Heart of Darkness*. This paragraph is a philosophical approach, which assumes the reader is familiar with the novel. It focuses on theme and how the development of the character is used to illustrate that theme. The ending of the paragraph presents an insight that invites the reader to "stay tuned."

Do this now. Write the body of your essay. Time yourself. Allow 15–20 minutes to complete this task.

Sample Student Essays

Here are two actual student essays that are followed by a rubric and comments on each essay.

Student Essay A

The journey taken by Edna in Kate Chopin's <u>The Awakening</u> exemplifies the journey that is a very common feature in many works of literature. This journey is not a commonplace journey; it is one that brings about development and change in the story's main character. In <u>The Awakening</u>, the spiritual journey that Edna takes changes the way she thinks, acts, and lives. The ramifications of her journey change her life.   5

The story takes place in New Orleans around the turn of the century. The women of society were treated as possessions, either of their fathers or their husbands, or even of their religion. The story's protagonist, Edna, is introduced as the respectable wife. She is a good mother and is faithful to her husband. The   10 family vacations for the summer in Grand Isle. While there, Edna befriends Robert who every summer devotes himself to being an attendant to one of the married women, Edna being his current choice. While there, she undergoes a series of "awakenings" which begin her journey. One such push was Edna's learning to swim. Although she was previously afraid of the water and of swimming, one day   15 she tried, and is successful. Her newfound ability signifies the steps she is taking towards no longer being a possession. It is one of the first signs that Edna is ready to break free and to be her own person. The water gives her a sense of freedom, and she relishes this sensation.

Edna's growing love for Robert alerts her of the journey upon which she has unknowingly embarked. After Robert leaves, giving very short notice, she misses him tremendously. She realizes that she is in love with him but has no such love for her husband, Leonce. While Robert gives into her every whim, Leonce only cares about Edna as if she were his possession. He does not consider her feelings and emotions, only his own. He leaves the family often to go into the city for work, sending candy and chocolates to Edna and her children in order to compensate for his absence. He constantly neglects Edna's emotional needs, and as a result, intensifies the strength of her journey. However, Leonce is not the only person who sees Edna merely as a possession. Even Robert, who is in love with her, feels that Edna belongs to Leonce. Because he knows that she cannot be his, Robert refuses to let their relationship progress any further than it has, and the only way for him to achieve this is to go away and cut off contact with Edna.

When the family returns to their home in New Orleans, Edna is not content with her life and begins to neglect performing some of her expected activities and duties, such as entertaining the wives of her husband's clients. Edna's refusal to accompany her husband on a business trip is the pinnacle of her journey. Leonce is shocked and appalled by her noncompliance, but he feels that she is going through a phase and will soon come to her senses.

While her husband is gone, Edna's children are sent to live with their grandmother. During this time, Edna is free and independent. She meets a variety of new people who she begins to spend time with. One of these people is Alcee Arobin, who becomes her lover. This relationship is important in Edna's journey because it represents a further rift from her previous life as a possession. More and more, Edna becomes her own person. Moreover, although he tries to make her his own possession as well, Edna refuses to let Alcee have the upper hand in their relationship. She refuses to let anyone control her life ever again. She even goes so far as to close up her house and rent a much smaller place to dwell in. Edna's actions come as a shock to many people, especially her husband, but she is really just trying to assert her individuality. However, no one understands what she is going through. In fact, many people, including her husband, blame her behavior on mental illness. Edna realizes that she cannot continue to live in this manner.

At the novel's conclusion, Edna decides to commit suicide. She swims into the ocean and drowns herself. It is fitting that she chooses the ocean, the place where she feels she has the most freedom, to end the journey. Edna decides that she would rather not live at all than to live a life where she cannot be her own person.

Student Essay B

It is easy to interpret the novel, <u>Things Fall Apart</u>, as a denouncement of white colonization, or simply as a detailed portrayal of African culture. But that would be all too banal; it has already been said and done by many authors. What makes this novel distinctive is the development and depiction of Okonkwo's journey through life and how his journey effects the novel's themes.

Given Okonkwo's rugged personality, he encounters many conflicts on his journey to self-awareness. Okonkwo clashes with his father, his wives, his children, his village, and perhaps every other character, but his greatest struggle is with himself. It seems as if Okonkwo's enemy is his father's flaws, but in reality, Okonkwo's hidden enemy is his fear of his father's reflection upon himself. Okonkwo spends his whole life on a journey away from the values of his father, so much up to the point where he ruins his life as well as the lives of those around him. His tragic flaw is his obsessive aversion to his father's laid back character. Okonkwo is so engulfed by his life's mission to become a rejection of his father's character, that he fails to see Unoka's positive traits such as tenderness, wisdom, and a passion for life, which Okonkwo lacks.

10

15

Even though Okonkwo is the protagonist in this book, he is also the antagonist; clearly, he is on a trip to disaster. He has not journeyed inside himself to understand what makes him act the way he does. He is extremely rash and explosive and does not think twice about throwing a fatal punch. He foolishly thinks that his aggressiveness is the only way for a man to act; it is this misconception that ultimately ruins him. Unfortunately for Okonkwo, he never realizes his flaw, and in the end, it is as if he cannot flee his father's reflection, for just like his father, he dies with shame and disgrace.

20

He had the ambition; he had the intelligence; he had the passion; but he had all of these for the wrong reasons. Perhaps <u>Things Fall Apart</u> portrays Okonkwo's lack of development rather than his development through time. From his early youth he forms this strong aversion to weakness and ineptitude, and this controls all his actions throughout his life. In actuality, the fact that he is totally ruled by this fear of ineptitude underscores how internally weak Okonkwo is. In the end, when he realizes that there is no possible way to triumph, that he cannot control people with his violent actions, and that he cannot control his fate, what does he do? He gives up and commits the most cowardly act of suicide.

25

30

Note: With specific reference to the 6-point rubric, we will use the following abbreviations to indicate into which column the comment would fall: **T = thesis, E = evidence, C = complexity, S = sophistication.**

Rating the Student Essays

Student Essay A

This is essay is rated within the high-range for several reasons:

- It presents a defensible thesis that addresses all aspects of the prompt with a clear indication of a line of reasoning. T
- It is highly detailed (lines 13–14, 25–26, 34–35). E
- It demonstrates strong topic adherence (lines 5–6, 14–15, 20, 36–37, 50–51). E/C
- There is strong integration of specifics to support the thesis (lines 16–17, 29–32, 42–43). E/C
- There is perceptive character analysis (lines 33–36, 49–51). C
- There is clear linear development of the essay (lines 9, 13–14, 33, 39, 48). C/S
- The essay is frequently repetitive and needs echo words. S
- There are some syntax and diction errors. S

This is an example of an essay that makes the jump into the high-range area because of its organization, its use of detail, and its insights. It's obvious that the writer thoroughly understands the work and presents various specifics to support the thesis. The diction and syntax are, at times, not as mature as would be found in more sophisticated essays.

Student Essay B

Student Essay B is a mid-range essay for the following reasons:

- It addresses the prompt with a defensible thesis and indicates a line of reasoning. T
- It identifies character and theme. T
- It refers to the character's journeys but does not really develop any of them (paragraphs 2–3). E/C
- There are many generalizations that need more specific support (lines 10–16, 25–27). E/C
- It does contain several perceptive insights that are unevenly developed. C/S
- The essay loses its clear connection to the prompt at times (paragraph 4). T/S
- The diction and syntax, although adequate, lack a maturity seen in higher-level papers. S

This mid-range essay demonstrates that the writer understands the prompt. This is obviously a first draft in need of further revision. As it stands, it relies too heavily on generalizations.

Final Comments

Warning! Although the free-response essay may appear to be the easiest and most accessible on the exam, it is fraught with danger. The worst danger is relying on vague references and general statements that are not supported by specific details or lines. In addition, you have to develop the organizational pattern of the essay and control its progression. All too often the essays read like capsule summaries of the plots.

Your lifesaver in this essay situation is preparation. We say this again because it bears repeating:

- Review full-length works you've read during the year.
- Choose a minimum of five works you've connected with.
- Classify the five works to ensure a broad spectrum of types, literary movements, and themes.
- Isolate several *pivotal* scenes, moments, or episodes from each of the five works and examine the suitability of those scenes for a variety of questions.
- Select quotations and details from these pivotal scenes.
- If necessary, reread only the pivotal scenes before you take the exam.

Rapid Review

- Remember the pitfalls of the free-response essay: vagueness and plot summary.
- Choose AP-level full-length novels or plays that you thoroughly recall and understand.
- Generally, use this year's material.
- Familiarize yourself with sample free-response prompts.
- Anticipate free-response prompts.

- Develop specific review materials for several full-length works.
- Practice applying your knowledge to a variety of prompts.
- Highlight the prompt to make certain you are addressing the requirements of the question.
- Do not waste time looking at the suggested works. Choose from your own memory bank.
- Plan the essay thoroughly before you begin writing.
- Briefly chart your response. Fill in with concrete details and quotes, if possible.
- Write an engaging opening paragraph that reflects the question's requirements.
- Stay on topic.
- *Avoid plot summary.*
- Include transitions and echo words.
- Review our models and rubrics for self-evaluation.
- Share your ideas with others.

Steps to Achieving Six Points for the AP English Literature Exam Essays

I. (Row A, 1 pt.) The thesis

    A. Clearly address the elements of the essay prompt.

    B. Structure your argument by drawing from the text.

    Note: An essential requirement of this section is a "defensible interpretation." This is a phrase used for the 1-point Thesis component for all three essays.

    C. Make sure your argument is clear and logical.

II. (Row B, 4 pts.) Using evidence and providing commentary

    A. Provide specific evidence to support ALL claims in your line of reasoning.

        1. For prose and poetry arguments, you will supply specific, direct evidence from the text.

        2. For the literary argument, you will draw from specific scenes, characterizations, and settings.

        3. Supporting ALL claims puts you in the best position to be receive either 3 or 4 points for this section. While incorporation of developed commentary and literary elements will also be essential to scoring 4 points, the support of ALL claims establishes a strong foundation to achieve a 4.

    B. Consistently explain HOW the evidence supports your line of reasoning (Commentary).

        1. Demonstrate control of your argument by not merely presenting evidence but by also integrating clear connections between that material and the underlying reasoning.

        2. Establish a line of reasoning and be consistent. This is essential in putting you in the best possible position to gain all 4 points in this section. Point deductions result from the absence of a line of reasoning and inconsistent explanations of evidence.

    C. Explain how multiple literary elements of techniques contribute to a work's meaning.

        1. This rubric element applies directly to the poetry and prose essays. However, your integration of literary elements into the literary argument could very well help you achieve the demonstration of sophistication (Row C) by presenting a complex literary argument.

        2. Using multiple literary elements of techniques puts you in the best position to achieve 4 points in this section. Using one literary element or technique puts you in the 3-point range while using no elements or techniques drops you to 2 points or fewer.

III. (Row C, 1 pt.) Sophistication of thought and/or development of a complex literary argument

    A. To earn this point, you must demonstrate sophistication of thought by doing any of the following:

        1. Identifying and exploring complexities or tensions within the poem, passage, or selected work.

        2. Illuminating [your] interpretation by situating it within a broader context.

        3. Accounting for alternative interpretations of the poem, passage, or selected work.

        4. Employing a style that is consistently vivid and persuasive.

    B. The preceding criteria are consistent for all three essays.

Note: The requirement of "doing any one of the following" allows you to approach sophistication based on the specific text you are considering. In other words, the ambiguity in a poem might lead you to examine alternative interpretations, while an historically situated prose passage might call for placing the interpretation into a broader context.

    C. Demonstrate consistent development when you are incorporating any one of the preceding four opportunities.

Note: The final note of this "sophistication" (Row C) stipulates: This point should be awarded only if the sophistication of thought or complex understanding is part of the student's argument, not merely a phrase or reference. Therefore, you need to integrate this sophistication fully into your essay.

STEP 4

Review the Knowledge
You Need to Score High

Introduction to Review Section

Why a Review Section? Why Not Just Provide a Series of Practice Exams?

Since the AP Lit exam is the culminating, evaluative tool for your high school English career, it would be wonderful if it could be truly representative of all that you have learned. But, it is only a 3-hour test. Therefore, it must of necessity be general, and it must be wide ranging enough to provide equity and opportunity for every student who takes the exam. What the test makers assume about the students who take the AP Lit exam is a common background of terminology and skills.

The following three chapters are not a replacement for your serious in-class study and practice. Instead, they provide a resource for terminology and skills when you need clarification or explanation. We want the information to enhance your analytical skills and to present you with direction you might not have considered.

CHAPTER 8

Comprehensive Review—Prose

IN THIS CHAPTER

Summary: A brief review of terms and processes associated with prose analysis

Key Ideas
- ✪ Understand the components of a narrative
- ✪ Explore various types of novels
- ✪ Learn literary terminology related to analysis
- ✪ Understand various levels of interpretation

Introduction to Prose

Our desire to know ourselves and others, to explore the unknown mysteries of existence, to make sense out of chaos, and to connect with our own kind are all primary reasons for engaging in the process of literary analysis.

The benefits to self and society that result from this interaction include a sense of wonder at the glory of humanity's imagination, a sense of excitement at the prospect of intellectual challenge, and a sense of connection with the universe.

You have already engaged in these lofty experiences. This section will provide a brief review of terms and processes associated with the study of literature. Included are some suggested activities for you to try which will help you prepare for the exam.

What Is Prose?

As you know, prose is the written equivalent of the spoken language. It is written in words, phrases, sentences, paragraphs, and chapters. It utilizes punctuation, grammar, and vocabulary to develop its message. Prose is made up of fiction and nonfiction. For the AP Lit exam, you are required to be well read in the areas of:

- Fiction, which includes:
  - Novels
  - Short stories
- Nonfiction, which includes:
  - Essays
  - Autobiographies and biographies
  - Speeches
  - Journals
  - Articles

Note: A brief word about drama. Since this section is a review of prose designed to prepare you for the AP Lit exam, it is not feasible to address every literary distinction and definition. Therefore, we wish to stress the following:

- Specific terminology can be found in the Glossary at the back of this book.
- All the techniques examined for prose can be used to analyze drama as well.
- The overlapping nature of the analytical skills makes them suitable for prose, poetry, and drama.

Five Aspects of Every Narrative

There is a certain degree of universality regarding definitions of terms when analyzing literature. For clarity and understanding, you should be aware of the following terms.

Plot

The plot is a series of episodes in a *narrative* carried out by the *characters*. Here are the primary terms related to plot. You should be familiar with all of them. Obviously each work manipulates these concepts in its own unique way.

- *Initial incident:* the event that puts the story in gear.
- *Rising action:* the series of complications in the narrative.
- *The climax:* the highest point of interest, action, or tension. More subtly, it is a turning point in the protagonist's behavior or thoughts.
- *Falling action:* the series of events occurring after the climax.
- *Denouement:* the resolution that ties up the loose ends of the plot.

These form the skeleton of a discussion about plot. But there are also other elements that add to your comprehension.

- *Foreshadowing:* hints at future events.
- *Flashbacks:* cut or piece a prior scene into the present situation.
- *In medias res:* literally, to be in the middle. This is a device that places the reader immediately into the action.

- *Subplot:* secondary plot that explores ideas that are different from the main story line.
- *Parallel plot:* a secondary story line that mimics the main plot.

Setting

Traditionally, setting is the time and place of a work, but it is also so much more. Setting is not accidental. It is a vital part of the narrative, and it can serve many functions. You should consider setting in light of the following:

- *General:* to underscore the universality of the work ("The Open Boat").
- *Specific:* to create a definitive ambiance that impacts on the work's possibilities (*The Kite Runner*).
- *Character or foil:* in relation to the protagonist (*Brave New World*).
- *Limiting factor:* to allow the plot, character, and theme to develop (*Lord of the Flies*).
- To *reveal style* (*To the Lighthouse*).
- To *reveal character* (*Hedda Gabler*).
- To *reveal theme* (*Heart of Darkness*).

Your Turn

Choose a literary text you've read during the past two years and examine a particularly effective setting.

1. Jot down the major specifics of the setting.

2. Identify the function(s) of that setting.

Title: _____

Setting: _____

_____

Details/Specifics   **Function(s)**

_____   _____

_____   _____

_____   _____

_____   _____

_____   _____

_____   _____

Character

Character development can be both simple and complex. The author has a variety of methods from which to choose. Here's a mnemonic device that may help you analyze character: Use the word **STAR**.

- *S*—what the character *says*;
- *T*—what the character *thinks*;
- *A*—how the character *acts* and interacts; and
- *R*—how the character *reacts*.

Traditionally, characters carry out the plot, and it is around the characters that the plot revolves and the theme is developed. There can be many types of characters in a given work:

- *Protagonist:* the main character who is the central focus of the story. For example, Hamlet is the eponymous protagonist.
- *Antagonist:* the opposing force. It does not always have to be a person. For example, the sea or the fish in *The Old Man and the Sea*.
- *Major:* the character or characters who play a significant role in the work.
- *Minor:* the characters who are utilized for a specific purpose, such as moving the plot along or contrasting with a major character.
- *Dynamic:* refers to characters who undergo major changes, such as Jane Eyre.
- *Static:* generally refers to characters who remain the same throughout the story. For instance, Brutus in *Julius Caesar* always considers himself to be an "honorable man."
- *Stereotype:* a character who is used to represent a class or a group.
- *Foil:* a character who provides the opportunity for comparison and contrast. For example, in Shakespeare's *Julius Caesar*, Brutus and Cassius are foils for each other.

Character as Hero

Once again, you may encounter many variations on the concept of hero:

"Be consistent and persistent in maintaining a literary journal. Students who do this have greater recall of information that they can incorporate into their literary essays."
—Charles V.
    AP teacher

- Aristotelian tragic hero:
  - Of noble birth; larger than life
  - Basically good
  - Exhibits a fatal flaw
  - Makes error in judgment
  - Possesses hubris (excessive arrogance or pride) which causes the error in judgment
  - Brings about his own downfall
  - Has a moment of realization, an epiphany
  - Lives and suffers
  - Examples: Creon in *Antigone*, Oedipus in *Oedipus*, Jason in *Medea*

- Classical hero: a variation on the tragic hero:
  - Examples: Macbeth in *Macbeth*, Lear in *King Lear*, Hamlet in *Hamlet*

- Romantic hero:
  - Larger than life
  - Charismatic
  - Possesses an air of mystery
  - "Saves the day" or the heroine

- Embodies freedom, adventure, and idealism
- Often outside the law
- Examples: Robin Hood, James Bond

- Modern hero:
  - May be everyman
  - Has human weaknesses
  - Caught in the ironies of the human condition
  - Struggles for insight
  - Examples: Willy Loman in *Death of a Salesman*, Offred in *The Handmaid's Tale*, Oscar Wao in *The Brief Wondrous Life of Oscar Wao*

- Hemingway hero:
  - Brave
  - Endures
  - Maintains a sense of humor
  - Exhibits grace under pressure
  - Examples: Santiago in *The Old Man and the Sea*, Jake Barnes in *The Sun Also Rises*

- Antihero: Protagonist is notably lacking in heroic qualities:
  - Examples: Meursault in *The Stranger*, Randall McMurphy in *One Flew Over the Cuckoo's Nest*, Okonkwo in *Things Fall Apart*

Theme

Theme is the main idea, the moving force, what it's all about, the "why" behind the "what," the universal concept or comment, the big picture, the major insight, the *raison d'être*. But theme is much more than a simple checklist. And, we cringe each time we hear, "What is the theme?" Remember, the enlightened, complex mind questions, ponders, responds. A literary work evolves and can be validly interpreted in so many ways that it would be a disservice to limit it to any single, exclusive theme.

Keeping an open mind, understand that the following is an overview of ways of assessing themes. All elements of a literary work point toward the development of the theme. Therefore, you will apply all that you have been learning and practicing in your search for a discernible, supportable theme.

Motif In its most general sense, motif is the repetition of an image. It may be closely connected to symbol, or it may be a thematic restatement.

The following is a preparation process for discovering and analyzing the function of motif. You can try this with any work.

- Isolate some general motifs you've noticed in a work.
- Provide specific examples to illustrate the motif.
- Draw inferences from your observations.

These rough inferences may lead you to a better understanding of character and theme. The following is a sample worksheet that uses the above process to analyze motif in Tennessee Williams's *A Streetcar Named Desire*.

Motif in *A Streetcar Named Desire*

MOTIF	EXAMPLE	THEMATIC IMPLICATIONS
Color	White woods (Blanche DuBois) Blue piano Red pajamas—Stanley Allan Grey	Red/white/blue = American theme Blue/gray—Civil War? Rape of Old South? Destruction of a way of life
Music	The blues "Only a Paper Moon" (if you believed in me) Captive maiden	Loss/sorrow, betrayal Lack of reality—insanity Control/slavery

Animals	Blanche:
	   fine feathered/wildcat
	   trapped bird/tiger
	   moth to light
	Stanley:
	   rooster/pig
	   ape
	   goat/Capricorn
		ego/id
		duality
		self-destruction
		
		survival of the fittest
		Darwinism/primitivism
		Dionysian—rape

Here's another way to work through an idea about theme. Sometimes it's easier to input a theme and then prove it with support from a work. If you can defend an idea with several specifics, you probably have identified a theme. Let's look at Shakespeare's *Hamlet*:

Hamlet

POSSIBLE THEME	EVIDENCE
What is, is not	1. Hamlet is not mad, only north-northwest. 2. Polonius is not Claudius in Gertrude's chamber. 3. Ophelia is not disinterested in Hamlet's overtures. 4. Rosencrantz and Guildenstern are not Hamlet's "friends."
Vengeance	1. Old Hamlet's charge to Hamlet to redress his murder. 2. Laertes's vow to avenge his father's death. 3. Fortinbras's victory to avenge his father.

Obviously, we have provided the organization in our samples, but these two techniques are solid, reliable processes. They will work on the exam, too, especially as you interrelate ideas for your essays or identify points that may be the topic of multiple-choice questions.

Keep a section in your notes where you enter important motifs, images, and so on and their implications from works you study. These concrete details will be invaluable when you write the free-response essay. Keep in mind that motif, imagery, symbol, and theme build on one another and are interrelated.

Point of View

Point of view is the method the author utilizes to tell the story. It is the vantage point from which the narrative is told. You've had practice with this in both reading and writing.

- *First person*: The narrator is the story's protagonist. (I went to the store.)
- *Third-person objective*: The narrator is an onlooker reporting the story. (She went to the store.)
- *Third-person omniscient*: The narrator reports the story and provides information unknown to the character(s). (She went to the store unaware that in three minutes she would meet her long-lost mother selling apples on the corner.)
- *Stream of consciousness*: This is a narrative technique that places the reader in the mind and thought processes of the narrator, no matter how random and spontaneous that may be (e.g., James Joyce's *Ulysses*).
- *Chorus*: Ancient Greek plays employed a chorus as a narrative device. The chorus, as needed, could be a character, an assembly, the playwright's voice, the audience, an omniscient forecaster. This function can be seen in modern works as well.
- *Stage manager*: This technique utilizes a character who comments omnisciently (e.g., *Our Town*, *The Glass Menagerie*).
- *Interior monologue*: This technique reflects the inner thoughts of the character.

    Note: In modern literature, authors often use multiple forms of narration. For example, in *As I Lay Dying* by William Faulkner, every chapter has a different narrator.

Types of Novels

There are many types of novels you will encounter during your study of English literature. Some novels exhibit several qualities. A few of the most common genres are:

- *Epistolary*: These novels utilize the convention of letter writing and are among the earliest novel forms (e.g., *Pamela*, *Dracula*, *The Color Purple*).
- *Picaresque*: This early, episodic novel form concentrates on the misadventures of a young rogue (e.g., *Huckleberry Finn*, *Don Quixote*, *Tom Jones*, *Candide*).
- *Autobiographical*: This readily identifiable type is always told in the first person and allows the reader to directly interact with the protagonist (e.g., *David Copperfield*, *Catcher in the Rye*).
- *Gothic*: This type of novel is concerned with the macabre, supernatural, and exotic (e.g., *Frankenstein*, *Beloved*, *Dr. Jekyll and Mr. Hyde*).
- *Historical*: This form is grounded in a real context and relies heavily on setting and factual detail (e.g., *A Tale of Two Cities*, *War and Peace*).
- *Romantic*: This novel form is idealistic, imaginative, and adventuresome. The romantic hero is the cornerstone of the novel, which often includes exotic locales (e.g., *Wuthering Heights*, *Madame Bovary*).
- *Allegorical*: This type of novel is representative and symbolic. It operates on at least two levels. Its specifics correspond to another concept (e.g., *Animal Farm*, *The Handmaid's Tale*, *Lord of the Flies*).

Consider this. *Jane Eyre* has elements of all these types, as do many other novels. List and loosely categorize some of the major novels you've read.

_____

_____

_____

_____

_____

Literary Terminology

Literary analysis assumes the working knowledge of a common vocabulary.

The Kaleidoscope of Literary Meaning

Literary meaning is developed and revealed through various devices and techniques. What follows is a brief listing of those terms and devices most often used in prose, poetry, and drama.

- *Allusion*: An allusion is a reference to another work, concept, or situation which generally enhances the meaning of the work that is citing it. There are many types of allusions, and they may be implicit or explicit, highly limited or broadly developed. Often, modern readers may miss the context of a particular reference because they have a limited frame of reference. A few common categories of allusion follow:
  - *Mythological allusions*: These often cite specific characters. Common allusions might refer to the beauty of Aphrodite or the power of Zeus. "She followed like Niobe, all tears" (*Hamlet*). Sometimes the entire work may refer to a mythological event. The play *Desire Under the Elms* is a sustained allusion to the Phaedra legend, as well as the Oedipal myth.
  - *Biblical allusions*: These references may deal with circumstances as familiar as "the mark of Cain," "the fall from paradise," "the tribulations of Job," or "destruction by flood or fire." A character may have the "strength of Samson" or the "loyalty of Ruth."
  - *Historical allusions*: These kinds of allusions might refer to major historical events, such as Napoleon meeting his Waterloo or Nixon dealing with Watergate.
  - *Literary allusions*: Often works will refer to other well-known pieces. For example, *West Side Story* expects you to think of *Romeo and Juliet*. To describe a character as "quixotic" refers to Cervantes's great novel *Don Quixote*.
  - *Political allusions*: These references would be sustained in works like *Gulliver's Travels* or *Alice in Wonderland*. They might also be used briefly. If a character were called the next Julius Caesar, we might sense that he would be betrayed in some manner. *The Crucible* is a historical allusion to the Salem witch trials and is also a statement about McCarthyism in the 1950s.
  - *Contemporary allusions*: These are often lost when the current context is no longer in the public eye. For example, the Kardashians, TikTok, or "BoJack Horseman" may not remain in vogue, and, therefore, references to them would lose their effectiveness.

- _Ambiguity_: This is the seemingly incongruous and contradictory interpretations of meaning in a work. James Joyce and William Faulkner utilize ambiguity often in their writing.
- _Allegory_: A work that operates on another level. The characters and events may be interpreted for both literal and symbolic meaning. For example, _Of Mice and Men_ by Steinbeck is an indictment of the exploitation of the masses and a call to unionism as well as a story of doomed friendship. Other allegorical works include _The Old Man and the Sea_ by Hemingway, _Animal Farm_ by Orwell, _Candide_ by Voltaire, and _Pilgrim's Progress_ by John Bunyan.
- _Parable_: A parable is an allegorical story that is intended to teach. It generally provides a moral lesson or illustrates a guiding principle. "The Nun's Priest's Tale" in _The Canterbury Tales_ by Chaucer is a parable about vanity and pride.
- _Symbol_: This is an image that also represents something else. Some symbols appear to be extremely specific. In Hawthorne's _The Scarlet Letter_ the scarlet letter is a symbol of Hester's impropriety. It can also represent Hester's pride, talent, responsibility, and shame. The reader should always be open to the broadest interpretation of the concept of symbol, whether about character, setting, situation, detail, or whatever. Another example of symbol is the splitting of the chestnut tree in _Jane Eyre_. Here Brontë symbolizes the breach in the relationship between Jane and Rochester. The caged parrot Methuselah in _The Poisonwood Bible_ by Barbara Kingsolver is a symbol of the failed Republic of Congo, since the bird has been trapped for so long that it doesn't know how to take care of itself.
- _Connotation_: This is the implication that is suggested by a word or phrase rather than the word or phrase's actual, literal meaning. For example, the use of "antique land" instead of "ancient land" brings a richer connotation to Shelley's "Ozymandias." The reader must be especially open to the varied levels of meaning in poetry.
- _Denotation_: The literal meaning of a word or phrase. If a reader is attempting to present a valid interpretation of a literary work, he or she must pay attention to both the denotation and the connotation of the language.
- _Tone_: Tone is difficult to define but is relatively easy to assess. It is a subtle feeling that the author creates through diction. The following is a short list of words often used to describe tone. Notice that they are adjectives.

bitter	objective	idyllic
sardonic	naive	compassionate
sarcastic	joyous	reverent
ironic	spiritual	lugubrious
mocking	wistful	elegiac
scornful	nostalgic	gothic
satiric	humorous	macabre
vituperative	mock-serious	reflective
scathing	pedantic	maudlin
confidential	didactic	sentimental
factual	inspiring	patriotic
informal	remorseful	jingoistic
facetious	disdainful	detached
critical	laudatory	

- _Transition_: Do not be fooled into thinking that "transition" is an unimportant term. An author will give you a road map through his or her story's journey, and one of the best indicators of direction is the transition word or phrase. Transitions help to move the reader smoothly from one part of the text to another. Below is a list of the most effective commonly used transitions:

and	also	as a result	after
but	besides	for example	although
for	consequently	in addition	because
nor	furthermore	in the same way	once
or	however	on the contrary	since
so	likewise	on the other hand	unless
yet	moreover	otherwise	until
	nonetheless	unlike the former	while
	similarly		
	still		
	therefore		

Prose Analysis

A word about this section: There are many processes that will help you to understand prose, poetry, and drama.

These approaches may not all be suitable for every work, but they certainly are worth considering as methods for responding to subtleties that are in the work.

Name Analysis

Consider your name. Did your folks have a specific reason for choosing it? Does it have a family significance or a special cultural meaning? What would you choose for your name and why? Remember, names and identity are closely linked.

Authors often choose names that bring another dimension to a character or place. A good reader is sensitive to the implications of names. Here are a few interesting names and observations about each:

- Oedipus—swollen foot, seeker of truth
- Billy Budd—simple, melodic, young growth, ready to bloom
- Jane Eyre—Janus/beginning, air, err, heir, ere, eerie, ire
- Helen Burns—fever, fervor, mythological inspiration
- Mr. Mason—the Masons are a secret fraternity; he holds the secret
- Stella—star, light
- Kurtz—short, curt
- Willy Loman—low man
- Oscar Wao—combines English and Spanish

Your Turn

Create your own listing of literary names and their interpretations and implications. (This could also include place names, etc.)

Literary Work	Name	Interpretations

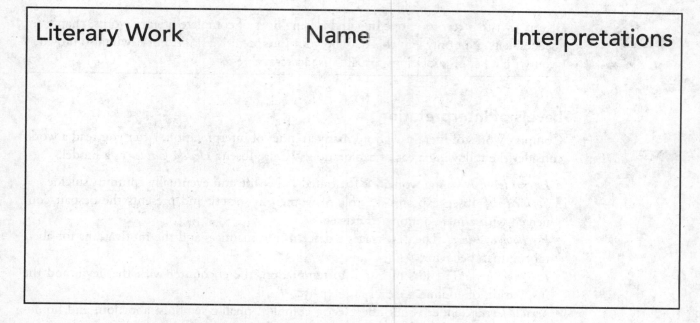

It's an Open-and-Closed Case

The first thing that catches your attention should be the title. By all means, consider it carefully. *David Copperfield* lets you know it will be a novel about character. *As I Lay Dying* involves plot and theme. *One Flew Over the Cuckoo's Nest* involves you immediately in symbol, character, and theme.

Authors place special emphasis on the first and last impressions they make on a reader. The opening and closing lines of chapters or scenes are, therefore, usually very significant and should be closely examined. (This is much like an establishing shot in a movie that sets up the audience for future developments.)

Here's the opening line from Chapter 1 of *Jane Eyre*:

There was no possibility of taking a walk that day.

Here are some implications of this one line: no independence, locked in, no sense of curiosity, outside force preventing a journey, not ready to leave. Obviously, the character is not ready to experience the outside world or to embark on her journey.

Contrast that with the last line of Chapter 1:

Four hands were laid upon me and I was borne upstairs.

This line introduces a spiritual level to the novel. It also implies that a new Jane will emerge, and indeed she does.

Take a look at one of the last lines of the novel:

We wended our way into the wood

This lovely, alliterative line completes the journey. Jane and Edward have come full circle as they stroll their way together.

In a Shakespearean play, often a couplet at the end of a scene or act will neatly summarize or foreshadow events. In *Julius Caesar*, for example:

And after this, let Caesar seat him sure
For we will shake him, or worse days endure (Julius Caesar)

Keep a written record of opening and closing lines of complete literary works, chapters, scenes, acts. Not only will this develop your interpretative skills, but it will also provide you with a list of quotations for later use in essays.

Levels of Interpretation

Complex works of literature afford many avenues of interpretation. After you read a work, consider the following areas of exploration. We use Ibsen's *Hedda Gabler* as a model.

- *Literal level*: A young woman is frustrated in her life and eventually commits suicide.
- *Social level*: Ibsen explores the role of women in society and presents the despair connected with a male-dominated existence.
- *Psychological level*: The play traces a descent into madness and the motivations for aberrant human behavior.
- *Religious level*: The loss of a soul to temptation, the encounter with the devil, and the inspiration of godliness are all in the play.
- *Sexual level*: Gender issues, the Electra complex, phallic symbols, abortion, and homosexuality are all developed and explored through numerous love triangles.
- *Political level*: The play could be read as a treatise on socialism. It denigrates capitalism and pays homage to the ideas of Marx's *Communist Manifesto*.

Obviously, you need to supply the evidence from the works to develop your interpretations in a concrete manner.

Note: A word about **subtext**:

Subtext refers to the implied meaning of a work or section of a work. It involves reading between the lines to discover subtle attitudes, comments, and observations within the piece. The exploration of subtext utilizes all of the interpretative skills you've been developing in your AP course.

Practice looking beyond the literal presentation of the plays, novels, and short stories you read. The following are richly suitable for such study:

Heart of Darkness	Joseph Conrad
Dubliners	James Joyce
The Grapes of Wrath	John Steinbeck
Les Miserables	Victor Hugo
The Kite Runner	Khaled Hosseini
Beloved	Toni Morrison

Final Comments

One of the more rewarding forms of preparation you can do involves developing a sensitivity to the words of a piece of literature.

Get a journal or set aside a section of your notebook for recording lines you respond to for their beauty, appeal, meaning, or relevance. For each work you read:

- Enter the lines.
- Identify the speaker and situation.

- Interpret, connect, comment, or reflect on your choice.
- Free-associate as well as relate the quotation to the original text.
- Make connections to other works you read.
- Project and expand on the lines.

For each full-length work, record at least ten references. Write these quotations out and include the page numbers so you can easily find them if you need to. Try to take them from throughout the work. Here is what is going to happen. Soon, you will automatically identify and respond to significant lines and passages. It will become second nature for you to identify lines of import and meaning in a work as you read. You will also begin to remember lines from a work and to connect them to important details, episodes, and themes. You will be able to understand and analyze a character in light of his or her own language. In other words, you will be interpreting literature based on text.

Rapid Review

- Every narrative is composed of plot, setting, character, theme, and point of view.
- Motifs develop characters and themes.
- Themes require specific illustrations to support them.
- There are many types of characters and heroes.
- There are many forms of narration.
- Novels may exhibit many characteristics.
- Meaning may be revealed via multiple approaches.
- Parables and allegories operate on symbolic levels. Connotations of words reveal the subtext of a work.
- Tone is a description of the attitude found in a piece of literature.
- Transitions aid movement and unity in a written work.
- Titles and names are important areas for analysis.
- First and last lines often carry great meaning in a work and demand careful attention.
- Works may be interpreted literally, socially, psychologically, sexually, politically, and so on.
- Quotations from works are an accurate way of understanding meaning and characterization. They also provide support for your interpretations.

Comprehensive Review—Poetry

IN THIS CHAPTER

Summary: Overview, including definitions, examples, and practice with poetic forms

Key Ideas
- ✪ Learn the differences between poetry and prose
- ✪ Understand the structure of poetry
- ✪ Explore various types of poetry
- ✪ Practice interpreting selected poems
- ✪ Compare and contrast given poems

Introduction to Poetry

Poetry—the very word inspires fear and trembling, and well it should because it deals with the intensity of human emotion and the experiences of life itself. But there is no reason to fear that which elevates, elucidates, edifies, and inspires. Poetry is a gift of language, like speech and song, and with familiarity comes pleasure and knowledge and comfort.

However, it may still be intimidating to read poetry. After all, we've been speaking and reading prose our entire lives. This review assumes that by the time you reach an AP-level literature course, you have some experience and facility with poetry. We provide you with definitions, examples, and practice with interpretation. Hopefully, you will provide the interest, diligence, and critical thinking necessary for a joyful and meaningful experience.

Remember our philosophy of firsts: First, we believe that you should read as much poetry as possible. Early in the year, pick up an anthology of poetry and read, read, read. Open to any page and read for pleasure and interest. Don't try to "study" the poems; just respond to them on an emotional level. Consider the following:

- Identify subjects that move you or engage you.
- Are there certain themes you respond to? Are there certain poets you like? List them and read more poetry by them.
- Are there certain types or styles of poems you enjoy? What do they seem to have in common?
- Are there images or lines you love? Keep a record of some of your favorites.

Make this a time to develop a personal taste for poetry. Use this random approach to experience a broad range of form and content. You should find that you are more comfortable with poetry simply because you have been discovering it at your own pace.

When you are comfortable and have honestly tried reading it for pleasure, it is time to approach it on a more analytical level.

The Structure of Poetry

What Makes Poetry Different from Prose?

How do you know when you're working with poetry and not prose? Simple. Just look at it. It's shorter; it's condensed; it's written in a different physical form. The following might help you to visualize the basic differences:

Prose	Poetry
Words	Syllables
Phrases	Feet
Sentences	Lines
Paragraphs	Stanzas
Chapters	Cantos

It should not be news to you when we say that poetry sounds different from prose. It is more musical, and it often relies on sound to convey meaning. In addition, it can employ meter, which provides rhythm. Did you know that poetry is from the ancient oral tradition of storytelling and song? Rhyme and meter made it easier for the bards to remember the story line. Try to imagine Homer in a dimly lit hall chanting the story of Odysseus.

As with prose, poetry also has its own jargon. Some of this lingo is specifically related to form and meter. The analysis of a poem's form and meter is termed **scansion**.

The Foot

The **foot** is the basic building block of poetry. It is composed of a pattern of syllables. These patterns create the meter of a poem. **Meter** is a pattern of beats or accents. We figure out this pattern by counting the stressed and unstressed syllables in a line. Unstressed syllables are indicated with a ˘, and stressed syllables are indicated with a ´.

There are five common patterns that are used repeatedly in English poetry. They are:

- The *iamb*   ˘ ´   (tŏ dáy) (bĕ cáuse)
- The *trochee*   ´ ˘   (háp pў) (líght lў)
- The *anapest*   ˘ ˘ ´   (ŏb vĭ oús) (rĕ gŭ lár)
- The *dactyl*   ´ ˘ ˘   (cĭg ă reŕte) (íń tĕr rŭpt)
- The *spondee*   ´ ´   (dówn tówn) (slíp shód)

The Line

Unlike the prose sentence, which is determined by subject, verb, and punctuation, the poetic line is measured by the number of feet it contains.

- 1 foot   monometer
- 2 feet   dimeter
- 3 feet   trimeter
- 4 feet   tetrameter
- 5 feet   pentameter
- 6 feet   hexameter
- 7 feet   heptameter
- 8 feet   octameter
- 9 feet   nonometer

Your Turn

Now answer the following. How many stressed syllables are in a line of:

Iambic pentameter   _____
Dactylic trimeter   _____
Anapestic dimeter   _____
Spondaic monometer   _____
Trochaic tetrameter   _____

Note: Answers can be found at the end of the definition of "meter" in the Glossary of terms.

The Stanza

You should now understand that syllables form feet, feet form lines, and lines form stanzas. Stanzas also have names:

- 1 line   a line
- 2 lines   couplet
- 3 lines   tercet
- 4 lines   quatrain
- 5 lines   cinquain
- 6 lines   sestet
- 7 lines   septet
- 8 lines   octave

Your Turn

What is the total number that results from adding up all of the metric references in the following, make-believe poem?

- The poem is composed of 3 quatrains, 2 couplets, and 1 sestet.
- Each quatrain is written in iambic tetrameter.
- The couplets are dactylic dimeter.
- The sestet is trochaic trimeter.

The total number is _____.

Note: You can find the answer at the end of the definition of "rhythm" in the Glossary of terms.

You will never have to be this technical on the AP exam. However, you will probably find a question on meter, and technical terms may be included in the answer choices to the multiple-choice questions. In addition, sometimes in the poetry essay you may find an opportunity to use your knowledge of scansion, or your analysis of the rhyme and meter of the poem, to develop your essay. This can be very effective if it is linked to interpretation.

Rhyme

One of the first processes you should become familiar with concerns the identification of a poem's rhyme scheme. This is easily accomplished by assigning consecutive letters of the alphabet to each new sound at the end of a line of poetry. Traditionally, rhyme scheme is indicated with italicized, lowercase letters placed to the right of each line of the poem.

- *a* for the first
- *b* for the second
- *c* for the third
- *d, e,* and so forth

Try this with the opening stanza from "Peace" by George Herbert.

> *Sweet Peace, where dost thou dwell? I humbly crave,*
> *Let me once know.*
> *I sought thee in a secret cave,*
> *And asked if Peace were there.*
> *A hollow wind did seem to answer, "No,*
> *Go seek elsewhere."*

You may restart the scheme with each new stanza or continue throughout the poem. Remember, the purpose is to identify and establish a pattern and to consider if the pattern helps to develop sound and/or meaning. Here's what the rhyme scheme looks like for the above selection: *a b a c b c.*

When you analyze the pattern of the complete poem, you can conclude that there is a very regular structure to this poem which is consistent throughout. Perhaps the content will also reflect a regular development. Certainly the rhyme enhances the sound of the poem and helps it flow. From now on we will refer to rhyme scheme when we encounter a new poem.

The rhymes we have illustrated are called **end rhymes** and are the most common. **Masculine rhyme** is the most frequently used end rhyme. It occurs when the last stressed syllable of the rhyming words matches exactly. ("The play's the thing / Wherein I'll catch the conscience of the king.") However, there are **internal rhymes** as well. These rhymes occur within the line and add to the music of the poem. An example of this is *dreary*, in Poe's "The Raven" ("Once upon a midnight dreary, while I pondered, weak and weary"). **Feminine rhyme** involves two consecutive syllables of the rhyming words, with the first syllable stressed. ("The horses were prancing / as the clowns were dancing.")

Types of Poetry

Because of its personal nature, poetry has evolved into many different forms, each with its own unique purpose and components. What follows is an examination of the most often encountered forms.

KEY IDEA

Most poetry falls into one of two major categories. ***Narrative poetry*** tells a story. ***Lyric poetry*** presents a personal impression.

The Ballad

The ***ballad*** is one of the earliest poetic forms. It is a narrative that was originally spoken or sung and has often changed over time. It usually:

- Is simple.
- Employs dialogue, repetition, minor characterization.
- Is written in quatrains.
- Has a basic rhyme scheme, primarily *a b c b*.
- Has a refrain which adds to its songlike quality.
- Is composed of two lines of iambic tetrameter which alternate with two lines of iambic trimeter.

The subject matter of ballads varies considerably. Frequently, ballads deal with the events in the life of a folk hero, like Robin Hood. Sometimes they retell historical events. The supernatural, disasters, good and evil, love and loss are all topics found in traditional ballads.

The following is a typical folk ballad. Read this poem out loud. Listen to the music as you read. Get involved in the story. Imagine the scene. Try to capture the dialect or sound of the Scottish burr.

Bonny Barbara Allan
by Anonymous

It was in and about the Martinmas* time,
When the green leaves were falling,
That Sir John Graeme, in the West Country,
Fell in love with Barbara Allan.

He sent his man down through the town,   5
To the place where she was dwelling:
"O haste and come to my master dear,
Gin ye be Barbara Allan."

Slowly, slowly rose she up,
To the place where he was lying,   10
And when she drew the curtain by:
"Young man I think you're dying."

"O it's I'm sick, and very, very sick,
And 'tis a' for Barbara Allan.'
O the better for me ye's never be,   15
Though your heart's blood were a-spilling.

"O dinna ye mind, young man," said she,
"When ye was in the tavern a drinking,

---

* St. Martin's Day, commemorates the funeral of St. Martin, also known as old Halloween Eve, the end of harvest.

That ye made the healths gae round and round,
And slighted Barbara Allan?"   20

He turned his face unto the wall,
And death was with him dealing:
"Adieu, adieu, my dear friends all,
And be kind to Barbara Allan."

And slowly, slowly raise she up,   25
And slowly, slowly left him,
And sighing said, she could not stay,
Since death of life had reft him.

She had not gane a mile or twa,
When she heard the dead-bell ringing,   30
And every jow* that the dead bell geid,
It cried, "Woe to Barbara Allan."

"O mother, mother, make my bed!
O make it saft and narrow!
Since my love died for me to-day,   35
I'll die for him to-morrow."

---

* Tolling of a bell.

After you've read the ballad, consider the following:

1. Check the rhyme scheme and stanza form. You should notice it is written in quatrains. The rhyme scheme is a little tricky here; it depends on pronunciation and is what is called a ***forced rhyme***. If you soften the "g" sound in the word "falling," it more closely rhymes with "Allan." Try this throughout the ballad, recognizing that the spoken word can be altered and stretched to fit the intention of rhyme. This falls under the category of "poetic license."

2. Follow the plot of the narrative. Poor Barbara Allan, poor Sir John. They are a classic example of thwarted young lovers, a literary pattern as old as Antigone and Haemon or Romeo and Juliet. Love, unrequited love, and dying for love are all universal themes in literature.

3. Observe the use of repetition and how it unifies the poem by sound and structure. "Barbara Allan / Slowly, slowly / Adieu, adieu / Slowly, slowly / Mother, mother."

4. Notice that dialogue is incorporated into the poem for characterization and plot development.

Don't be too inflexible when checking rhyme or meter. Remember, never sacrifice meaning for form. You're smart; you can make intellectual leaps.

Here are some wonderfully wicked and enjoyable ballads to read:

"Sir Patrick Spens"—the tragic end of a loyal sailor
"The Twa Corbies"—the irony of life and nature
"Edward"—a wicked, wicked, bloody tale

"Robin Hood"—still a great, grand adventure
"Lord Randall"—sex, lies, and death in ancient England
"Get Up and Bar the Door"—a humorous battle of the sexes
"La Belle Dame Sans Merci"—John Keats's fabulous tale of a demon lover
"Ballad of Birmingham"—Dudley Randall's recounting of the bombing of a church in Birmingham, Alabama, in 1963

Have you read ballads? Traditional or modern? List them here. Jot down a few details or lines to remind you of important points. If you're musical, try singing one out loud.

_____

_____

_____

_____

_____

The Lyric

Lyric poetry is highly personal and emotional. It can be as simple as a sensory impression or as elevated as an ode or elegy. Subjective and melodious, it is often reflective in tone.

The following is an example of a lyric:

A Red, Red Rose
by Robert Burns

O my luve's like a red, red rose,
That's newly sprung in June;
O my luve's like the melodie
That's sweetly played in tune.

As fair art thou, my bonnie lass,   5
So deep in luve am I;
And I will luve thee still, my dear,
Till a' the seas gang dry.

Till a' the seas gang dry, my dear,
And the rocks melt wi' the sun: 10
O I will luve thee still, my dear,
While the sands o' life shall run.

And fare the weel, my only luve,
And fare the weel awhile!
And I will come again, my luve,   15
Though it were ten thousand mile.

Now answer the following questions:

1. The stanza form is _____

2. The rhyme scheme is _____

3. The meter of line 6 is _____

4. The first stanza depends on similes. Underline them. _____

5. Cite assonance in stanza one. _____

6. Line 8 is an example of _____

7. Highlight alliteration in the poem. _____

8. Did you recognize iambic trimeter? How about hyperbole? _____

The following are wonderful lyric poems. Read a few.

Edna St. Vincent Millay—"Childhood Is the Kingdom Where Nobody Dies"
Emily Dickinson—"Wild Nights, Wild Nights"
Dylan Thomas—"Fern Hill"
Matthew Arnold—"Dover Beach"
Andrew Marvell—"To His Coy Mistress"
Carol Ann Duffy—"Syntax"
Elizabeth Alexander—"Praise for the Day"
Louise Glück—"Vita Nova"

The Ode

The *ode* is a formal lyric poem that addresses subjects of elevated stature. One of the most beautiful odes in English literature is by Percy Bysshe Shelley.

Ode to the West Wind

O wild West Wind, thou breath of Autumn's being,
Thou, from whose unseen presence the leaves dead
Are driven, like ghosts from an enchanter fleeing,

Yellow, and black, and pale, and hectic red,   5
Pestilence-stricken multitudes: O thou,
Who chariotest to their dark wintry bed

The wingéd seeds, where they lie cold and low,
Each like a corpse within the grave, until
Thine azure sister of the Spring shall blow   10

Her clarion* o'er the dreaming earth, and fill
(Driving sweet buds like flocks to feed in air)
With living hues and odors plain and hill:

Wild Spirit, which art moving everywhere;
Destroyer and preserver; hear, oh, hear!

        2   15

Thou on whose stream, mid the steep sky's commotion,
Loose clouds like earth's decaying leaves are shed,
Shook from the tangled boughs of Heaven and Ocean,

Angels of rain and lightning: there are spread
On the blue surface of thine aery surge,   20
Like the bright hair uplifted from the head

*Melodious trumpet call

Of some fierce Maenad,* even from the dim verge
Of the horizon to the zenith's height,
The locks of the approaching storm. Thou dirge

Of the dying year, to which this closing night   25
Will be the dome of a vast sepulcher,
Vaulted with all thy congregated might

Of vapors, from whose solid atmosphere
Black rain, and fire, and hail will burst: oh, hear!

3

Thou who didst waken from his summer dreams
The blue Mediterranean, where he lay,   30
Lulled by the coil of his crystalline streams

Beside a pumice isle in Baiae's† bay,
And saw in sleep old palaces and towers
Quivering within the wave's intenser day,

All overgrown with azure moss and flowers   35
So sweet, the sense faints picturing them! Thou
For whose path the Atlantic's level powers

Cleave themselves into chasms, while far below
The sea-blooms and the oozy woods which wear
The sapless foliage of the ocean, know   40

Thy voice, and suddenly grow gray with fear,
And tremble and despoil themselves: oh, hear!

4

If I were a dead leaf thou mightest bear;
If I were a swift cloud to fly with thee;
A wave to pant beneath thy power, and share   45

The impulse of thy strength, only less free
Than thou, O uncontrollable! If even
I were as in my boyhood, and could be

The comrade of thy wanderings over Heaven,
As then, when to outstrip thy skiey speed   50
Scarce seem a vision; I would ne'er have striven

As thus with thee in prayer in my sore need.
Oh, lift me as a wave, a leave, a cloud!
I fall upon the thorns of life! I bleed!

---

*Frenzied dancer
†A village near Naples, Italy

A heavy weight of hours has chained and bowed   55
One too like thee: tameless, and swift, and proud.

5

Make me thy lyre,* even as the forest is:
What if my leaves are falling like its own!
The tumult of thy mighty harmonies

Will take from both a deep, autumnal tone,   60
Sweet though in sadness. Be thou, Spirit fierce,
My spirit! Be thou me, impetuous one!

Drive my dead thoughts over the universe
Like withered leaves to quicken a new birth!
And, by the incantation of this verse,   65

Scatter, as from an unextinguished hearth
Ashes and sparks, my words among mankind!
Be through my lips to unawakened earth

The trumpet of a prophecy! O Wind,   70
If Winter comes, can Spring be far behind?

———————

*Small, harplike instrument

    As always, read the poem carefully. (Find a private place and read it aloud. You'll be carried away by the beauty of the sounds and imagery.) Now answer the following questions.

1. Look at the configuration of the poem. It is divided into five sections. What function might each section serve? _____

2. Count the lines in each section. How many? _____ Name the two stanza forms you encountered. _____

3. Check the rhyme scheme. Did you come up with *a b a b c b c d c d e d e e*? The first four tercets are written in a form called *terza rima*. Notice how this rhyme scheme interweaves the stanzas and creates unity throughout the poem. Did it cross your mind that each section might be a variation on the sonnet form? _____

4. Check the meter. You should notice that it is very irregular. (Freedom of form was a tenet of the Romantic Movement.)

5. Stanza one: Did you catch the *apostrophe*? The direct address to the wind places us in the poem's situation and provides the subject of the ode. Highlight the *alliteration* and trace the similes in line 3. _____

6. Stanza two: What are the "pestilence-stricken multitudes"? In addition to leaves, could they be the races of man? _____

7. Stanza three: See how the enjambment pulls you into this line. Find the simile. _____ Alliteration can be seen in "azure," "sister," "Spring," "shall."

8. Stanza four: What images are presented? _____ Locate the simile. _____ Find the contrast between life and death. _____ Highlight the personification.

9. Identify the essential paradox of the poem and life itself in the couplet.

We are not going to take you through the poem line by line. You may isolate those lines that speak to you. Here are a few of our favorites that are worth a second look:

- Lines 29–31
- Lines 35–42 for assonance
- Lines 53–54
- Lines 55–56
- Lines 57–70

You should be able to follow the development of ideas through the five sections. Were you aware of:

- The land imagery in section 1?
- The air imagery in section 2?
- The water imagery in section 3?
- The comparison of the poet to the wind in section 4?
- The appeal for the spirit of the wind to be the poet's spirit in section 5?

After you have read the poem, followed the organization, recognized the devices and images, you still have to interpret what you've read.

This ode has many possibilities. One interpretation linked it with the French Revolution and Shelley's understanding of the destructive regeneration associated with it. Another valid reading focuses on Shelley's loss of faith in the Romantic Movement. He asks for inspiration to breathe life into his work again. Try to propose other interpretations for this "Ode to the West Wind."

Here is a brief list of some odes you may want to consider:

"Ode on Intimations of Immortality"—William Wordsworth
"Ode to My Socks"—Pablo Neruda
"Homage to My Hips"—Lucille Clifton
"Ode on a Grecian Urn"—John Keats
"Ode to Silence"—Edna St. Vincent Millay
"Ode to Dirt"—Sharon Olds

The Elegy

The *elegy* is a formal lyric poem written in honor of one who has died. *Elegiac* is the adjective that describes a work lamenting any serious loss.

One of the most famous elegies is by Percy Bysshe Shelley. It was written to mourn the loss of John Keats. Here is the first stanza of "Adonais." It contains all the elements of an elegy.

Adonais*

I weep for Adonais—he is dead!
O, weep for Adonais! Though our tears
Thaw not the frost which binds so dear a head!
And thou, sad Hour, selected from all years
To mourn our loss, rouse thy obscure compeers,   5
And teach them thine own sorrow, say: "With me
Died Adonais; till the Future dares
Forget the Past, his fate and fame shall be
An echo and a light unto eternity!"

_____

* An elegy on the death of John Keats, author of "Endymion," "Hyperion," etc.

Read this stanza several times. Try it aloud. Get carried away by the emotion. Respond to the imagery. Listen to the sounds; let the meter and rhyme guide you through. Consider the following:

1. Adonais, Shelley's name for Keats, is derived from Adonis. This is a mythological allusion to associate Keats with love and beauty. (The meter will tell you how to pronounce Adonais.)

2. Check the rhyme scheme. Did you come up with *a b a b b c b c c*? See how the last two lines are rhymed to set this idea apart.

3. Line 1 contains a major *caesura* in the form of a dash. This forces the reader to pause and consider the depth of emotion and the finality of the event. The words that follow are also set off by the caesura and emphasized by the exclamation point. Notice that the meter is not interrupted by the caesura. (˘ ´ ˘ ´ ˘ ´ ˘ ´ ˘ ´ is perfect iambic pentameter.) This line is a complete thought which is concluded by punctuation and is an example of an *end-stopped line*.

4. Line 2 utilizes repetition to intensify the sense of loss. Here the caesura is an exclamation point. Notice that the last three words of the line fulfill the meter of iambic pentameter but do not express a complete thought as did line 1. The thought continues into line 3. This is an example of *enjambment*.

5. Lines 2 and 3 contain *alliteration* ("Though," "tears," "Thaw," "the") and *consonance* ("not," "frost," continuing into line 4 with "thou").

6. Line 3 contains *imagery* and *metaphor*. What does the frost represent? _____

_____

7. Line 4 contains an *apostrophe*, which is a direct address to the sad Hour, which is personified. To what event does the "sad Hour" refer? _____

_____

8. Lines 4, 5, and 6 incorporate *assonance*. The vowel sounds provide a painful tone through "ow" sounds ("thou," "Hour," "our," "rouse," "sorrow").

9. Notice how the enjambment in lines 7–9 speeds the stanza to the final thought. This helps the pacing of the poem.

10. Reread the poem. Choose images and lines you respond to.

Have you read any elegies? List them here. Jot down the poet, title, and any images and lines you like. Add your own thoughts about the poem.

_____

_____

_____

Following is a list of some of the most beautiful elegies in the English language. Make it a point to read several. You won't be sorry.

"Elegy for Jane" by Theodore Roethke—a teacher's lament for his student.
"Elegy in a Country Church Yard" by Thomas Gray—a reflective look at what might have been.
"When Lilacs Last in the Dooryard Bloomed" and "O Captain, My Captain" by Walt Whitman—tributes to Abraham Lincoln.
"In Memory of W. B. Yeats" by W. H. Auden—a poet's homage to a great writer.
"Lycidas" by John Milton on the death of a college friend.
"Timer" by Tony Harrison reflects on the death of his mother.
"Song for the Last Act" by Louise Bogen on the death of someone she cares for deeply.
"Minstrel Man" by Langston Hughes laments the stereotype of the minstrel slave.
"Candle in the Wind" by Elton John mourns the death of Princess Diana.

The Dramatic Monologue

The *dramatic monologue* relates an episode in a speaker's life through a conversational format that reveals the character of the speaker.

Robert Browning is the acknowledged master of the dramatic monologue. The following is an example of both the dramatic monologue and Browning's skill as a poet.

Porphyria's Lover

The rain set early in tonight,
    The sullen wind was soon awake.
It tore the elm-tops down for spite,
    And did its worst to vex the lake:
    I listened with heart fit to break.   5
When glided in Porphyria; straight
    She shut the cold out and the storm,
And kneeled and made the cheerless grate
    Blaze up, and all the cottage warm;
    Which done, she rose, and from her form   10
Withdrew the dripping cloak and shawl,
    And laid her soiled gloves by, untied
Her hat and let the damp hair fall,
    And, last, she sat down by my side
    And called me. When no voice replied,   15
She put my arm about her waist,
    And made her smooth white shoulder bare,
And all her yellow hair displaced,
    And, stooping, made my cheek lie there,
    And spread, o'er all, her yellow hair,   20

Murmuring how she loved me—she
    Too weak, for all her heart's endeavor,
To set its struggling passion free
    From pride, and vainer ties desever,
    And give herself to me forever.   25
But passion sometimes would prevail,
    Nor could tonight's gay feast restrain
A sudden thought of one so pale
    For love of her, and all in vain:
    So, she was come through wind and rain.   30
Be sure I looked up at her eyes
    Happy and proud; at last I knew
Porphyria worshipped me: surprise
    Made my heart swell, and still it grew
    While I debated what to do.   35
That moment she was mine, mine, fair,
    Perfectly pure and good: I found
A thing to do, and all her hair
    In one long yellow string I wound
    Three times her little throat around,   40
And strangled her. No pain felt she;
    I am quite sure she felt no pain.
As a shut bud that holds a bee,
    I warily oped her lids: again
    Laughed the blue eyes without a stain.   45
And I untightened next the tress
    About her neck; her cheek once more
Blushed bright beneath my burning kiss:
    I propped her head up as before,
    Only, this time my shoulder bore   50
Her head, which droops upon it still:
    The smiling rosy little head,
So glad it has its utmost will,
    That all it scorned at once is fled,
    And I, its love, am gained instead!   55
Porphyria's love: she guessed not how
    Her darling one wish would be heard.
And thus we sit together now,
    And all night long we have not stirred,
    And yet God has not said a word!   60

Read the poem aloud, or have someone read it to you. Try for a conversational tone.

1. Concentrate on following the storyline. (Were you surprised by the concluding events?)

2. Once you know the "story," look closely at the poem for all the clues concerning character and episode.

3. Automatically check for the relationship between form and content. Quickly scan for rhyme scheme and meter. You should notice a definite presence of rhyme in an unusual form *a b a b b c d c d d e f e f f*, etc. You should be able to recognize that the meter is iambic tetrameter. Rather than scan the entire poem, try lines throughout to see if a pattern exists.

4. *Lines 1–5:* What does the setting indicate or foreshadow? _____

_____

Lines 6–9: What diction and imagery is associated with Porphyria?

_____

Lines 10–12: Why are we told her gloves were soiled?

_____

Lines 20–25. Try to understand what the narrator is telling you here.

This reveals what is important to him. _____

Lines 30–37: Have you found the turning point? _____

Remember, literary analysis is like unraveling a mystery. Find motivational and psycho-logical reasons for the narrator's behavior. _____

_____

Line 41: Notice how the caesura emphasizes the finality of the event. You are forced to confront the murder directly because of the starkness of the syntax. This is followed by the narrator's justification.

Line 43: Did you catch the simile? It's a little tricky to spot when "as" is the first word.

_____

Line 55: What character trait is revealed by the narrator? _____

_____

Lines 59–60: Notice how the rhyming couplet accentuates the final thought and sets it off from the previous lines. Interpret the last line. Did you see that the last two lines are end-stopped, whereas the majority of the poem utilizes enjambment to create a conversational tone? _____

_____

5. Did you enjoy this poem? Did you feel as if you were being spoken to directly? _____

_____

The AP often uses dramatic monologues because they can be very rich in narrative detail and characterization. This is a form you should become familiar with by read-ing several from different times and authors. Try one of these: Robert Browning —"My Last Duchess," "The Soliloquy of the Spanish Cloister," "Andrea Del Sarto"; Alfred Lord Tennyson —"Ulysses," T. S. Eliot—"The Love Song of J. Alfred Prufrock," Ai—"Killing Floor," Federico Garcia Lorca—"The Unfaithful Housewife," Joshua McCarter Simpson—"No, Master, Never!," Alice Moore Dunbar-Nelson—"I Sit and Sew."

How many dramatic monologues have you read? List them here and add details and lines that were of interest and/or importance to you.

_____

_____

_____

_____

_____

The Sonnet

The **sonnet** is the most popular fixed form in poetry. It is usually written in iambic pentameter and is always made up of 14 lines. There are two basic sonnet forms: the *Italian* or *Petrarchan* sonnet, named after Petrarch, the poet who created it, and the *English* or *Shakespearean* sonnet, named after the poet who perfected it. Each adheres to a strict rhyme scheme and stanza form.

The subject matter of sonnets varies greatly, from expressions of love to philosophical considerations, religious declarations, or political criticisms. The sonnet is highly polished, and the strictness of its form complements the complexity of its subject matter. As you know by now, we like to explore the relationship between form and function. The sonnet effectively integrates these two concepts.

Let's compare the two forms more closely. The **Italian sonnet** is divided into an octave and a sestet. The rhyme scheme is:

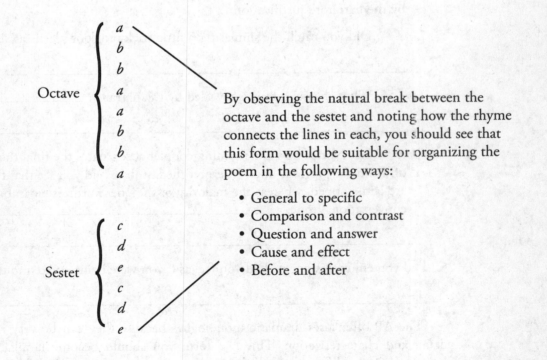

Octave
- a
- b
- b
- a
- a
- b
- b
- a

Sestet
- c
- d
- e
- c
- d
- e

By observing the natural break between the octave and the sestet and noting how the rhyme connects the lines in each, you should see that this form would be suitable for organizing the poem in the following ways:

- General to specific
- Comparison and contrast
- Question and answer
- Cause and effect
- Before and after

The **Shakespearean sonnet** has a different rhyme scheme and stanza form:

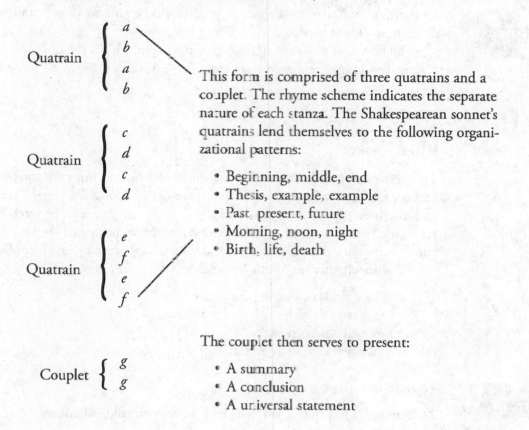

Quatrain
- a
- b
- a
- b

This form is comprised of three quatrains and a couplet. The rhyme scheme indicates the separate nature of each stanza. The Shakespearean sonnet's quatrains lend themselves to the following organizational patterns:

Quatrain
- c
- d
- c
- d

- Beginning, middle, end
- Thesis, example, example
- Past, present, future
- Morning, noon, night
- Birth, life, death

Quatrain
- e
- f
- e
- f

The couplet then serves to present:

Couplet
- g
- g

- A summary
- A conclusion
- A universal statement

Modern sonnets often vary rhyme and stanza form, but they will always have 14 lines.

For more practice with the sonnet, see Poems for Comparison and Contrast in this chapter. We recommend you read sonnets written by Shakespeare, Milton, Wordsworth, e e cummings, Edna St. Vincent Millay, and Keats. You might also want to examine some late twentieth and early twenty-first century sonnets, such as "Tapestry" by Amy Foreman, "America" by Clause McKay, "Potpourri" by Joseph Salem, and "Petrarch on West 115th Street" by Marion Shore.

The Villanelle

The **villanelle** is a fixed form in poetry. It has six stanzas: five tercets, and a final quatrain. It utilizes two refrains: The first and last lines of the first stanza alternate as the last line of the next four stanzas and then form a final couplet in the quatrain.

As an example, read: "Do Not Go Gentle Into That Good Night" by Dylan Thomas. Other villanelles that are worth a close reading include "The Art of Losing" by Elizabeth Bishop and "The Waking" by Theodore Roethke.

Interpretation of Poetry

KEY IDEA

Interpretation is not license for you to say just anything. Your comments/analysis/interpretation must be based on the given text.

How Do I Begin to Interpret Poetry?

To thoroughly understand a poem, you should be able to view it and read it from three different angles or viewpoints.

The first level is the *literal reading* of the poem. This is the discovery of what the poem is actually saying. For this, you only use the text:

- Vocabulary
- Structure
- Imagery
- Poetic devices

The *second level* builds on the first and draws conclusions from the connotation of the form and content and the interpretation of symbols. The *third level* refers to your own reading and interpretation of the poem. Here, you apply the processes of levels one and two, and you bring your own context or frame of reference to the poem. Your only restriction is that your interpretation is grounded in, and can be supported by, the text of the poem itself.

To illustrate this approach, let's analyze a very simple poem.

> Where ships of purple gently toss
> On seas of daffodil,
> Fantastic sailors mingle
> And then, the wharf is still.

1. Read it.

2. Respond. (You like it; you hate it. It leaves you cold. Whatever.)

3. Check rhyme and meter. We can see there is some rhyme, and the meter is iambic and predominantly trimeter. The first and third lines are irregular. (If this does not prove to be critical to your interpretation of the poem, move on.)

4. Check the vocabulary and syntax. Are there any words you are not familiar with?

5. Look for poetic devices and imagery.

6. Highlight, circle, connect key images and words.

7. Begin to draw inferences from the adjectives, phrases, verbs.

As an example, we have provided the following notes:

Movement

- Toss
- Mingle   } **Progression**
- Still

Images

- Ships
- Seas   } **Literally nautical**
- Sailors   } **Figuratively on a dock**
- Wharf

Syntax

- Ships of purple = purple ships (Where or when do you see purple ships?)
- Seas of daffodil = daffodil seas (When would seas be yellow?)
- Fantastic sailors = sailors of fantasy = clouds moving, birds flying (What might they be?)
- Wharf is still = place is quiet = ?

Put your observations together and formulate your interpretation. Write it below.

_____

_____

_____

Some students have said that they saw a field of flowers, bees and butterflies, a coronation, a celebration, and/or a royal event. These are all valid interpretations. Remember, this is only a simple exercise to acquaint you with the approaches you can use to analyze complex poetry. By the way, Emily Dickinson was writing about a sunset over Boston harbor.

Poetry for Analysis

This section will walk you through the analysis of several poems, presenting the poetry and a series of directed questions for you to consider. For maximum benefit, work with a highlighter and refer often to the poem. *Always* read the entire poem before you begin the analysis.

The Snake
by D. H. Lawrence

A snake came to my water-trough
On a hot, hot day, and I in pyjamas for the heat
To drink there.

In the deep, strange-scented shade of the great dark carobtree
I came down the steps with my pitcher   5
And must wait, must stand and wait, for there he was at the trough
    before me.

He reached down from a fissure in the earth-wall in the gloom
And trailed his yellow-brown slackness soft-bellied down, over the
    edge of the stone trough,   10
And rested his throat upon the stone bottom,
And where the water had dripped from the tap, in a small clearness,
He sipped with his straight mouth,
Softly drank through his straight gums, into his slack long body,
Silently.   15

Someone was before me at my water-trough,
And I, like a second comer, waiting
He lifted his head from his drinking, as cattle do,
And looked at me vaguely, as drinking cattle do,

And flickered his two-forked tongue from his lips, and mused a   20
     moment,
And stooped and drank a little more,
Being earth-brown, earth-golden from the burning bowels of the earth
On the day of Sicilian July, with Etna smoking.

The voice of my education said to me   25
He must be killed,
For in Sicily the black, black snakes are innocent, the gold are
     venomous.

The voice in me said, If you were a man
You would take a stick and break him now, and finish him off.   30

But must I confess how I liked him,
How glad I was he had come like a guest in quiet, to drink at my
     water-trough
And depart peaceful, pacified, and thankless,
Into the burning bowels of this earth?   35

Was it cowardice, that I dared not kill him?
Was it perversity, that I longed to talk to him?
Was it humility, to feel so honoured?
I felt so honoured.

And yet those voices: 40
If you were not afraid, you would kill him!
And truly I was afraid, I was most afraid,
But even so, honoured still more
That he should seek my hospitality
From out the dark door of the secret earth.   45

He drank enough
And lifted his head, dreamily, as one who has drunken,
And flickered his tongue like a forked night on the air, so black,
Seeming to lick his lips,
And looked around like a god, unseeing, into the air,   50
And slowly turned his head,
And slowly, very slowly, as if thrice a dream,
Proceeded to draw his slow length curving round
And climb again the broken bank of my wall-face.

And as he put his head into that dreadful hole,   55
And as he slowly drew up, snake-easing his shoulders, and entered
     farther,
A sort of horror, a sort of protest against his withdrawing into that
     horrid black hole,
Deliberately going into blackness, and slowly drawing himself   60
     after,
Overcame me now his back was turned.

I looked round, I put down my pitcher,
I picked up a clumsy log
And threw it at the water-trough with a clatter.   65

I think it did not hit him,
But suddenly that part of him that was left behind convulsed in
      undignified haste.
Writhed like lightning, and was gone
Into the black hole, the earth-lipped fissure in the wall-front,   70
At which, in the intense still noon, I stared with fascination.

And immediately I regretted it.
I thought how paltry, how vulgar, what a mean act!
I despised myself and the voices of my accursed human education.
And I thought of the albatross,   75
And I wished he would come back, my snake.

For he seemed to me again like a king,
Like a king in exile, uncrowned in the underworld,
Now due to be crowned again.
And so, I missed my chance with one of the lords   80
Of life.
And I have something to expiate:
A pettiness.

1. Since there is no regular rhyme scheme or length of lines or stanza form, we may conclude that this is *free verse*. _____ Yes _____ No

2. After reading the poem, you should be able to determine the situation, which is
   _____, and the speaker, who is
   _____.

3. The first stanza establishes the conflict, which is _____
   _____.

4. Find evidence of the developing conflict in lines 4–6. _____

5. Find examples of alliteration and assonance in lines 7–13. Notice how the sounds are appropriate for a snake rather than just random sounds.

6. Read line 12 aloud. Hear how slowly and "long" the sounds are, like the body of the snake itself.

7. Circle or highlight the imagery in lines 16–24. _____
   Notice how the scene is intensifying.

8. Restate the speaker's position in lines 25–28. _____

9. In lines 31–38, identify the conflict and the thematic ideas of the poem. Highlight them.

10. Identify the opposition facing the speaker in lines 36–39. State it. _____

_____

11. In lines 46–54, highlight the similes presented. Explore the nature of a snake and the connotation associated with one. _____

12. Interpret the setting as presented in lines 55–62. _____

13. The poem breaks at line 63. Highlight the change in the speaker at this point. Who is to blame for this action? _____

14. In line 75 there is a reference or allusion to the "Rime of the Ancient Mariner" by Coleridge, which is a poem in which a man learns remorse and the meaning of life as the result of a cruel, spontaneous act. Is this a suitable comparison for this poem's circumstances? Why? _____

15. Identify the similes and metaphor in lines 66–71. _____

16. Elaborate on the final confession of the speaker. May we conclude that the poem is a modern dramatic monologue? _____

After you have considered these ideas, expand your own observations. Might the entire poem be a metaphor? Can it be symbolic of other pettinesses? Can you interpret this poem socially, religiously, politically, psychologically, sexually?

The following poem is particularly suitable for the interpretation of symbolism. Apply what you have learned and reviewed and respond to this sample.

The Sick Rose
by William Blake

O Rose, Thou Art Sick!
The Invisible Worm
That flies in the night
In the howling Storm,

Has found out thy bed
Of Crimson joy,
And his dark secret love
Does thy life destroy.

Try your hand at interpreting this poem:

1. Literally

2. Sexually

3. Philosophically

4. Religiously

5. Politically

Apply the following thematic concepts to the poem:

1. Passion

2. Deceit

3. Betrayal

4. Corruption

5. Disease

6. Madness

Interesting, isn't it, how much can be found or felt in a few lines. Read other poems by Blake, such as "Songs of Innocence" and "Songs of Experience."

Poems for Comparison and Contrast

In the past, the AP would occasionally present compare and contrast selections of two poems. While these essays are no longer given on the exam, comparing and contrasting two poems offers a valuable, if secondary, exercise. This type of question can provide you with a chance to really explore ideas.

Following are two poems suitable for this kind of analysis. Read each poem carefully. Take a minute to look at them and allow a few ideas to take shape in your mind. Then plan your approach logically. Remember, form and content are your guidelines.

She Walks in Beauty
by Lord Byron

She walks in Beauty, like the night
    Of cloudless climes and starry skies;
And all that's best of dark and bright
    Meet in her aspect and her eyes:
Thus mellowed to that tender light   5
    Which heaven to gaudy day denies.

One shade the more, one ray the less,
    Had half impaired the nameless grace
Which waves in every raven tress,
    Or softly lightens o'er her face;   10
Where thoughts serenely sweet express,
    How pure, how dear their dwelling-place.

And on that cheek, and o'er that brow,
  So soft, so calm, yet eloquent,
The smiles that win, the tints that glow,   15
  But tell of days in goodness spent,
A mind at peace with all below,
  A heart whose love is innocent!

Sonnet 130
by William Shakespeare

My mistress' eyes are nothing like the sun;
Coral is far more red than her lips' red;
If snow be white, why then her breasts are dun;
If hairs be wires, black wires grow on her head.
I have seen roses damasked red and white,   5
But no such roses see I in her cheeks;
And in some perfumes is there more delight
Than in the breath that from my mistress reeks.
I love to hear her speak, yet well I know
That music hath a far more pleasing sound;   10
I grant I never saw a goddess go:
My mistress, when she walks, treads on the ground.
And yet, by heaven, I think my love as rare
As any she belied with false compare.

It is essential that you read each poem again, marking, highlighting, connecting, etc. those points you will develop. List or chart your findings before you begin to write your essay.

Common Elements

- Both have the same topic—to a lover
- Both use similes: "She Walks"—"like the night"; "Sonnet 130"—"nothing like the sun"
- Both rely on nature imagery: "She Walks"—"starry skies"; "Sonnet 130"—"Coral, roses"
- Both deal with light or dark
- Both include references to lover's hair: "She Walks"—"raven tress"; "Sonnet 130"—"black wires"
- Both appeal to the senses: "She Walks"—"raven tress"; "Sonnet 130"—perfume, roses, music, garlic stink
- Both use alliteration: "She Walks"—"cloudless climes"; "Sonnet 130"—"goddess go"

Differences

- Form: "She Walks" lyric, has sestets; "Sonnet 130," 12 + 2 (3 quatrains and couplet)
- Kind of love: "She Walks" serious and adoring; "Sonnet 130"—critical and humorous
- Diction: "She Walks"—positive; "Sonnet 130"—negative
- Ending: "She Walks"—adoring; "Sonnet 130"—realistic
- Tone: "She Walks"—idyllic; "Sonnet 130"—realistic

"Practice. Practice. Practice."
—Martha W.
  AP teacher

Rapid Review

- Poetry has its own form.
- The foot, line, and stanza are the building blocks of poetry.
- Meter and rhyme are part of the sound of poetry.
- There are many types of rhyme forms.
- There are many types of poetic feet. They may be iambic, trochaic, anapestic, dactylic, or spondaic.
- There are several stanza forms.
- Narrative poetry tells stories.
- Ballads are simple narratives.
- Lyric poetry is subjective and emotional.
- Odes are formal lyrics that honor something or someone.
- Elegies are lyrics that mourn a loss.
- Dramatic monologues converse with the reader as they reveal events.
- The sonnet is a 14-line form of poetry.
- The villanelle is a fixed form that depends on refrains.
- Levels of interpretation depend on the literal and figurative meaning of poems.
- Symbols provide for many levels of interpretation.

CHAPTER 10

A Practical Approach— PLOTSUMAR

IN THIS CHAPTER

Summary: The culmination of applying the knowledge of the previous chapters to the poetry and prose essays

Key Ideas

✪ Learn a variety of approaches to examine poetry and prose
✪ Understand to look for how an author delivers meaning
✪ Explore how to avoid clichéd responses to applying literary technique
✪ Incorporate how techniques enhance the author's meaning
✪ Practice using PLOTSUMAR on a sample poem

Introduction to PLOTSUMAR

When writing AP poetry and prose essays, students naturally look at a work for its subject matter. Many are not sure what to say beyond the general meaning of the poem or passage. The AP essays are more often asking for *how* a poem/passage means rather than *what* a poem/passage means. By analyzing how a poem/passage arrives at meaning, a student is able to achieve deeper interpretations of the poem/passage.

The following is one way to make sure you examine how the writer goes about delivering meaning beyond the basic message. The following approach, called PLOTSUMAR, guides students through how the author goes about presenting the subject. What is PLOTSUMAR, you ask? It is a cheesy but handy acronymic device formulated to help you remember what to do on your essays. Certainly a student can draw on other approaches beyond PLOTSUMAR. For example, a work's title can often serve as a fine instrument for further investigation. However, PLOTSUMAR offers truly reliable approach to analysis. Remember, if you use PLOTSUMAR, you will always have something to write.

P Perspective: What is the narrator's view? Does that view evolve? Disintegrate? Is the narrator's perspective/tone different from the author's?

L Language: What is the language like? How does it fit with the subject matter? Is it ironic? How does it affect and, more important, effect meaning? Change a reader's outlook?

O Omissions: Every writer must make choices to create maximum effect in limited space. What is left out of the work? Why?

T Technique: Be aware of the employment of literary devices such as metaphor, simile, alliteration, assonance, consonance, metonymy, synecdoche, personification. More important, discuss the effect they have on the work, and don't say they make the work more interesting or vivid. Have an idea behind the application of the technique.

S Sound: Are there any strange or different sounds in the work and to what effect?

U Unusual: Is there any unusual phrasing or syntax? Do certain lines stand out? Are there paradoxes, puns, or oxymorons? What effect do they have on the work?

M Mechanics: Look for any distinguishing punctuation or capitalization and think about what effect they have on the work. Are there patterns you can discern in this punctuation or capitalization? If not, can any insight be drawn from the apparent randomness?

A Ambiguity: What lines have an unclear meaning? Don't ignore these lines, but address them head on, suggesting the various interpretations and what they reveal about the work. Why did the author make these lines or elements ambiguous? What might they mean?

R Repetition: Are lines, phrases, or words repeated? To what effect? Repetition does not have to be exact and precise. One line, phrase, or word can sound a good deal like another, creating an echo effect. Certain words and lines have a way of resonating throughout the entire work. Keep in mind their effect.

PLOTSUMAR in Action

The most useful part of preparing for the AP English Literature exam is it gives you a marvelous opportunity for intellectual growth. You are learning to discover greater meaning through the nuances of language. Within every word sits an idea and the relationships between those words can expand and enrich one idea or they can introduce a multitude of ideas. PLOTSUMAR helps you scour those places where ideas hide. Now you need to be able to express those ideas in a sophisticated way that can lead you to insight. Obviously, there can be no one methodology to finding meaning from a poem, just as a doctor cannot have merely one test to discover what is wrong with a patient. But the following are a series of approaches that should help you. The *What not to say* comments indicate the common responses and clichés that are devoid of meaning and do not advance an essay. The *What to consider* comments are designed to move a reader from identifying an approach an author employs to how that approach enhances meaning.

P Perspective

Narrators, Characters, and Points-of-View

What not to say: The first-person narrator allows the reader to get an insider understanding. **OR** The third-person narrator gives the reader a broader viewer of what is going on. **OR** The omniscient narrator knows everything that is going on. **OR** The two characters offer different points-of-view.

What to consider: First off, figure out how many viewpoints are being presented in the poem/passage. Sometimes, a single narrator appears. In that case, recognize whether the narrator employs a first- or third-person voice, or even a second person voice, using "you" to speak directly to another character or the reader. Do not dismiss other characters who are not the narrator. Their viewpoints can be presented through dialogue, their reactions . . . even their manners. The interactions among narrator and multiple characters can present a multitude of perspectives. Whenever a reader is struggling about what to say beyond the basic content of the passage, the narrative perspective is great opportunity to speak about how the author is making meaning.

L Language

Diction and Imagery

What not to say: The imagery makes the reader feel like she is right in the middle of the action.

What to consider: Look to organize diction in a work according to subject or theme. Try to be as specific in these categories as possible. For example, instead of saying nature imagery, see if the diction fits in a small subset like water imagery. In addition, if you can cluster that diction into a sentence by using parentheses to present both the argument and evidence, the essay will gain greater force through this concision. To demonstrate, here is a sentence employing this approach: *The water imagery ("soak," "riptide," "waves," and "plunge") suggests the character is metaphorically drowning.*

O Omissions

The Unnamed and the Unmentioned

What not to say: The author has left out this information because it is not relevant.

What to consider: An author can choose to not identify a character by more than her position (e.g., a doctor) or a relationship (e.g., a daughter). The reasons could well be to impose universal qualities on the character, but could as likely be to heighten the importance of that position or relationship. The absence of what would often be key information—such as what caused a breakup or why someone is dying—can speak to a narrator's focus or obsession. It can speak to a narrator's or character's unwillingness to focus on anything else but the situation at hand. Simply put, a narrator/character can be too wrapped up in some pressing business or emotion to offer anything more; it might be a psychological block. Furthermore, what is unnamed or unmentioned can hover over work as something that could be anywhere from too obvious or too awful to mention.

T Technique

Personification

What not to say: The personification gives human quality to the object.

What to consider: Since personification gives human qualities to some element of the poem, decide whether those qualities reflect on the narrator, a character, or a sensibility within the poem. The mood or tone of a poem or a particular stanza can often be expressed through this personification. Similarly, personification can give the personified object a menacing or luminous quality that will pervade the stanza or the entire poem.

S Sound

Assonance

What not to say: The use of assonance makes the poem flow better.

What to consider: The use of *o, oo, ou, ow* can dramatically slow the pace and at times present a mournful mood, an oratorical flourish, a pronounced tone. In general, long, hard vowels can slow the pace and generate a more commanding sound in the narrator, while soft, short vowels can quicken the pace, and at times lighten the tone.

Consonance

What not to say: The use of consonance makes the reader more into the poem and makes the poem sound better.

What to consider: Letters like *t*, *p*, and *d* can often create harder sound effects, sometimes giving the work a staccato quality. But again, decide how these harder sounds affect meaning in the poem (reinforce, undermine, etc.). Letters like *f, l, s,* and w can create softer effects and therefore can help underscore a particular mood. Naturally, unless you characterize that mood and further develop meaning, your reference to consonance is useless.

U Unusual

Paradoxes, Oxymorons, Puns

What not to say: The paradoxes make the poem more complicated.

What to consider: Paradoxes can often reveal that the author is working on multiple levels. Find those levels through both the paradox and the overall sensibility of the poem, and characterize those levels with as much penetration as you can muster. Paradoxes can also express anything from an author's ambivalence to a character's desire to have something both ways. Most paradoxes have a physical quality to them (clear opposites generally demand sensory perceptions), so they can function symbolically and serve as the poles between which the poem ranges. Finally, on a stylistic level, consider that through paradoxes or oxymorons the narrator has employed extremes to convey his messages; that might give you some clues about anything from his psychological state to the poem's social context. As you grow more sensitive to paradoxes and oxymorons, you will become increasingly aware of words that have double meanings in the context of poems. Those words are so useful and powerful because they tend to achieve much of what has been described previously with the conflict readily apparent.

M Mechanics

Punctuation: Question Marks, Parentheses, Dashes, Ellipses, etc.

What not to say: Any statement that describes the punctuation marks without delineating either their isolated alterations of meaning or their larger contextual purposes.

What to consider:

- **Parentheses** can present asides revealing, often telling, even confessional information. They can also qualify or undermine the surrounding information.
- **Dashes** can serve many of the same purposes as parentheses, yet they can offer a dramatic pause right before anything from an external revelation or internal epiphany.
- **Ellipses** often demonstrate the disjointedness of either thought or action within a poem. They can connote fragmentation, reminiscences, fading visions, and haunting qualities.
- **Question marks** can often characterize the outlook of the narrator, whether he is ambivalent, philosophical, childlike, distracted, exasperated. Questions can also serve to set an agenda or establish a theme.
- **Exclamation points** can go beyond mere excitement. They can connote giddiness, madness, mockery, anger, frustration. Always be aware that exclamation points are an attention-getting device, either summoned by the narrator or the author.
- **Capitalization** of abstract nouns can signal personification or the development of symbolism. If the capitalization is arbitrary throughout the poem, that could reflect the instability of the narrator or the randomness of the thoughts/actions.

A Ambiguity

What not to say: The ambiguity leads to confusion in the work.

What to consider: Most of the time, if you find a passage ambiguous, it is not because you have read poorly. The author is employing ambiguity for higher purposes such as to reveal an irresolvable conflict, to depict torn allegiances, to expose faulty logic, to uncover rising dissatisfaction, to render a clouding of belief, to demonstrate an erosion of faith, to underscore the irony of a situation, to introduce uncertainty into what was once definite.

R Repetition

What not to say: Repetition emphasizes the author's point.

What to consider: Repetition could serve to express any of the following: obsession, preoccupation, unbridled joy, a pause in thought, an affirmation, a moment of realization, a mockery, a rallying cry, a sob. Yes, the possibilities are large, but if the purpose of repetition is not readily apparent, start with this list. And if this list doesn't help, consider the meaning of the passage and look how the repetition undermines, reinforces, or distracts from that message. Repetition can just be there for rhythm, but if that's the case, you probably shouldn't be writing about it, unless you are leading to a larger point (such as "the repetition and the monosyllabic diction give the work a childlike quality").

Applying PLOTSUMAR to a Poem

Below is a typical poetry essay on the AP Literature exam. Read over the prompt and the poem and look for ways you might be able to apply PLOTSUMAR to the work. After you are done, look at the next page for some ideas of how PLOTSUMAR can directly serve in poetry and prose analysis.

Question 2
Suggested time—40 minutes

Read carefully the following poem by Matthew Arnold. Then write an essay analyzing how Arnold employs literary technique to develop complex meaning through the speaker. You may wish to consider such elements as setting, consonance, pacing, allusion, tone, and symbolism.

Dover Beach

The sea is calm to-night.
The tide is full, the moon lies fair
Upon the straits; on the French coast the light
Gleams and is gone; the cliffs of England stand;
Glimmering and vast, out in the tranquil bay.   5
Come to the window, sweet is the night-air!
Only, from the long line of spray
Where the sea meets the moon-blanched land,
Listen! you hear the grating roar
Of pebbles which the waves draw back, and fling,   10
At their return, up the high strand,
Begin, and cease, and then again begin,
With tremulous cadence slow, and bring
The eternal note of sadness in.

Sophocles long ago   15
Heard it on the Aegean, and it brought
Into his mind the turbid ebb and flow
Of human misery; we
Find also in the sound a thought,
Hearing it by this distant northern sea.   20

The Sea of Faith
Was once, too, at the full, and round earth's shore
Lay like the folds of a bright girdle furled.
But now I only hear
Its melancholy, long, withdrawing roar,   25
Retreating, to the breath
Of the night-wind, down the vast edges drear
And naked shingles of the world.

Ah, love, let us be true
To one another! for the world, which seems   30
To lie before us like a land of dreams,
So various, so beautiful, so new,
Hath really neither joy, nor love, nor light,
Nor certitude, nor peace, nor help for pain;
And we are here as on a darkling plain   35
Swept with confused alarms of struggle and flight,
Where ignorant armies clash by night.

P Perspective: What is the narrator's view? Does that view evolve? Disintegrate? Is the narrator's perspective/tone different from the author's?

L Language: What is the language like? How does it fit with the subject matter? Is it ironic? How does it affect and, more important, effect meaning? Change a reader's outlook?

O Omissions: Every writer must make choices to create maximum effect in limited space. What is left out of the work? Why?

T Technique: Be aware of the employment of literary devices such as metaphor, simile, alliteration, assonance, consonance, metonymy, synecdoche, personification. More important, discuss the effect they have on the work, and don't say they make the work more interesting or vivid. Have an idea behind the application of the technique.

S Sound: Are there any strange or different sounds in the work and to what effect?

U Unusual: Is there any unusual phrasing or syntax? Do certain lines stand out? Are there paradoxes, puns, or oxymorons? What effect do they have on the work?

M Mechanics: Look for any distinguishing punctuation or capitalization and think about what effect they have on the work. Are there any patterns you can discern in this punctuation or capitalization? If not, can any insight be drawn from the apparent randomness?

A Ambiguity: What lines have an unclear meaning? Don't ignore these lines, but address them head on, suggesting the various interpretations and what they reveal about the work. Why did the author make these lines or elements ambiguous? What might they mean?

R Repetition: Are lines, phrases, or words repeated? To what effect? Repetition does not have to be exact and precise. One line, phrase, or word can sound a good deal like another, creating an echo effect. Certain words and lines have a way of resonating throughout the entire work. Keep in mind their effect.

PLOTSUMAR Techniques

The poem "Dover Beach" focuses on how the narrator comes to the realization that the world is a dark and unstable place without the comforting assurances of religion. The narrator's only source of solace seems to be in the knowledge that he can be with his beloved in this bewildering world.

The following are examples how PLOTSUMAR can be applied to this poem. Using all of the elements of PLOTSUMAR as presented here would be too much material for one timed essay. Therefore, look at these commentaries as varied paths of exploration that might help you incorporate how the author goes about delivering meaning in the process of conveying what that meaning is.

Perspective

If you use no other element from PLOTSUMAR, an essay should always include perspective, since it forces the writer to consider the point-of-view of the narrator (and often other characters) when investigating the layers of meaning conveyed in the poem or passage.

In this poem, the perspective of the narrator allows the reader to follow the evolving thought process as he looks out onto Dover Beach one evening. While he initially (in the first five lines) focuses on the loveliness of the evening and the view across the English Channel to the French coast, he begins to actively listen to the sea as he brings his beloved to the window to hear the "grating roar / Of pebbles" (lines 9–10) along the coastline. By the end of the first stanza, he becomes aware of the "eternal note of sadness" entering.

That the second stanza alludes to Sophocles and the Aegean Sea indicates that the narrator sees this sadness as part of a larger historical continuum and connects the tragic Greek playwright's experiences to that which he now experiences on England's shores. In the third stanza, the narrator becomes even more cerebral—not only comparing the sea to the Aegean that Sophocles encountered, but now connecting it to the deterioration of religious belief in his time. This stanza underscores that the narrator uses this view out the window as an opportunity to ruminate about the history of misery and the deterioration of spiritual faith in his time.

Drawing on the perspective of the narrator, the reader understands that the final stanza combines the personal connection of the first stanza, as he returns to directly addressing his beloved, with the more disturbing intimations of stanzas two and three. Even as he embraces his beloved as his one source of comfort, the narrator acknowledges his emerging awareness that the potentially wonderful qualities of the world have a much darker and more disturbing reality.

Finally, students delving into this viewpoint should acknowledge how the narrator encourages the reader to take on the perspective of the beloved. When she is called over to the window (line 6), so is the reader; this call to engage with the reader is repeated when the narrator asks his beloved to "Listen!" (line 9). The perspective of the narrator addressing a nameless person allows the reader to come along for the journey and return to the role of both observer and participant in the final stanza when the narrator calls on his beloved once again.

Language

A good way to approach language in a work is to explore patterns. After the serene opening five lines, the poem shifts to using increasingly regressive and dispiriting language. For example, a reader in this poem could recognize diction that focuses on a deliberateness of motion ("grating," "slow," "turbid," "withdrawing") or diction that points to a depressing outlook ("sadness," "misery," "melancholy," "drear," "darkling").

Omission

In this poem, the reader is merely presented with a moment in time in which the narrator describes his thoughts when he is looking out a window onto Dover Beach. We do not know who the narrator is, what he does for a living, or what his plans are. We do not know anything about the person whom he calls to the window, who will be referred to throughout this commentary as his "beloved," although even that description is a stretch, since it could be a relative or friend. The reader has no context of what brought the narrator to this crisis, to the depressing conclusion at the poem's end. The reader is encountering the narrator at that moment when he has come to an epiphany about the state of the world. The reader is given no perspective on what led the narrator to this conclusion.

Technique

"Dover Beach" is heavy on literary devices. The **conceit** (extended metaphor) of "Sea of Faith" gives force and scale to the impact of religion on human history. The **simile** of "like the folds of a bright girdle furled" (line 23) demonstrates how religion—like a girdle—kept everything in place and compact. Another simile—"like a land of dreams" (line 31)—demonstrates how the narrator's former perception of the world was illusory, perhaps even naïve. That "Sea of Faith" can also function as a **symbol** with the tide leaving the shore demonstrating a diminishment in belief in God. Furthermore, the pebbles being drawn back by the waves serves as a **pathetic fallacy** (objects attributed to human emotions), since roiling of the pebbles as they are pushed away speak to a human experience of being tossed around by larger forces.

The **allusion** to Sophocles (line 15) hints to the tragic vision that will conclude the poem and presents a continuum of "human misery" (line 18). The allusion to Greek civilization connects the moment at Dover Beach to a high point in world culture. As such, Arnold indicates that even in the best of times, this eternal note of sadness exists and has been part of mankind throughout his existence. By recognizing that an important artist like Sophocles heard this sadness, the narrator indicates that individuals might have to listen carefully to identify it. Furthermore, in relating the Aegean to "this distant northern sea," Arnold has drawn its own British civilization into this loftier context. Such suffering is cyclical ("the turbid ebb and flow of human misery"), but in those rhythms is a confirmation of its role in a larger continuum.

Sound

While "Dover Beach" has other fine sound devices, this discussion will be limited to single highly effective examples of consonance and assonance. For consonance, "Lay like the folds of a bright girdle furled" (line 23) demonstrates how the employment of *l*s throughout and *d*s in the back of words can slow the pacing and match the lovely tightness of the image with the compact limits of consonants. More important, the use of assonance in line 25—"Its melancholy, long, withdrawing roar"—slows down the pacing of the poem through the elongated vowel sounds. The effect of the consonance and assonance so near to each other echoes the rhythmic cadence of the tides.

Unusual

The situation of the poem is in itself unusual in that the narrator used his stay by Dover Beach as an opportunity to see how religion has receded during that time and has left the world unstable . . . full of confusion and darkness. This viewpoint is further established by the strange term "naked shingles" (line 28), indicating the construction of this world is exposed and vulnerable.

Mechanics

Compared to most prose and poems, "Dover Beach" has limited use of the more eye-catching forms of capitalization and punctuation. What it does have, however, is very useful. For example, the capitalization of "Sea of Faith" in line 21 will establish the extended metaphor (conceit) of comparing religion to the tides. Furthermore, the Sea of Faith takes on symbolic qualities of being this larger force turning in another direction. The use of exclamation points at three key moments in the poem (lines 6, 9, and 30) provide greater insight in the dynamic between the narrator and his beloved. The first two exclamation marks serve as requests from the narrator to his beloved. The exclamations reveal an intensity in the narrator's connection to tides. The exclamation that opens the final stanza ("Ah, love, let us be true / To one another!") reveals a more desperate speaker, clinging to his beloved, in light of the depressing conclusions he arrives at in the poem's last five lines.

Ambiguity

The last three lines of the poem are a central source of ambiguity "And we are here as on a darkling plain / Swept with confused alarms of struggle and flight, / Where ignorant armies clash by night." The ambiguity of those lines reflects the disorientation of the narrator, with a "darkling plain," "confused alarms," and "ignorant armies" clashing "by night." The language emphasizes the absence of clarity. The reader should not shy away from interpreting this confusing jumble. Instead, the bewildering chaos of this description should be embraced. The reader can speak to how the narrator puts all of us in the hypothetical "as on a darkling plain" and then presents a vision marked by panic, retreats, and combat. Ultimately, those last three lines indicate no one is clear on what exactly is transpiring; however, all of us sense the situation is troubling.

Repetition

For much of the poem, the repetitions are more thematic than language based. The narrator's repeated calls to his beloved that open the poem and initiate the final stanza reveal the central figure as one who needs to seek comfort in the process of lurching toward disturbing insights. Yet in the final stanza, repetition takes over in the form of anaphora, giving the poem a rhythmic and rhetorical punch that concludes the poem. A figure of speech in which words or phrases are repeated to create cadences that can build in sonic effect, anaphora rises first with "So various, so beautiful, so new" (line 32) and is immediately countered by "neither joy, nor love, nor light, / Nor certitude, nor peace, nor help for pain" (lines 33–34). This use of repetition reveals a narrator rapidly ticking off what he once believed compared to what he now perceives as a reality. The sharpness of this repetition pounding into the rhythms of the poem's ending indicates how intensely this stark contrast has pounded away at the reader.

Rapid Review

- Perspective serves as a reliable source of analysis for every piece of poetry and prose.
- Multiple perspectives (including the narrator's and the author's) can be in a piece.
- Omissions speak to the choices an author makes.
- Literary techniques can be broad, varied, and flexible, ranging from allusion to zoomorphism.
- Sound devices often affect pacing and mood.
- Unusual elements in poetry and prose often call attention to the complexity, strangeness, or awkwardness of a situation.
- Mechanics can often be discerned simply by scanning the work.
- The frequency of specific mechanical elements (capitalization, punctuation, etc.) often reflects a sensibility embedded in the work.
- Ambiguity is an element the reader should embrace rather than avoid.
- Use ambiguity to explore multiple interpretations of a particular word, phrase, or sentence.
- Repetition can often reflect the psychological state of a speaker or a narrator.
- Repetition can also be used to establish the tones and rhythms of a piece.

STEP 5

5

Build Your Test-Taking Confidence

Practice Exam 1
Practice Exam 2

PRACTICE EXAM 1
ANSWER SHEET FOR MULTIPLE-CHOICE QUESTIONS

1. _____   20. _____   39. _____

2. _____   21. _____   40. _____

3. _____   22. _____   41. _____

4. _____   23. _____   42. _____

5. _____   24. _____   43. _____

6. _____   25. _____   44. _____

7. _____   26. _____   45. _____

8. _____   27. _____   46. _____

9. _____   28. _____   47. _____

10. _____   29. _____   48. _____

11. _____   30. _____   49. _____

12. _____   31. _____   50. _____

13. _____   32. _____   51. _____

14. _____   33. _____   52. _____

15. _____   34. _____   53. _____

16. _____   35. _____   54. _____

17. _____   36. _____   55. _____

18. _____   37. _____

19. _____   38. _____

"I need to honestly time myself on the practice exams, or else I don't really concentrate the way I should."
—Carol K.
  AP student

I _____ did _____ did not complete this part of the test in the allotted 1 hour.

I had _____ correct answers. I had _____ incorrect answers. I left _____ blank.

I have carefully reviewed the explanations of the answers, and I think I need to work on the following types of questions:

PRACTICE EXAM 1
ADVANCED PLACEMENT ENGLISH LITERATURE

Section I

Total time—1 hour

Questions 1–12 are based on a careful reading of the following 2015 poem by Juan Felipe Herrera.

Almost Livin' Almost Dyin'
by Juan Felipe Herrera

for all the dead
& hear my streets
with ragged beats & the beats
are too beat to live so the graves push out with
hands that cannot touch the makers of light & the   5
sun flames down through the roofs & the roots that slide
to one side & the whistlin' fires of the cops & the cops
in the shops do what they gotta do & your body's
on the fence & your ID's in the air & the shots
get fired & the gas in the face & the tanks   10
on your blood & the innocence all around & the
spillin' & the grillin' & the grinnin' & the game of Race
no one wanted & the same every day so U fire &
eat the smoke thru your long bones & the short mace
& the day? This last sweet Swisher[1] day that turns to love   15
& no one knows how it came or what it is or what it says
or what it was or what for or from what gate
is it open is it locked can U pull it back to your life
filled with bitter juice & demon angel eyes even though
you pray & pray mama says you gotta sing she says   20
you got wings but from what skies from where could
they rise what are the things the no-things called love
how can its power be fixed or grasped so the beats
keep on blowin' keep on flyin' & the moon tracks your bed
where you are alone or maybe dead & the truth   25
carves you carves you & calls you back still alive
cry cry the candles by the last four trees still soaked
in Michael Brown[2] red and Officer Liu[3] red and
Officer Ramos[4] red and Eric Garner[5] whose
last words were not words they were just breath   30
askin' for breath they were just burnin' like me like
we are all still burnin' can you hear me
can you can you feel me swaggin' tall & driving low &
talkin' fine & hollerin' from my corner crime & fryin'
against the wall   35

almost livin' almost dyin'
almost livin' almost dyin'

---

[1]**Swisher day:** local day set aside for fun, games, and celebration
[2]**Michael Brown:** an unarmed black teenager shot and killed in 2014 by a white police officer
[3]**Officer Liu:** slain NYC police officer
[4]**Officer Ramos:** slain NYC police officer
[5]**Eric Garner:** killed by NYC police officers while being arrested for selling single cigarettes; remembered for crying out, "I can't breathe."

1. The pace of this poem can best be described as
   A. processional
   B. breathless
   C. contemplative
   D. ambling
   E. steady

2. The effect of using the ampersand throughout the poem is to
   A. set up a hyperbole
   B. direct the reader's attention to the next item in a list
   C. gives the impression of person who doesn't care about language
   D. act like a quickening heartbeat
   E. act as a symbol of the neighborhood's character

3. Lines 1 to the beginning of line 15 is a recounting of
   A. a street fair
   B. a robbery of a local grocery store
   C. a confrontation between neighborhood young men and police
   D. the life around a low-income, urban neighborhood
   E. a conflict between rival gangs

4. The speaker is most probably
   A. an onlooker from outside the community
   B. a reporter for a national newspaper
   C. the mother of one of the young men
   D. a politician
   E. a young person who lives in the neighborhood

5. The poem contains examples of all of the following literary devices *except*
   A. internal rhyme
   B. alliteration
   C. metaphor
   D. repetition
   E. synecdoche

6. Lines 15–18 indicate the speaker's
   A. longing for a life that is filled with love
   B. hoping for his mother to rescue him
   C. giving up any hope for the future
   D. blaming life's uncertainty on "the system"
   E. believing he will have a better life in the future

7. The pace and rhythm of the poem is created primarily with a combination of
   A. playful imagery, repetition, ampersands
   B. similes and repetition
   C. appeals to emotions, metaphors
   D. single syllable words, no punctuation, repetition
   E. ampersands, extended analogy

8. Lines 18–26 can best be summarized as:
   A. Love can conquer violence.
   B. There is no real escape from this life of violence and fear.
   C. Hope lies in prayer.
   D. There is no truth.
   E. Enjoy life as it comes.

9. "Its" in line 23 refers to
   A. angel eyes (19)
   B. wings (21)
   C. skies (21)
   D. love (22)
   E. no-things (22)

10. In the context of the poem, "you" in line 33 can best be understood to be
    A. the speaker
    B. the friends of the speaker
    C. those in power
    D. the speaker's mother
    E. neighborhood rivals

11. "we all are still burnin'" in line 32 can best be interpreted to mean
A. Nothing is able to end the fear and violence.
B. There eventually will be a rebellion.
C. The deaths of those mentioned in lines 28 and 29 should be avenged.
D. Only love can save the speaker.
E. Hope lies in remembering those who have lost their lives to violence.

12. The last six lines of the poem are a(n)
A. accusation
B. litany
C. eulogy
D. promise
E. plea

Carefully read the following passages and answer the questions that follow. Questions 13–25 are based on the following passage.

Bleak House
by Charles Dickens (1853)

Excerpt from Chapter 1—"In Chancery"

LONDON. Michaelmas Term lately over, and the Lord Chancellor sitting in Lincoln's Inn Hall. Implacable November weather. As much mud in the streets as if the waters had but newly retired from the face of the earth, and it would not be wonderful to meet a Megalosaurus, forty feet long or so, waddling like an elephantine lizard up Holborn Hill. Smoke lowering down from chimney-pots, making a soft black drizzle, with flakes of soot in it as big as full-grown 5 snowflakes—gone into mourning, one might imagine, for the death of the sun. Dogs, undistinguishable in mire. Horses, scarcely better; splashed to their very blinkers. Foot passengers, jostling one another's umbrellas in a general infection of ill-temper, and losing their foot-hold at street-corners, where tens of thousands of other foot passengers have been slipping and sliding since the day broke (if the day ever broke), adding new deposits to the crust upon 10 crust of mud, sticking at those points tenaciously to the pavement, and accumulating at compound interest.

Fog everywhere. Fog up the river, where it flows among green aits and meadows; fog down the river, where it rolls defiled among the tiers of shipping and the waterside pollutions of a great (and dirty) city. Fog on the Essex marshes, fog on the Kentish heights. Fog creeping into the 15 cabooses of collier-brigs; fog lying out on the yards, and hovering in the rigging of great ships; fog drooping on the gunwales of barges and small boats. Fog in the eyes and throats of ancient Greenwich pensioners, wheezing by the firesides of their wards; fog in the stem and bowl of the afternoon pipe of the wrathful skipper, down in his close cabin; fog cruelly pinching the toes and fingers of his shivering little 'prentice boy on deck. Chance people on the bridges peeping over 20 the parapets into a nether sky of fog, with fog all round them, as if they were up in a balloon, and hanging in the misty clouds.

Gas* looming through the fog in divers places in the streets, much as the sun may, from the spongey fields, be seen to loom by husbandman and ploughboy. Most of the shops lighted two hours before their time—as the gas seems to know, for it has a haggard and unwilling look. 25

The raw afternoon is rawest, and the dense fog is densest, and the muddy streets are muddiest near that leaden-headed old obstruction, appropriate ornament for the threshold of a leaden-headed old corporation, Temple Bar. And hard by Temple Bar, in Lincoln's Inn Hall, at the very heart of the fog, sits the Lord High Chancellor in his High Court of Chancery.

---

* (23) *gas:* gas lights

Never can there come fog too thick, never can there come mud and mire too deep, to assort   30
with the groping and floundering condition which this High Court of Chancery, most pestilent of
hoary sinners, holds this day in the sight of heaven and earth.

On such an afternoon, if ever, the Lord High Chancellor ought to be sitting here—as here he
is—with a foggy glory round his head, softly fenced in with crimson cloth and curtains,
addressed by a large advocate with great whiskers, a little voice, and an interminable brief, and   35
outwardly directing his contemplation to the lantern in the roof, where he can see nothing but
fog. On such an afternoon some score of members of the High Court of Chancery bar ought to be
—as here they are—mistily engaged in one of the ten thousand stages of an endless cause,
tripping one another up on slippery precedents, groping knee-deep in technicalities, running their
goat-hair and horse-hair* warded heads against walls of words and making a pretence of equity   40
with serious faces, as players might. On such an afternoon the various solicitors in the cause,
some two or three of whom have inherited it from their fathers, who made a fortune by it, ought
to be—as are they not?—ranged in a line, in a long matted well (but you might look in vain for
truth at the bottom of it) between the registrar's red table and the silk gowns, with bills, cross-bills,
answers, rejoinders, injunctions, affidavits, issues, references to masters, masters' reports,   45
mountains of costly nonsense, piled before them. Well may the court be dim, with wasting
candles here and there; well may the fog hang heavy in it, as if it would never get out; well may
the stained-glass windows lose their colour and admit no light of day into the place; well may the
uninitiated from the streets, who peep in through the glass panes in the door, be deterred from
entrance by its owlish aspect and by the drawl, languidly echoing to the roof from the padded   50
dais where the Lord High Chancellor looks into the lantern that has no light in it and where the
attendant wigs are all stuck in a fog-bank! This is the Court of Chancery, which has its decaying
houses and its blighted lands in every shire, which has its worn-out lunatic in every madhouse
and its dead in every churchyard, which has its ruined suitor with his slipshod heels and
threadbare dress borrowing and begging through the round of every man's acquaintance, which   55
gives to monied might the means abundantly of wearying out the right, which so exhausts
finances, patience, courage, hope, so overthrows the brain and breaks the heart, that there is not
an honourable man among its practitioners who would not give—who does not often give—the
warning, "Suffer any wrong that can be done you rather than come here!"

---

*(40) *goat-hair and horse-hair warded heads*: wigs worn by members of the court

13. In context, "Implacable November weather" [line 2] serves as
A. the major theme of the passage
B. the introduction to the extinction imagery
C. a contrast to the tone of the passage
D. the introduction to the controlling metaphor of the passage
E. personification of "Michaelmas Term"

14. The juxtaposition of "Megalosaurus" [line 3] with London town has as its purpose
A. indicating a natural disaster
B. foreshadowing an outdated legal system
C. reinforcing the animalistic nature of man
D. indicating the magnitude of London's poverty
E. revealing the onslaught of civil unrest

15. "Gone into mourning" in line 6 refers to
A. snow-flakes
B. smoke
C. death of the sun
D. flakes of soot
E. drizzle

16. In the context of the passage, "death of the sun" [line 6] can be seen as parallel to the
A. philandering of the Lord High Chancellor
B. degradation of London
C. indifference of the wealthy class
D. blighted lands
E. corruption of justice

17. "For it has a haggard and unwilling look" [line 25] refers to
    A. the fog
    B. the gas
    C. the shops
    D. the husbandman and ploughboy
    E. the sun

18. The purpose of lines 26–29 is to
    A. provide the major shift in the subject
    B. solidify the implacable nature of November weather
    C. reemphasize the nature of the fog
    D. proceed from setting to theme
    E. foreshadow a religious conversion

19. The attitude of the speaker in lines 26–29 can best be described as
    A. self-serving platitude
    B. vitriolic indictment
    C. disconsolate resignation
    D. unfounded aspiration
    E. pathetic desperation

20. Lines 37–41, beginning with "On such an afternoon" and ending with "as players might," reinforce which of the following lines?
    A. 4–6
    B. 13–15
    C. 17–20
    D. 23–25
    E. 30–32

21. The imagery created in lines 46–52 serves to
    A. emphasize the poverty of London
    B. reinforce the crowded court condition
    C. characterize the role of lawyers in the court
    D. reveal the author's attitude toward his subject
    E. separate the exterior from the interior

22. One could best summarize lines 52–59 with which of the following statements?
    A. The court system is not just
    B. The court system needs to be revised
    C. The lawyers are corrupt
    D. The court system has the support of the attorneys
    E. The courts exist only to help the poor

23. The second and last paragraphs are primarily developed through the use of
    A. comparison and contrast
    B. simple sentences
    C. parallel structure
    D. rhetorical questions
    E. animal imagery

24. The organization of the passage moves from
    A. past to present
    B. positive to negative
    C. cause to effect
    D. general to specific
    E. literal to figurative

25. The overall tone of the passage can best be described as
    A. remorseful and resigned
    B. outraged and exhortative
    C. scathing and bitter
    D. victimized and vengeful
    E. dispassionate and objective

Questions 26–36 are based on the following poem.

The Writer
by Richard Wilbur (1969)

In her room at the prow of the house
Where light breaks, and the windows are tossed with linden,
My daughter is writing a story.

I pause in the stairwell, hearing
From her shut door a commotion of typewriter-keys   5
Like a chain hauled over a gunwale.

Young as she is, the stuff
Of her life is a great cargo, and some of it heavy:
I wish her a lucky passage.

But now it is she who pauses,   10
As if to reject my thought and its easy figure.
A stillness greatens, in which

The whole house seems to be thinking,
And then she is at it again with a bunched clamor
Of strokes, and again is silent.   15

I remember the dazed starling
Which was trapped in that very room, two years ago;
How we stole in, lifted a sash

And retreated, not to affright it;
And how for a helpless hour, through the crack in the door,   20
We watched this sleek, wild, dark

And iridescent creature
Batter against the brilliance, drop like a glove
To the hard floor, or the desk-top,

And wait then, humped and bloody,   25
For the wits to try it again; and how our spirits
Rose when, suddenly sure,

It lifted off from a chair-back,
Beating a smooth course for the right window
And clearing the sill of the world.   30

It is always a matter, my darling,
Of life or death, as I had forgotten. I wish
What I wished you before, but harder.

26. The last line of the poem "What I wished you before, but harder" implies that
   A. the speaker loves his daughter more than at the beginning of the poem
   B. the speaker realizes the intensity of life's challenges
   C. the speaker cannot be as creative as she
   D. the speaker feels he has failed her
   E. the daughter will never be a successful writer

27. Which of the following is used to develop the poem?
   A. cause and effect
   B. argument
   C. general to specific examples
   D. definition
   E. parallel analogy

28. Line 13 is an example of
   A. allusion
   B. alliteration
   C. personification
   D. simile
   E. apostrophe

29. "A smooth course for the right window" in line 29 parallels line(s)
   A. 1
   B. 5–6
   C. 8
   D. 9
   E. 11

30. The poem breaks after line
   A. 3
   B. 6
   C. 8
   D. 15
   E. 27

31. The final stanza serves all the following purposes *except*
   A. to restate the theme
   B. to reemphasize the father's love for his daughter
   C. to solidify the daughter's character
   D. to connect the two major sections of the poem
   E. to allow the father to be more sympathetic

32. Stanzas 1–3 include all the following analogies *except*
   A. the house as a ship
   B. the daughter's room as a ship's cabin
   C. life's problems as a ship's cargo
   D. writing as a safe harbor
   E. life as a sea journey

33. The father's sensitivity is supported by line(s)
   A. 3
   B. 4
   C. 11
   D. 19
   E. 21–22

34. Contrasts developed in the poem include all the following *except*
   A. stillness and clamor
   B. house and cargo
   C. bird and daughter
   D. life and/or death
   E. light and dark

35. According to the poem, the daughter, as young as she is, has
   A. endured hardships
   B. published her writing
   C. fought for her independence
   D. saved a starling
   E. left home and returned

36. The poet alludes to all the following as part of the process of a creative life *except*
   A. "Batter against the brilliance"
   B. "drop like a glove to the hard floor"
   C. "clearing the sill of the world"
   D. "the wits to try it again"
   E. "Beating a smooth course for the right window"

Questions 37–47 are based on the following passage.

Jane Eyre
by Charlotte Brontë (1847)

Miss Temple got up, took her hand and . . . returned to her own seat: as she resumed
it, I heard her sigh low. She was pensive a few minutes, then rousing herself, she
said cheerfully:—

"But you two are my visitors to-night; I must treat you as such." She rang her bell.

"Barbara," she said to the servant who answered it, "I have not yet had tea; bring   5
the tray, and place cups for these two young ladies."

And a tray was soon brought. How pretty, to my eyes, did the china and bright
teapot look, placed on the little round table near the fire! How fragrant was the steam of the
beverage, and the scent of the toast! of which, however, I, to my dismay (for I was
beginning to be hungry), discerned only a very small portion: Miss Temple discerned it   10
too:—

"Barbara," said she, "can you not bring a little more bread and butter? There is not
enough for three."

Barbara went out: she returned soon:—

"Madam, Mrs. Harden says she has sent up the usual quantity."   15

Mrs. Harden, be it observed, was the housekeeper: a woman after Mr.
Brocklehurst's own heart, made up of equal parts of whalebone and iron.

"Oh, very well!" returned Miss Temple; "we must make it do, Barbara, I
suppose." And as the girl withdrew, she added, smiling, "Fortunately, I have it in my
power to supply deficiencies for this once."   20

Having invited Helen and me to approach the table, and placed before each of us a
cup of tea with one delicious but thin morsel of toast; she got up, unlocked a drawer, and
taking from it a parcel wrapped in paper, disclosed presently to our eyes a good-sized
seed-cake.

"I meant to give each of you some of this to take with you," said she; "but as there   25
is so little toast, you must have it now," and she proceeded to cut slices with a generous
hand.

We feasted that evening as on nectar and ambrosia; and not the least delight of the
entertainment was the smile of gratification with which our hostess regarded us, as we
satisfied our famished appetites on the delicate fare she liberally supplied. Tea over and the   30
tray removed, she again summoned us to the fire; we sat one on each side of her, and now a
conversation followed between her and Helen, which it was indeed a privilege to be
admitted to hear.

Miss Temple had always something of serenity in her air, of state in her mien, of
refined propriety in her language, which precluded deviation into the ardent, the excited, the   35
eager: something which chastened the pleasure of those who looked on her and listened to
her, by a controlling sense of awe; and such was my feeling now: but as to Helen Burns, I
was struck with wonder.

The refreshing meal, the brilliant fire, the presence and kindness of her beloved
instructress, or, perhaps, more than all these, something in her own unique mind, had   40
roused her powers within her. They woke, they kindled: first, they glowed in the bright tint
of her cheek, which till this hour I had never seen but pale and bloodless; then they shone in

the liquid lustre of her eyes, which had suddenly acquired a beauty more singular than that
of Miss Temple's—a beauty neither of fine colour nor long eyelash, nor pencilled brow,
but of meaning, of movement, of radiance. Then her soul sat on her lips, and language   45
flowed, from what source I cannot tell: has a girl of fourteen a heart large enough, vigorous
enough to hold the swelling spring of pure, full, fervid eloquence? Such was the
characteristic of Helen's discourse on that, to me, memorable evening; her spirit seemed
hastening to live within a very brief span as much as many live during a protracted
existence.   50

     They conversed of things I had never heard of ! Of nations and times past; of
countries far away: of secrets of nature discovered or guessed at: they spoke of books: how
many they had read! What stores of knowledge they possessed! They seemed so
familiar with French names and French authors: but my amazement reached its climax
when Miss Temple asked Helen if she sometimes snatched a moment to recall the Latin her   55
father had taught her, and taking a book from a shelf, bade her read and construe a page of
"Virgil"; and Helen obeyed, my organ of Veneration expanding at every sounding line.
She had scarcely finished ere the bell announced bedtime: no delay could be admitted;
Miss Temple embraced us both, saying, as she drew us to her heart:—
     "God bless you, my children!"   60
     Well has Solomon said—"Better is a dinner of herbs where love is, than a stalled ox
and hatred therewith."

37. From the passage, it can be concluded that
Mrs. Harden is
A. in love with Mr. Brocklehurst
B. generous with the girls
C. a confidante of Miss Temple's
D. strong-willed and inflexible
E. Miss Temple's superior

38. Religious imagery in this passage is developed
by all the following *except*
A. Miss Temple's name
B. feasting on nectar and ambrosia
C. the taking of tea and toast
D. Miss Temple's benediction
E. being summoned to sit by the fire

39. The "smile of gratification with which our
hostess regarded us" (line 29) indicates that
Miss Temple derives pleasure from
A. having power over the girls
B. being a role model for the girls
C. keeping secrets
D. outsmarting the girls
E. providing for the girls

40. For the speaker, the most nourishing part of
the evening was
A. the seed cake
B. the tea and toast
C. the company of an adult
D. the conversation
E. the brilliant fire

41. ". . . her spirit seemed hastening to live within
a very brief span as much as many live during
a protracted existence" (lines 48–49) is an
example of
A. circular reasoning
B. satire
C. foreshadowing
D. denouement
E. digression

42. The reader can infer from lines 45– 47 ("Then
her soul sat on her lips . . . eloquence") that
A. Helen has traveled the world
B. Helen likes to show off intellectually
C. Miss Temple has been tutoring Helen
D. the speaker is afraid of Helen
E. Helen is an instrument of divine
inspiration

43. The last sentence of the passage may be best interpreted to mean
A. It is better to be rich than poor
B. Everything in moderation
C. The greatest of all riches is love
D. Denial of riches leads to love
F. Riches lead to hatred

44. The tone developed in the passage is best described as
A. amused indifference
B. subdued admiration
C. pedantic
D. reverent wonder
E. remorseful

45. The reader may infer all the following *except* that
A. the evening has transformed Helen
B. the speaker is observant of and sensitive to human nature
C. the evening is in contrast to their daily lives
D. Miss Temple will save the two children
E. love of learning is important to the speaker

46. The description of Miss Temple in lines 34–38 reveals her to be a woman of
A. religious fervor
B. restraint and reservation
C. passionate beliefs
D. submissive inclinations
E. dominating sensibilities

47. Based on the passage, all the following can be inferred about Jane's character *except that* she is
A. cognizant of her limitations
B. a great observer
C. of an inquisitive nature
D. highly impressionable
E. religious

Questions 48–55 are based on a careful reading of the following 2011 poem by Tracy K. Smith.

The Good Life
by Tracy K. Smith

When some people talk about money
They speak as if it were a mysterious lover
Who went out to buy milk and never
Came back, and it makes me nostalgic
For the years I lived on coffee and bread,   5
Hungry all the time, walking to work on payday
Like a woman journeying for water
From a village without a well, then living
One or two nights like everyone else
On roast chicken and red wine.   10

48. This poem is an example of
  A. a ballad
  B. free verse
  C. a sonnet
  D. blank verse
  E. rhymed verse

49. In line 2, "it" refers to
  A. "The Good Life"
  B. milk
  C. mysterious lover
  D. coffee and bread
  E. money

50. The tone of the poem can best be described as
  A. formal and didactic
  B. uncaring and suspicious
  C. informal and satirical
  D. brusque and patronizing
  E. casual and conversational

51. Lines 2–4 are developed using
  A. personification
  B. hyperbole
  C. allusion
  D. alliteration
  E. onomatopoeia

52. Line 5 is an indication that the speaker is speaking about her
  A. future
  B. present condition
  C. past
  D. nightmares
  E. fears

53. Examples of similes are found in all of the following lines *except*
  A. 2
  B. 5
  C. 6
  D. 7
  E. 9

54. Based on the poem as a whole, the title "The Good Life" can best be described as
  A. accusatory
  B. sentimental
  C. mournful
  D. sarcastic
  E. hopeful

55. In context, the reader can infer that the speaker is
  A. bitter
  B. indigent
  C. successful
  D. envious
  E. indifferent

END OF SECTION I

Section II

Total time—2 hours

Question 1

(Suggested time 40 minutes. This question counts as one-third of the total score for Section II.)

The following is the 1973 short story "The Flowers" by Alice Walker. Carefully read the passage. Then, in a well-written essay analyze how Walker uses literary elements and techniques to convey the complex meaning of "The Flowers" and how she prepares the reader for the ending of this short story.

In your response you should do the following:

- Respond to the prompt with a thesis that presents an assertion that requires defense and support.
- Select and use evidence to support your line of reasoning.
- Explain how the evidence supports your line of reasoning.
- Use appropriate grammar and punctuation in communicating your argument.

The Flowers
by Alice Walker

It seemed to Myop as she skipped lightly from her house to pigpen to smokehouse that the days had never been as beautiful as these. The air held a keenness that made her nose twitch. The harvesting of the corn and cotton, peanuts and squash, made each day a golden surprise that caused excited little tremors to run up her jaws.

Myop carried a short, knobby stick. She struck out at random at chickens she liked, 5 and worked out the beat of a song on the fence around the pigpen. She felt light and good in the warm sun. She was ten, and nothing existed for her but her song, the stick clutched in her dark brown hand, and the tat-de-ta-ta-ta of accompaniment.

Turning her back on the rusty boards of her family's sharecropper cabin, Myop walked along the fence till it ran into the stream made by the spring. Around the spring, 10 where the family got drinking water, silver ferns and wildflowers grew. Along the shallow banks pigs rooted. Myop watched the tiny white bubbles disrupt the thin black scale of soil and the water that silently rose and slid away down the stream.

She had explored the woods behind the house many times. Often, in late autumn, her mother took her to gather nuts among the fallen leaves. Today she made her own path, 15 bouncing this way and that way, vaguely keeping an eye out for snakes. She found, in addition to various common but pretty ferns and leaves, an armful of strange blue flowers with velvety ridges and a sweetsuds bush full of the brown, fragrant buds.

By twelve o'clock, her arms laden with sprigs of her findings, she was a mile or more from home. She had often been as far before, but the strangeness of the land made it not as 20 pleasant as her usual haunts. It seemed gloomy in the little cove in which she found herself. The air was damp, the silence close and deep.

Myop began to circle back to the house, back to the peacefulness of the morning.

It was then she stepped smack into his eyes. Her heel became lodged in the broken ridge between brow and nose, and she reached down quickly, unafraid, to free herself. It was 25 only when she saw his naked grin that she gave a little yelp of surprise. He had been a tall man. From feet to neck covered a long space. His head lay beside him. When she pushed back the leaves and layers of earth and debris Myop saw that he'd had large white teeth, all of them cracked or broken, long fingers, and very big bones. All his clothes had rotted away

except some threads of blue denim from his overalls. The buckles of the overalls had turned 30
green.

Myop gazed around the spot with interest. Very near where she'd stepped into the
head was a wild pink rose. As she picked it to add to her bundle she noticed a raised mound, a
ring, around the rose's root. It was the rotted remains of a noose, a bit of shredding plow-line,
now blending benignly into the soil. Around the overhanging limb of a great spreading 35
oak clung another piece, frayed, rotted, bleached, and frazzled—barely there—but spinning
restlessly in the breeze. Myop laid down her flowers.

And the summer was over.

Question 2

(Suggested time 40 minutes. This question counts as one-third of the total score for Section II.)

In his 1957 poem "The Naked and the Nude," Robert Graves contemplates the distinguishing differences
between the complex connotations of the two main words in the title. Read the poem carefully. Then, in a
well-written essay, analyze how Graves uses poetic elements and techniques to portray these differences.

In your response you should do the following:

- Respond to the prompt with a thesis that presents an assertion that requires defense and support.
- Select and use evidence to support your line of reasoning.
- Explain how the evidence supports your line of reasoning.
- Use appropriate grammar and punctuation in communicating your argument.

The Naked and the Nude
by Robert Graves

For me, the naked and the nude
(By lexicographers construed
As synonyms that should express
The same deficiency of dress
Or shelter) stand as wide apart   5
As love from lies, or truth from art.

Lovers without reproach will gaze
On bodies naked and ablaze;
The Hippocratic eye will see
In nakedness, anatomy;   10
And naked shines the Goddess when
She mounts her lion among men.

The nude are bold; the nude are sly
To hold each treasonable eye.
While draping by a showman's trick   15
Their dishabille in rhetoric,
They grin a mock-religious grin
Of scorn at those of naked skin.

The naked, therefore, who compete
Against the nude may know defeat;
Yet when they both together tread
The briary pastures of the dead,
By Gorgons with long whips pursued,
How naked go the sometime nude!

20

Question 3

(Suggested time 40 minutes. This question counts as one-third of the total score for Section II.)

Often in your study of literature you encounter a character or group that intentionally dissembles in order to advance a specific agenda. Either from your own reading or from the list below, choose a work of fiction in which intentional dissembling occurs. Then, in a well-written essay analyze how the complex nature of the deceit or misrepresentation contributes to the development of the character or to the interpretation of the work as a whole. Do not merely summarize.

In your response you should do the following:

• Respond to the prompt with a thesis that presents an assertion that requires defense and support.
• Select and use evidence to support your line of reasoning.
• Explain how the evidence supports your line of reasoning.
• Use appropriate grammar and punctuation in communicating your argument.

The Adventures of Huckleberry Finn	*Hamlet*
Oedipus	*The Brief Wondrous Life of Oscar Wao*
Jane Eyre	*King Lear*
The Scarlet Letter	*The Great Gatsby*
Heart of Darkness	*Crime and Punishment*
Brave New World	*Things Fall Apart*
Beloved	*The Importance of Being Earnest*
A Streetcar Named Desire	*1984*
Major Barbara	*The Handmaid's Tale*

END OF SECTION II

ANSWERS TO MULTIPLE-CHOICE QUESTIONS

Answer Key

1. B	20. E	39. E
2. D	21. D	40. D
3. C	22. A	41. C
4. E	23. C	42. E
5. E	24. E	43. C
6. A	25. C	44. D
7. D	26. B	45. D
8. B	27. E	46. B
9. D	28. C	47. E
10. C	29. D	48. B
11. A	30. D	49. E
12. E	31. C	50. E
13. D	32. D	51. A
14. B	33. D	52. C
15. A	34. B	53. B
16. E	35. A	54. D
17. B	36. B	55. C
18. A	37. D	
19. B	38. E	

Answers and Explanations

Almost Livin Almost Dyin
by Jose Felipe Herrera

1. **B.** The lack of internal and end punctuation, single syllable words, and the use of ampersands create a quick, relentless movement from one word to another and one line to another.

2. **D.** The ampersand acts like the sound of a heart monitor. The quickening pace is pushed forward with this sign. It is the heartbeat of the world that is portrayed in the poem.

3. **C.** The event described is like a filmed police chase in the movies. It's quite visual: from the rooftops to the fence climbing, to the chase through the neighborhood.

4. **E.** The poem is not objective and reportorial. It is told from the vantage point of experience, not from the perspective of a caring parent or a politician seeking office. It is the story of a passionate insider.

5. **E.** Internal rhyme (6, 20, 21), alliteration (6, 7, 27), metaphor (4, 5, 19), and repetition (7, 26, 30) are all included in the construction of the poem. Synecdoche is not.

6. **A.** "This last sweet Swisher day that turns to love" is a nostalgic plea for hope. It is not asking for help or to lay blame.

7. **D.** There is nothing playful about or in this poem. Its pace, rhythm, beat are hard, fast, and furious. This is constructed with diction and syntax that forces the momentum.

8. **A.** A close look at the diction and imagery ("bitter, demon, alone, death, the truth carves you") negates any feeling of hope, love, truth, or joy.

9. **D.** This is a predictable question related to antecedents. In this case, "its" refers to "love" in line 22.

10. **C.** This is a plea for those who have power to do the right thing so that love and hope may survive. None of the other choices has this ability.

11. **A.** The key to the meaning lies in consideration of ALL and EACH of the words in this line. For the speaker, burning was, is, and will always be without end. For the speaker, this applies to himself and everyone he knows. Love and hope are not a possibility as things now stand.

12. **E.** When the speaker says "can you hear me / can you feel me," he is pleading for a way to regain hope and love, some way to delete almost.

Bleak House
by Charles Dickens

13. **D.** All of the weather images illustrate and reinforce the conditions that exist within the legal system.

14. **B.** The image of an extinct, gigantic, lumbering creature in the midst of London is as out of place as the efficacy of the court system that Dickens describes in the passage.

15. **A.** This is another basic reference question. The image is one of smoke-flakes wearing black for mourning.

16. **E.** The key here is "In the context of the passage." The death of the sun symbolizes the end of enlightenment, warmth, hope, and nurturing—all of which are characteristic of the High Court of Chancery.

17. **B.** This is a basic antecedent question. You need to trace "it" back to "gas."

18. **A.** The author takes the two major images and combines them (fog:court).

19. **B.** The deliberate repetition and diction (for example: "leaden-headed," "obstruction") is evidence of the bitter accusation.

20. **E.** "Mud," "mire," "groping," and "floundering" are echoed by "endless cause," "tripping," "slippery," and "knee-deep."

21. **D.** Phrases such as "court be dim," "wasting candles," "admit no light of day," "lantern that has no light" all reveal the author's attitude toward the court.

22. **A.** The listing of the effects of the court on the people specifically indicate how justice is not being served. There is no direct call for revision of the court in this passage.

23. **C.** In paragraph 2 the repetition of "fog," and the repetition of "On such," "Well may," and "which has" in the last paragraph, all serve to

tightly structure both the description and the indictment presented in the excerpt.

24. E. The excerpt begins with a specific description of London in November and progresses to a symbolic depiction of the Court of Chancery.

25. C. The previous questions should have pointed you toward this answer. There is no resignation in the author. He rails against the system (A). While it is obvious the writer is outraged, he does not call for action on the part of the reader (B). We may infer that he has been victimized, but there is no evidence of that in this excerpt (D). His sarcasm, diction, and imagery reveal a subjective point of view (E).

The Writer
by Richard Wilbur

26. B. The entire poem hinges on the speaker's epiphany about life and creativity, which occurs in the last stanza. It is this realization that points to choice B. Choice A is silly and should be eliminated immediately. There is no discussion of the daughter's talent, which eliminates choice E. Although C and D sound plausible and may even be insights raised by the reader, once again there is no concrete evidence in the poem to support these choices.

27. E. The careful reader should recognize that the poem introduces a new idea in lines 16–30, and he or she should question the reason for this. It is obvious that the episode of the starling is meant to parallel the intensity of the creative process the daughter is experiencing.

28. C. The house is personified as "thinking." This is a question that is really a freebie if you've done your preparation. The answer depends on your knowledge of simple terms and your ability to identify examples of them in a work.

29. D. A question of this type demands that you actually refer to the passage. (You might try highlighting or underlining to emphasize line 29 and the various choices. This will prevent you from losing your place or focus.) Use the process of elimination until you find an "echo" word or phrase. In line 9, "passage" parallels "course" and points to choice D. It is a good

idea to follow the choices in order for clarity and continuity because each rereading may give you help with another question.

30. D. Question 2 may help you with this answer. Skim the poem from line 1 until you strike a new idea—the dazed bird. The answer has to be D. A, B, and C all describe the daughter and are on topic, while line 27 refers to the previous idea, in this case, the starling introduced earlier.

31. C. The perceptive reader will understand that the stanza is not about the daughter at all, whereas each of the other ideas is valid and can be supported in the context of the stanza.

32. D. The use of nautical terms dominates the first section of the poem, establishing the concept of life as a sea journey or passage. The words, "prow" (line 1), "gunwale" (line 6), and "great cargo" (line 8) all support choices A, B, C, and E. The only image not stated concerns writing as a safe harbor.

33. D. This is essentially a reading question and one you should find easy to answer. Start with the first choice and work your way through each of the others. Highlight or underline lines, look for concrete evidence, and eliminate unsupported choices. Line 19 indicates the sensitivity shown by the father's consideration for the trapped bird.

34. B. This type of question is more complicated than the others because there are many steps involved in finding the answer. Don't just rely on memory. Actually circle or highlight the contrasts as you skim the poem. You may have a quick flash. If so, look immediately to prove it. If you can't, you have your answer. In this case, B. To illustrate the process, here are the images that prove that the other choices are contained in the poem.
A. Line 5: commotion; line 12: stillness
C. Lines 22–23: the implied analogy of child and bird
D. Line 32: life and death
E. Line 2: light breaks; line 21: dark

35. A. This simple reading question is a giveaway. Stanza three tells the reader that "the stuff of her life is a great cargo, and some of it heavy." You should be able to interpret the metaphor as life's difficulties.

36. B. All the choices, with the exception of B, reflect the need to persist in order to achieve a goal—freedom and creation. Only B is grounded to the hard floor.

Jane Eyre
by Charlotte Brontë

37. **D.** The answer is obvious if you carefully read lines 15–17. A heart made up of whalebones and iron is synonymous with strong-willed and inflexible.
38. **E.** Temple, feasting, food of the gods, and benediction can all imply religious connotations. Tea and toast can be a direct allusion to taking communion. Being asked to "come sit by the fire" is simply a request, nothing more.
39. **E.** "Gratification" involves thankfulness. And, in this case, Miss Temple is pleased that she is able to give the girls some special foods during their visit.
40. **D.** This is a metaphorical construction. With it, Jane lets the reader know that having the opportunity to be part of engaging and exciting conversation was like food for her mind and soul.
41. **C.** This is one of those questions that assumes the student is familiar with the definitions of specific terms. "Seemed hastening" is almost a literal flag waving in front of the reader's eyes signaling that something will happen in the future.
42. **E.** Helen's "soul sitting on her lips," her "secret sources of language," and her "purity and radiance" all relate to the realm of the divine.
43. **C.** Herbs are simple and of small quantity. An ox, on the other hand, is overwhelmingly large and overabundant. Love is better than hate. This analogy is straightforward and obvious.
44. **D.** If you read the passage carefully, Jane's wonder and deference are apparent. Look at lines 39–50 to see her sense of awe. Look at line 38. It clearly states Jane's wonder at Helen.
45. **D.** There is nothing in this passage that indicates either of the two girls needs to be saved.
46. **B.** "Serenity," "state in her mien," "refined propriety" in lines 34–35 are synonymous

with one who is restrained. The remainder of the lines illustrates and supports this characterization.
47. **E.** Although there is considerable religious diction and imagery in the passage, none of it directly relates to Jane's character and her being a religious person.

The Good Life
by Tracy K. Smith

48. **B.** This short poem does not have a rhyme scheme nor a regular meter. This is generally termed free verse. If you have any doubt about the definitions of the other choices, you should review them in Chapter 9 of this book.
49. **E.** You can count on questions asking you to locate a pronoun's antecedent. In this case, it is "money" in line 1. If you have any doubts, just exchange "it" with any of the other choices.
50. **E.** The details and diction are common, ordinary, and simple. Informal is a possibility, but the word "it's" paired with is not. None of the other choices is supported in the text.
51. **A.** The speaker gives "money" the qualities of a living being. This question assumes you have a working knowledge of literary devices. Take a few minutes to review them in the glossary of this book.
52. **C.** "For the years I lived . . ." is written in the past tense. Make certain you are familiar with verbs and their tenses. Choices D and E are not supported in this line.
53. **B.** Line 5 simply states a factual situation. The other lines cited contain or further develop a comparison using "like" or "as."
54. **D.** Remember what sarcasm means: an ironic indication of bitterness or contempt. The diction, subject matter, and literary devices are used to convey a tough life lived by the speaker. To title the poem "The Good Life" is sarcastic and quite the opposite of what is portrayed in the poem.
55. **C.** The key to this answer is in line 4. It is the word "nostalgic." This relates to remembering the past, and it is further developed in line 5.

Rating the Essay Section

Rubrics for "The Flowers" by Alice Walker

A high-range score (5, 6):

- Thesis indicates complete understanding and support of the prompt with an indication of the line of reasoning.
- Analyzes appropriate literary techniques that illustrate how Walker prepares the reader for the ending of the story.
- Thoroughly explores the contrasts/complexities inherent in the story.
- Fully presents Myop's character.
- Recognizes the underlying theme related to prejudice and innocence. (Very much related to sophistication.)
- Responds insightfully to image, diction, and setting.
- Presents suitable and unique interpretations of the text.
- Demonstrates a mature, sophisticated writing style.

A mid-range score (3, 4):

- The thesis refers accurately to the prompt and indicates the probable line of reasoning.
- Utilizes appropriate devices in the analysis of Walker's preparation for the surprise ending.
- Adequately supports the thesis with appropriate evidence.
- Uses obvious references and details.
- May miss the subtleties of the story.
- Inferences are based on an acceptable reading of the text.
- Demonstrates writing that is adequate to convey the writer's intent.
- May exhibit a few errors in syntax and/or diction.

Sample Student Essays

Student Essay A

". . . the days had never been as beautiful as these . . . each day a golden surprise." Surprise is the element Alice Walker presents in her story "The Flowers." It is at the heart of the meaning of this story which is driven forward by imagery, setting, and diction.

In the beginning of the story, Walker utilizes diction that creates an atmosphere of euphoric childhood innocence. Myop, the main character, "skipped lightly." Walker describes the harvests, which evince "excited little tremors" in Myop as she anticipates the new day.

This jocund diction continues into the second paragraph. Specifically, Myop feels "light and good" in the heat of the warm sun. In addition, ten year old Myop creates her own world in which nothing exists "but her song." In line 8, the use of onomatopaeia, "tat-de-ta-ta-ta" reinforces the idea of a happy, carefree youth.

Paragraph three, however, marks a small yet significant shift in the passage. Walker begins the paragraph with "Turning her back on the rusty boards of her family's sharecropper cabin, Myop . . ." Myop's world is not behind her, but moves forward to the familiar woods.

5

10

15

As the story progresses, there is a significant shift in paragraphs four
and five. Walker begins to prepare the reader for her profound conclusion. While   20
Myop has often explored the woods behind the house with her mother, today she
sets out alone and "made her own path." As she walks through the woods, she
cautiously keeps an eye out for snakes. The solitude of her journey, and the
possibility of danger, builds suspense and prepares the reader for the dark
surprise of the ending.

The diction of paragraphs four and five also contributes to the sudden   25
shift in the passage. While the diction in the beginning was blithe, describing
"beautiful," the language in paragraph five is negative, foreshadowing the
conclusion. Specifically, Myop is disoriented by the, "strangeness of the land"
It was "not as pleasant" as her usual expeditions. Furthermore, words such as
"gloomy" and "damp" reiterate the dark setting and prepare the reader for the   30
grotesque conclusion of the story.

Paragraph six, which is only one sentence long, marks a brief transition
into the ending of the passage. Myop wants to return to her house, to the
"peacefulness of the morning." But, while she was able to turn her back on the
reality of her poverty, she will not be able to ignore the next truth that hits her.   35

"Stepping smack into his eyes," Myop encounters death, but is unafraid
as she "frees herself." She is filled with innocent curiosity and gazes "around
the spot with interest." Ironically, as she picks her "wild pink rose," a symbol of
beauty, she spots the noose and has her epiphany.

The transition in image, setting, and diction all propel Walker's theme—   40
the coming of age. In the last paragraph Myop picks up the flowers and places
her bouquet in front of the lynched man. It is as if she is at a funeral, as if she
has sobered from her carefree state to one of realization. For, in the last line, the
images of the beginning are finally crushed. Myop can no longer return to the
world of flower-gathering or sun-lit skipping. For Myop, the "summer is over."   45

Note: With specific reference to the 6-point rubric, we will use the following abbreviations
to indicate into which column the comment would fall: **T = thesis, E = evidence, C =
complexity, S = sophistication**.

This is a high-ranking essay for the following reasons:

- Thesis presents a defensible assertion with a clear relationship to the prompt and an indi-
  cation of the line of reasoning. T
- Cites appropriate details to support the thesis: E
  - Imagery (lines 15, 25–30, 36) E
  - Diction (lines 5–6, 10, 30) E
  - Setting (lines 1, 15–16) E
- Thoroughly explores contrasts (lines 12, 16–17, 45). E/C
- Presents unique insights into the underlying theme (lines 16–17, 22–23, 41–43). C/S
- Adheres well to topic; exhibits transitions and connective tissue. S
- Has a definite, clear progression of thought and a strong writer's voice. S

This high-ranking essay presents a solid, mature, and insightful discussion and analysis of Myop's "epiphany" and how Walker prepares the reader for it.

Student Essay B

In the short story "The Flowers" by Alice Walker, the author conveys the meaning of the story and prepares the reader for the ending by using various literary techniques. Some of these are symbol, narrative pace, and style.

The narrative pace starts out as slow and relaxed as Myop explores the land around her family's sharecropper cabin. Every little detail is described creating an image of the blissful summer day. Myop's exuberance is portrayed through diction such as "skipped lightly," "she felt light and good," "bouncing," and "she was singing." Her innocence is shown by the way she is able to block out everything but her happiness and her song. The colors used in the beginning of the story further form the image that is being set up because they are earthy yet shiny colors such as "golden," "silver," and "dark brown."

The fifth paragraph is a transition of narrative pace. The diction and tone change from peaceful and relaxed to tense and dark. Diction such as "strangeness" and "gloomy" take over. When describing the new atmosphere, Walker uses syntax like "the air was damp, the silence close and deep."

From here, the story continues to darken and reaches a climax when Myop steps on a dead man's face. She then discovers his body—in parts and decaying. Walker's use of colors suddenly changes too. Now, "blue," "green," and "wild pink" are used. Although these colors can be seen as positive, in this story, they represent "rotting." Myop finds the noose as she picks up a flower. Such irony.

The last paragraph/sentence is brief and compact. It simply reads, "And the summer was over." The summer can be seen as a symbol of Myop's innocence. With the end of her summer, when she lays down her flowers, her innocence is gone forever. She can no longer exist "for nothing but her song." She had seen death in the midst of her paradise.

This is a mid-range essay (3, 4) for the following reasons:

- Presents a defensible thesis based on the prompt and indicates a probable line pf reasoning. T
- Makes an adequate, expedient presentation of the details in developing the thesis. E
- Illustrates an understanding of the selected literary devices used in the story, but does not fully link or expand them with regard to the thesis (lines 9–10, 14–15). E
- Has unsupported interpretation in lines 18–19. C
- In many places, the syntax resembles a list because ideas are not fully developed (lines 16–20). S

This mid-range essay addresses the prompt and provides details to support the thesis. While the writer obviously understood both the story and the author's process, the subtleties are not fully explored and the syntax lacks fluidity.

Rubrics for "The Naked and the Nude" by Robert Graves

A high-range score (5, 6):

- Thesis presents a defensible assertion related to the prompt and indicates the line of reasoning.
- Analysis demonstrates a complete understanding of the requirements for discussing the differences in connotation between "naked" and "nude."
- Recognizes and identifies the many differences between the two words.
- Analyzes how Graves uses appropriate literary techniques to present a coherent distinction between the two words.
- Responds to the irony in the final stanza.
- Perceives Graves's tone and preference for one of the words.
- Interprets allusions, images, symbols, etc.
- Uses smooth transitions and clear connective tissue.
- Demonstrates a mature writing style.

A mid-range score (3, 4):

- Presents a thesis with a defensible assertion related to the prompt and a probable line of reasoning.
- Adequately supports the thesis with appropriate evidence.
- Is less adept at interpreting the poem.
- May not be sensitive to the complex allusions and images or vocabulary.
- Demonstrates writing that is adequate to convey the writer's intent, may have minor errors in syntax and diction.

Sample Student Essays

Student Essay A

Many people tend to use the words "naked" and "nude" interchangeably. Yet Robert Graves objects to this misconception in his poem "The Naked and the Nude." Although both words mean "without clothes," Graves interprets them differently with regard to their connotations. He points out that "naked" refers to the body itself, whereas, "nude" refers to a personality or state of mind. Through his use of various allusions and imagery, Graves contrasts the two synonyms.

Graves dedicates one stanza apiece to explain his perception of each word. When describing the "naked," Graves uses several classical allusions. He points out that "the Hippocratic eye will see in nakedness, anatomy." Likewise, "naked shines the Goddess when she mounts her lion among men." It's clear that nakedness only refers to the naked body. However, Graves uses allusions to deception and trickery to explain his concept of the nude. He says, "the nude are bold, the nude are sly . . . they grin a mock-religious grin of scorn at those of naked skin." The concept of nude seems to be more of a cunning state of mind—"being naked with attitude."

The poet uses these details to create a certain imagery that clearly explains this discrepancy. His use of classical allusions creates images of peace, beauty, and spirituality which imply the inherent beauty of the human body on a physical level.

5

10

15

Yet, the imagery created by the second set of details does not deal with the physical body. Graves explains that the nude have a cunning state of mind, "while draping by a showman's trick their dishabille in rhetoric." 20

The contrast described in the poem, body versus mind, is reinforced when Graves tells us that the naked are physical bodies that are admired by "Lovers without reproach" and men of medicine. The nude, however, are more than that; they "are sly" and "hold each treasonable eye." The writer concludes that the naked, therefore, who compete against the nude may know defeat because the nude are more complex and cynical. 25

Graves's final stanza transfers the vulnerability of the naked to the nude. When treading "the briary patches of the dead," the nude will not have artifice to protect them from the Gorgons' whips—they will be the naked as well as the nude. 30

Note: With specific reference to the 6-point rubric, we will use the following abbreviations to indicate into which column the comment would fall: **T = thesis, E = evidence, C = complexity, S = sophistication**.

This is a high-ranking essay for the following reasons:

- Thesis states a defensible assertion clearly related to the prompt and indicates a line of reasoning. T
- Immediately presents an accurate distinction between "naked" and "nude" (lines 4–5). E/C
- Utilizes allusion and imagery correctly and links examples to meaning (lines 8–11, 12–15, 17–18). E/C
- Reinforces the contrast throughout the essay (lines 16, 22, 29–30). E
- Indicates perceptive, subtle analysis (lines 20–21, 29). E/C
- Is well organized. S
- Demonstrates a mature writing style. S

This essay is indicative of a confident writer and thinker. The paper is well focused, and it exhibits the writer's facility with literary terminology and analysis.

Student Essay B

The poem "The Naked and the Nude" written by Robert Graves explicitly shows how connotations can change the meaning of a thought or statement through images and other poetic devices. Those who are "naked" and those who are "nude" are not, according to the poem, in the same state of undress.

The speaker of the poem describes the differences between the naked and the nude using a variety of images and descriptions. He feels that one who is naked is hiding nothing while one who is nude is a picture of deception and art. The images of "Lovers without reproach will gaze on bodies naked and ablaze" depicts the honesty and truth that is given with love. Also the "Hippocratic eye will see in nakedness, anatomy." When this "eye" sees a naked person it is seeing what is really there and not what could be held in the deception of a person who is nude. 5 10

Although the naked are personified as "love" and "truth," when they "compete against the nude they may know defeat." This statement shows how those who are naked can sometimes be deceived and beaten by those who are artful liars. However, when it comes to the life after death, those who have been nude will also be naked, meaning that no matter what they were in life, when they die there will be no hiding behind the art of the body. Also, the facade that was built in life to hide from the truth will not work when it comes to the end. 15

Tone is another device that is used to convey the different connotations of naked and nude. When those who are naked are being discussed, the tone is not only positive, it presents an image of those who are happy with their position in life. For example, nakedness is linked with words such as "love," "truth," "shines," and "Goddess." However, when the speaker directs his attention on the nude, the tone is just the opposite. Nude is associated with "scorn," "showman," and "mock-religious." The speaker's tone in the descriptions of the two states of undress presents a clear difference in the connotations of the two words in the title of the poem. 25

The style and structure of the poem also contribute to conveying the two different connotations of naked and nude. The simple rhyme scheme shows how simplistic those who are naked can be as opposed to the deception and intricacies of those who are nude. The four stanza's each have a theme that it conveys. The first stanza 30 exhibits the differences between the naked and the nude. The second stanza has the theme of the freedom of the naked, while the third shows the deception of the nude. The fourth and final stanza reinforces the theme that everyone will be naked after death.

This is a mid-range essay for the following reasons:

- Accurately addresses the prompt with a defensible assertion and an indication of a probable prompt. T
- Understands deception and artifice (lines 6–7). E
- Refers to suitable textual material to support the thesis (lines 8–9, 22–24). E
- Demonstrates an ability to handle literary analysis (19–25, 27–29). E
- Adheres to the implied line of reasoning. T/E/C
- Has several awkward sentences and punctuation and agreement errors (lines 10–11, 13–29, and 30). S
- Uses transitions and connective tissue. S

It's obvious that the writer of this mid-range essay understands both the prompt and process of literary analysis. The second half of the paper is not as strong as the first. Perhaps, this writer was feeling the time pressure.

Rubrics for the Free-Response Essay

A high-range score (5, 6):

- Clearly incorporates a chosen work of fiction into the thesis that addresses the prompt and provides an indication of the line of reasoning.
- Chooses an appropriate novel or play.
- Effectively and coherently addresses the intentional dissembling of a character or group.
- Effectively and coherently analyzes how the dissembling contributes to character development.

- Effectively and coherently analyzes how the dissembling contributes to the meaning of the work.
- Uses references insightfully to support and illustrate the dissembling.
- Thoroughly discusses the character's nature and its relation to the theme.
- Strongly adheres to the topic using transitions and a clear line of reasoning.
- Substantiates development of the thesis.
- Exhibits mature writing style.

A mid-range score (3, 4):

- Addresses the prompt with a defensible thesis and indicates a probable line of reasoning.
- Identifies the intentional dissembling of a character or group.
- Chooses an acceptable novel or play.
- Adequately addresses the prompt with respect to intentional dissembling and how it contributes to both character development and meaning.
- Uses obvious references to support the prompt.
- Discussion of the character's nature and its relation to the theme is less developed.
- Adheres to topic, but may have lapses in coherence.
- Discussion of the theme is less developed.
- Writing style is acceptable but may show lapses in syntax and/or diction.

Sample Student Essays

Student Essay A

"To thine own self be true," advises Polonius in Shakespeare's *Hamlet*. Too bad he doesn't follow his own counsel when he continually dissembles to advance his own position in Claudius's court. This deceitfulness is the cause of the destruction of the lives of his children, himself, and ultimately the kingdom. His seemingly minor deceits reinforce the theme of betrayal and deception in the play.   5

Our first impression of Polonius is a positive one when we see him supporting Laertes's desire to return to his studies in Paris. However, his fatherly advice, "to not be false to any man" is ironic because he has already hired Reynaldo to spy on his son. He tells Reynaldo to use a "bait of falsehood" to see if Laertes's friends will be faithful   10
and true. Polonius plans for this to include starting rumors and even malicious lies. Later in the play, Shakespeare has Rosencrantz and Guildenstern play out a parallel scene with Hamlet.

As with his son, Polonius seems to be genuinely concerned with the well-being of his daughter Ophelia. He tells her to reject the "love" letters and tokens from Hamlet   15
because he fears Hamlet only wants to take advantage of her and will not and cannot marry her. But soon we see the other side of this paternal scheme when Polonius willingly uses his daughter's emotional connections to Hamlet for his own purpose of furthering his service to Claudius. Hoping to prove that Hamlet's madness is caused by love sickness, he permits himself to advance his own agenda even though he has to   20
know that it will cause pain and distress for both Ophelia and Hamlet.

Inevitably, Polonius's dissembling leads to his own destruction. Ever the deceitful sycophant, he suggests to Claudius that he hide behind the arras in Gertrude's chamber in order to spy on both her and Hamlet. While eavesdropping, he cries out when he believes that Hamlet is attacking the Queen. Believing the voice to be that of Claudius, Hamlet thrusts his sword through the curtain, fatally wounding Polonius. Here, the irony lies in his death resulting from an attempt to protect Gertrude.

It is this act that is the catalyst for the subsequent tragic events: Ophelia's madness and death, Laertes's desire for revenge, and Hamlet's fleeing Denmark. The final tragedies of the play—the deaths of Ophelia, Laertes, Gertrude, Claudus, and Hamlet—are all the results of further dissembling which is foreshadowed by Polonius's deceit.

Although Polonius dies in Act III, he sets the foundation for the theme of deceit and murder throughout the remainder of the drama. Truly, something was rotten in the state of Denmark, and it was Polonius.

Note: With specific reference to the 6-point rubric, we will use the following abbreviations to indicate into which column the comment would fall: **T = thesis, E = evidence, C = complexity, S = sophistication**.

This is a high-range essay for the following reasons:

- Presents a clear thesis with a defensible assertion and an indication of a line of reasoning. T
- Exhibits solid evidence of knowledge of the chosen work. E
- Demonstrates the ability to garner insights from the work. C
- Uses appropriate illustrations and details (lines 8–9, paragraphs 3 and 4). E/C
- Uses strong connective tissue. S
- Demonstrates thorough development of ideas that are linked to the meaning of the work (lines 3–6, 11–13, 19–21). E/C/S
- Strongly adheres to topic and organization. S
- Uses mature vocabulary and syntax (lines 22–23, 28). S

This essay is in the high-range because of its clear voice and strong organization. (S) The introductory paragraph establishes the premise, which is fully supported in the body paragraphs. (E/C) Rather than a summary, the concluding paragraph makes an insightful final comment.

Student Essay B

Often, in literature, there is a gap between the appearance of a situation and the meaning of the truth behind it. In Shakespeare's *Hamlet*, the protagonist assumes the antic disposition as a means of investigating the veracity of the ghost's admonition, "The serpent that did sting thy father's life, now wears his crown." In addition to contributing to the psychological development of Hamlet's character, this deceit augments many of the important themes in the play. In a work whose main topic is the search for truth, Hamlet's misrepresentation acts as a warning to sift through the surface appearance of things to discover purpose in this world.   5

Throughout the play, nothing is really as it seems. Hamlet's feigned   10 madness is perhaps the most egregious example of this pattern. The melancholy Dane becomes a different man behind the mask of insanity. He is free to taunt Polonius regarding his lack of intelligence, or to scold his mother for her sexual improprieties, or to chastise Ophelia for her attempt to trick him. He is free to express himself without the fear of being held responsible for his insolence. This   15 is a psychological coping method for Hamlet to deal with the trauma of a father's death and a mother's betrayal. Hamlet represses his anger and is paralyzed by it. The course of the play is a struggle for Hamlet to overcome his repression and to deal with the problems before him. Pretending to be mad is symbolic of this inner struggle and Hamlet's shield from the world.   20

Many of the major themes in *Hamlet* are also embodied in Hamlet's misrepresentation. The pervading irony in the play is that the "madman" is really thinking rationally. He sees what others do not and recognizes that his father was killed at Claudius's hands. Hamlet is a man who can and does make plans to seek the truth, and he carries these plans out. Another major theme is that of appearance   25 versus reality. Connected to and with Hamlet's situation is a king who is a murderer, a mystery involving a ghost, a play within a play, a royal request which will turn into an invasion of Denmark, spying for proof of madness, fatherly advice to his children, and friends who are enemies. Each of these separately and all of them together enhance this theme of the play.   30

Hamlet is a search for truth. Through the protagonist's discovery of self and the revelation of Claudius's guilt, he embodies everyman's striving for understanding. Dissembling as a madman, Hamlet is able to work toward his goal of gaining authentic knowledge of past events and future battles.

This is a solid mid-range essay for the following reasons:

- Provides a clear thesis statement with a defensible assertion and an indicated line of reasoning. T
- Decisively identifies theme and character. C
- References are appropriate. E
- Indicates cause and effect with supporting details. E/C
- Uses inferences rather than plot. E/C

- Good use of connective tissue. S
- Uses strong vocabulary. S
- Uses parallel structure well. S

Here is a paper that shows great promise and strength in the first half, but it loses continuity and lacks development in the second half. It seems that the writer has run out of time and is anxious to complete the essay. This student is a real thinker, but appears to be trapped by time constraints.

PRACTICE EXAM 2
ANSWER SHEET FOR MULTIPLE-CHOICE QUESTIONS

1. _____

2. _____

3. _____

4. _____

5. _____

6. _____

7. _____

8. _____

9. _____

10. _____

11. _____

12. _____

13. _____

14. _____

15. _____

16. _____

17. _____

18. _____

19. _____

20. _____

21. _____

22. _____

23. _____

24. _____

25. _____

26. _____

27. _____

28. _____

29. _____

30. _____

31. _____

32. _____

33. _____

34. _____

35. _____

36. _____

37. _____

38. _____

39. _____

40. _____

41. _____

42. _____

43. _____

44. _____

45. _____

46. _____

47. _____

48. _____

49. _____

50. _____

51. _____

52. _____

53. _____

54. _____

55. _____

I _____ did _____ did not complete this part of the test in the allotted 1 hour.

I had _____ correct answers. I had _____ incorrect answers. I left _____ blank.

I have carefully reviewed the explanations of the answers, and I think I need to work on the following types of questions:

PRACTICE EXAM 2
ADVANCED PLACEMENT ENGLISH LITERATURE

Section I

Total time —1 hour

Carefully read the following passages and answer the questions that follow.
Questions 1–12 are based on the following passage from William Shakespeare's *Richard II*.

Act 5—Scene 5   Pomfret Castle
King Richard II:

I have been studying how I may compare
This prison where I live unto the world:
And for because the world is populous
And here is not a creature but myself,
I cannot do it; yet I'll hammer it out.   5
My brain I'll prove the female to my soul,
My soul the father; and these two beget
A generation of still-breeding thoughts,
And these same thoughts people this little world,
In humours like the people of this world,   10
For no thought is contented. The better sort,
As thoughts of things divine, are intermix'd
With scruples and do set the word itself
Against the word:
As thus, 'Come, little ones,' and then again,   15
'It is as hard to come as for a camel
To thread the postern of a small needle's eye.'
Thoughts tending to ambition, they do plot
Unlikely wonders; how these vain weak nails
May tear a passage through the flinty ribs   20
Of this hard world, my ragged prison walls,
And, for they cannot, die in their own pride.
Thoughts tending to content flatter themselves
That they are not the first of fortune's slaves,
Nor shall not be the last; like silly beggars   25
Who sitting in the stocks refuge their shame,
That many have and others must sit there;
And in this thought they find a kind of ease,
Bearing their own misfortunes on the back
Of such as have before endured the like.   30
Thus play I in one person many people,
And none contented: sometimes am I king;
Then treasons make me wish myself a beggar,
And so I am: then crushing penury
Persuades me I was better when a king: 35

Then am I king'd again: and by and by
Think that I am unking'd by Bolingbroke,
And straight am nothing: but whate'er I be,
Nor I nor any man that but man is
With nothing shall be pleased, till he be eased   40
With being nothing.

1. This passage is an example of
   A. an elegy
   B. a villanelle
   C. an ode
   D. free verse
   E. a soliloquy

2. The extended metaphor in this passage develops around
   A. royalty
   B. poverty
   C. fortune
   D. prison
   E. treason

3. In line 5, "yet I'll hammer it out" refers to Richard's
   A. aggression
   B. thought processes
   C. anger at his circumstances
   D. arrogance
   E. self-loathing

4. The conceit in lines 6–11 is based on
   A. sexuality
   B. psychology
   C. genealogy
   D. religion
   E. human nature

5. In line 10, "the people of this world" refers to Richard's
   A. still breeding thoughts
   B. brain and soul
   C. "humours"
   D. children
   E. royal subjects

6. Lines 10–22 are developed using each of the following *except*
   A. personification
   B. direct address
   C. simile
   D. hyperbole
   E. synecdoche

7. Richard attempts to comfort himself with the idea that
   A. others have and are enduring comparable hardships
   B. it is possible to escape his prison
   C. prayer will redeem him
   D. his offspring will carry on his legacy
   E. fortune or fate will intervene

8. The organization of this passage moves from
   A. past to present
   B. definition to an example
   C. specific circumstances to universal conclusion
   D. general principle to specific instances
   E. positive attitude to negative one

9. Lines 38–41 conclude the passage with an example of
   A. couplet
   B. personification
   C. epitaph
   D. paradox
   E. understatement

10. Richard's major epiphany occurs within lines
    A. 1–5
    B. 11–14
    C. 38–41
    D. 18–22
    E. 23–27

11. Contrasts developed in the passage include all
    of the following *except*
    A. freedom and imprisonment
    B. men and women
    C. wealth and poverty
    D. power and powerlessness
    E. past and present

12. The theme of isolation (lines 3–4) is reinforced
    by which of the following lines?
    A. 24–25
    B. 36–38
    C. 25–27
    D. 11–14
    E. 31–32

Questions 13–25 are based on a careful reading of the following passage from the opening of the 2018 novel *Split at the Root* by Leah Napolin.

Beginnings
by Leah Napolin

I want to start talking about developing my universe, the universe of my understanding in growing up. I feel, as I've said before, that I've lived many lives in different times and places.

I was born in a small Southern town in southwest Mississippi. My mother, following the traditional pattern of many southern women, returned home to birth me in 1941. The home I remembered most in my memories is our home in Woodville . . . I dream of it, in fact, at night. In fact, for many many years, up until probably the last ten, all of my dreams usually took place in that house or in the surrounding area. So, in a way, I guess, I have inhabited that home and that place in my sleep, for the most part of my life.   5

It was a strange house. It was built on top of a hill. It just spread out, it never went up—meaning that there were never any stories above the first story. The first part of the house was built in 1842 for the regional governor at that time, whose name was Johnson. They just kept adding on to the house. It kept spreading out, I guess you would say, like this large encompassing giant. It was an old-fashioned house. It had only one front door, but it had a side door off a big, rambling porch on the side. At times I still kind of occupy those rooms.   10

The front window of my room looked on to this wonderful rambling porch that I referred to a moment ago. It really was rambling in the sense that it began on one side of the house, went down the entire front, turned a corner, and went down the other side of the house and into a dining room which was in the old part of the house, which must have been, probably I would say, thirty feet long—very narrow, but thirty feet long. Probably about fifteen feet wide, thirty feet long. It was in this dining room that had a mahogany table that used to seat—oh, now that I'm counting, probably with all the leaves in it—at least 12 to 15 people.   15   20

But in that dining room, at that long mahogany table, I can—it certainly brings up many memories. Pleasant ones and ones that were not so pleasant. In fact, in some ways that dining room and who sat at what place at the table says a lot about, probably, the hierarchy, or who really obtained power in my family.   25

At this table, once my parents moved from New Orleans in 1951, my mother and father, myself, my brother and younger sister, who was just still an infant, moved to my mother's home which was still occupied by her mother, or should I say her stepmother—in this small town. Now, my grandmother, my step grandmother—who I called Mammy from a very early age—was a very controlling sort of person. She was never more than, I guess, never taller than about five foot two, probably wore a size 4-1/2 shoe. But was a real dynamo. I mean, you could just tell by her body language that she had a stiff back and did not walk with a lot of flow in her gait. It was pretty, not calculated, but it certainly—I can't imagine her dancing to a waltz, or any kind of melodic tune. But anyhow, she was a very strict, controlling sort of person. She changed her clothes every afternoon around 3 o'clock, to put a fresh frock on, with new earrings and necklace, and freshened up her face. And would have her demi-tasse cup of coffee. 35

To go back to the dining room, and how you could pretty much understand the power struggle, the power structure within my family, could be represented by this seating at the dining room table. My grandmother would sit at one end, my father would sit at another, my mother would sit at the left side of my grandmother. My younger sister would occupy the right side of my grandmother. And at the other end of the table where my father was, I would sit 40 on his right side and my brother would sit on the left. And it was kind of interesting, because my grandmother would always have a little dinner bell at the end of the table which she would jingle for Evalina or Lalice, one of the servants, to come in—if water was needed or if it was time for the next course to be served. And my mother really had no participation in this at all. My grandmother controlled the entire affair from beginning to end. Now, my father at the 45 other end would always carve whatever it might be—a lamb or a turkey or a ham. And I would have the plate on my side where he would start transferring the slices, the leg or the thigh, to the plate. And so he would sometimes say, "Weesie, why don't you go ahead and start serving the pieces people would like?" So that gave me some role in this whole affair. But I think it's very telling that, again, my mother, who was very passive and was completely controlled by her 50 stepmother, sat to the left of her and did not really participate at all.

30

13. The reader can infer from the first paragraph that the narrator
A. is a psychotherapy patient
B. has a background as a storyteller
C. is being interviewed by a journalist
D. has led a varied life
E. is presenting a lecture

14. Which of the following statements best conveys the effect of lines 6–7?
A. curiosity about what happened to cause the change in the narrator's dreams
B. fear for the well-being of the narrator
C. sympathy for the narrator's circumstances
D. desire to learn more about the narrator's mother
E. curiosity about Woodville

15. Paragraph 3 is primarily developed using
A. assonance
B. understatement
C. alliteration
D. sarcasm
E. metaphor

16. Which of the following lines contains an example of personification?
A. 1–2
B. 4–5
C. 12–13
D. 15–16
E. 28–30

17. One may conclude from the passage that the narrator
    A. sees her southern heritage as a burden
    B. will continue her connection to her heritage
    C. will rebel against her southern heritage
    D. will be rejected by her family
    E. envies the lifestyle of her grandmother

18. Lines 48–51 reveal that the narrator
    A. did not want to be her father's favorite
    B. was afraid of her "Mammy"
    C. apologized for the treatment of the "servants"
    D. was eager to be given responsibilities
    E. wanted to run away from this family

19. In line 32, the long dash is used to
    A. indicate the narrator's difficulty in beginning to talk about personal memories
    B. indicate the narrator's desire to remain in the past
    C. introduce her conflict with her mother
    D. emphasize the narrator's troubled childhood
    E. demonstrate the narrator's trouble with language

20. "But" in line 22 is used to
    A. indicate an incongruence between the dining room and the rest of the house
    B. progress from a descriptive passage to a personal narrative
    C. introduce the family dining situation
    D. introduce the narrator's feelings about living in the house
    E. emphasize the narrator's internal conflict with the house

21. The narrator's perspective throughout the passage can best be described as that of
    A. an investigative reporter
    B. an objective historian
    C. a bitter relative
    D. an involved memoirist
    E. a mourning grandchild

22. Based on the last paragraph, who of the following probably had the strongest influence on the narrator?
    A. grandmother
    B. father
    C. mother
    D. sister
    E. brother

23. The overall tone of the passage can best be described as
    A. reverent and uneasy
    B. sentimental and playful
    C. frank and thoughtful
    D. nostalgic and bewildered
    E. blunt and biting

24. Which statement best describes the narrative technique employed in the last paragraph?
    A. uses repetition to emphasize a point
    B. cites a specific example as the basis for a generalization
    C. uses negative diction to develop a feeling of alienation
    D. uses hyperbole to illustrate a paradox
    E. uses figurative language to build the characterization of the narrator

25. The effect of the last paragraph can most appropriately be stated as
    A. illustrating how controlling her father was
    B. speculating whether or not the family will stay together
    C. showing how the household help was treated
    D. introducing the narrator's central fear
    E. suggesting that the narrator will have a difficult relationship with her mother

Questions 26–40 are based on the following poem.

Love Poem
by John Frederick Nims (1982)

My clumsiest dear, whose hands shipwreck vases,
At whose quick touch all glasses chip and ring,
Whose palms are bulls in china, burs in linen,
And have no cunning with any soft thing

Except all ill-at-ease fidgeting people: 5
The refugee uncertain at the door
You make at home; deftly you steady
The drunk clambering on his undulant floor.

Unpredictable dear, the taxi drivers' terror,
Shrinking from far headlights pale as a dime   10
Yet leaping before red apoplectic streetcars—
Misfit in any space. And never on time.

A wrench in clocks and the solar system. Only
With words and people and love you move at ease.
In traffic of wit expertly manoeuvre   15
And keep us, all devotion, at your knees.

Forgetting your coffee spreading on our flannel,
Your lipstick grinning on our coat,
So gayly in love's unbreakable heaven
Our souls on glory of spilt bourbon float.   20

Be with me, darling, early and late. Smash glasses—
I will study wry music for your sake.
For should your hands drop white and empty
All the toys of the world would break.

26. As used in the second stanza, "undulant" most closely means
   A. polished
   B. inebriated
   C. wavy
   D. dirty
   E. cluttered

27. With reference to the title, the irony lies in the
   A. reversal of the speaker's thoughts
   B. absence of the beloved
   C. kindness of the lover
   D. enumeration of the lover's weaknesses
   E. wit of the lover

28. The image of "hands drop white and empty" (line 23) implies the
A. breaking of vases
B. death of the lover
C. lover's clumsy nature
D. spilt bourbon
E. smashed glasses

29. The word "only" in line 13 serves to
A. introduce a contrasting thought
B. indicate isolation
C. make the rhyme effective
D. indicate cause and effect
E. indicate passage of time

30. According to the poem, the lover is all the following *except*
A. clever
B. clumsy
C. playful
D. selfish
E. gracious

31. "Be with me, darling" (line 21) is an example of
A. hyperbole
B. personification
C. allusion
D. invective
E. apostrophe

32. The poem is essentially a
A. caricature
B. satire
C. narrative
D. character study
E. parable

33. Lines 7 and 8 illustrate an example of
A. enjambment
B. oxymoron
C. jargon
D. connotation
E. ambiguity

34. The tone of the poem is
A. effusive
B. elegiac
C. benevolent
D. didactic
E. adoring

35. The speaker's attitude toward his love is
A. critical
B. embarrassed
C. enthralled
D. impatient
E. ill-at-ease

36. "Toys of the world" in the last line of the poem may be best understood as a metaphor for
A. life's pleasures
B. youthful infatuations
C. shattered dreams
D. material objects
E. lovers of the world

37. "A wrench in clocks and the solar system" (line 13) can be best interpreted to mean
A. the speaker is uncomfortable
B. star-crossed lovers
C. being obsessive about time
D. the inability to face the future
E. being out of synch with established conventions

38. The poem is written in
A. iambic pentameter
B. free verse
C. quatrains
D. blank verse
E. epigrams

39. Line 3 includes an example of
A. metaphor
B. synecdoche
C. metonymy
D. simile
E. onomatopoeia

40. Line 20 employs
A. internal rhyme
B. cacophony
C. apostrophe
D. literary conceit
E. assonance

Questions 41–55 are based on the following passage.

Excerpt from *As I Lay Dying*, "Addie,"
by William Faulkner (1930)

In the afternoon when school was out and the last one had left with
his little dirty snuffling nose, instead of going home I would go down the hill
to the spring where I could be quiet and hate them. It would be quiet there then,
with the water bubbling up and away and the sun slanting quiet in the trees and
the quiet smelling of damp and rotting leaves and new earth, especially in the   5
early spring, for it was worst then.

I could just remember how my father used to say that the reason for living
was to get ready to stay dead for a long time. And when I would have to look at
them day after day, each with his and her secret and selfish thought, and blood
strange to each other blood and strange to mine, and think that this seemed to be the   10
only way I could get ready to stay dead, I would hate my father for having planted
me. I would look forward to the times when they faulted, so I could whip them.
When the switch fell I could feel it upon my flesh; when it welted and ridged it was
my blood that ran, and I would think with each blow of the switch: Now you are
aware of me! Now I am something in your secret and selfish life, who have marked   15
your blood with my own for ever and ever.

And so I took Anse. I saw him pass the school house three or four times before
I learned that he was driving four miles out of his way to do it. I noticed then how he
was beginning to hump—a tall man and young—so that he looked already like a tall
bird hunched in the cold weather, on the wagon seat.   20

In early spring it was worst. Sometimes I thought that I could not bear it,
lying in bed at night, with the wild geese going north and their honking coming faint
and high and wild out of the wild darkness, and during the day it would seem as though
I couldn't wait for the last one to go so I could go down to the spring. And so when I
looked up that day and saw Anse standing there in his Sunday clothes, turning his hat   25
round and round in his hands, I said:

"If you've got any womenfolks, why in the world dont they make you get your
hair cut?"

"I aint got none," he said. Then he said suddenly, driving his eyes at me like
two hounds in a strange yard: "That's what I come to see you about."   30

"And make you hold your shoulders up," I said. "You haven't got any? But
you've got a house. They tell me you've got a house and a good farm. And you live
there alone, doing for yourself, do you?" He just looked at me, turning the hat in his
hands. "A new house," I said. "Are you going to get married?"

And he said again, holding his eyes to mine: "That's what I come to see you   35
about."

Later he told me, "I aint got no people. So that wont be no worry to you. I
dont reckon you can say the same."

"No. I have people. In Jefferson."

His face fell a little. "Well, I got a little property. I'm forehanded; I got a   40
good honest name. I know how town folks are, but maybe when they talk to me . . . "

"They might listen," I said. "But they'll be hard to talk to." He was watching
my face. "They're in the cemetery."

"But your living kin," he said. "They'll be different."

"Will they?" I said. "I dont know. I never had any other kind."

So I took Anse.

41. The "geese" (line 22) are a symbolic representation of
A. Addie's desire to be part of a family
B. Addie's desire to be connected to nature
C. Addie's desire to be free
D. the children Addie teaches
E. the people in Jefferson

42. In the first paragraph, the reader learns all the following *except*
A. the point of view of the piece
B. the speaker's tone
C. the conflicts
D. the setting
E. the central event of the narration

43. In lines 29–44, the character of Anse is revealed by which of the following literary techniques?
A. colloquial diction
B. rhetorical questions
C. a shift in tense
D. omniscient point of view
E. humor

44. Figurative language is found in lines
A. 4 and 8
B. 23 and 25–26
C. 1 and 2
D. 19–20 and 29–30
E. 7–8 and 35

45. The concept of alienation is supported by all of the following *except*
A. "each with his and her secret and selfish thought"
B. "blood strange to each other blood and strange to mine"
C. "When the switch fell I could feel it upon my flesh"
D. "They're in the cemetery"
E. "I aint got no people"

46. Addie marries because
A. she is in love with Anse
B. it was expected of women
C. she thinks he will take her north
D. Anse presents himself at that particular time
E. she wants children

47. The reader can infer that Addie's role in the marriage will be
A. supportive
B. controlling
C. submissive
D. grateful
E. erotic

48. The repetition of the phrase "so I took Anse" serves to
A. further develop the setting
B. establish an ironic situation
C. highlight the importance of the event
D. support Addie's ambivalence
E. establish a matter-of-fact explanation of the relationship

49. In line 21, "In early spring it was worst," "it" refers to Addie's
A. restless nature
B. longing for Anse
C. sadistic tendencies
D. students' behavior
E. desire to be married

50. Addie whips the children primarily because
A. they talk back to her
B. she hates her job
C. she believes corporal punishment will make the children learn better
D. she wants them to know she is there
E. she sees no other way to control them

51. All of the following ideas are presented and supported in the passage *except*
    A. the relationship between life and death
    B. isolation and alienation
    C. freedom and commitment
    D. frustration and resignation
    E. hope and liberation

52. Addie's philosophy and behavior most likely come from
    A. her religious beliefs
    B. her father
    C. her childhood experiences
    D. her people in Jefferson
    E. her education

53. Which of the following images are contrasted in the passage?
    A. the hill . . . the spring (lines 2–3)
    B. water bubbling up . . . sun slanting (line 4)
    C. rotting leaves . . . new earth (line 5)
    D. welted . . . ridged (line 13)
    E. secret . . . selfish (line 15)

54. On an interpretive level, Addie associates quiet with all of the following *except*
    A. hatred
    B. innermost feelings
    C. escape
    D. nature
    E. death

55. Symbolically, "early spring" may represent
    A. bubbling water
    B. the blood
    C. "womenfolks"
    D. Addie's life force
    E. secret and selfish lives

END OF SECTION I

Section II

Total time—2 hours

Question 1

(Suggested time 40 minutes. This question counts as one-third of the total score for Section II.)

The following passage is the 1902 short story "Reginald's Choir Treat" by Saki. In this story Saki contrasts two complex philosophies of life. Carefully read the short story. Then, in a well-written essay analyze how Saki uses literary elements and techniques to convey these two viewpoints and which of them is preferred by the narrator.

In your response you should do the following:

- Respond to the prompt with a thesis that presents an assertion that requires defense and support.
- Select and use evidence to support your line of reasoning.
- Explain how the evidence supports your line of reasoning
- Use appropriate grammar and punctuation in communicating your argument.

Reginald's Choir Treat
by Saki

"Never," wrote Reginald to his most darling friend, "be a pioneer. It's the Early Christian that gets the fattest lion."

Reginald, in his way, was a pioneer.

None of the rest of his family had anything approaching Titian hair or a sense of humour, and they used primroses as a table decoration.   5

It follows that they never understood Reginald, who came down late to breakfast, and nibbled toast, and said disrespectful things about the universe. The family ate porridge, and believed in everything, even the weather forecast.

Therefore the family was relieved when the vicar's daughter undertook the reformation of Reginald. Her name was Anabel; it was the vicar's one extravagance. Anabel was   10
accounted a beauty and intellectually gifted: she never played tennis, and was reputed to have read Maeterlinck's "Life of a Bee." If you abstain from tennis and read Maeterlinck in a small country village, you are of necessity intellectual. Also she had been twice to Fecamp to pick up a good French accent from the Americans staying there; consequently she had a knowledge of the world which might be considered useful in dealings with a worldling.   15

Hence the congratulations in the family when Anabel undertook the reformation of the wayward member.

Anabel commenced operations by asking her unsuspecting pupil to tea in the vicarage garden; she believed in the healthy influence of natural surroundings, never having been in Sicily, where things are different.   20

And like every woman who has ever preached repentance to unregenerate youth, she dwelt on the sin of an empty life, which always seems so much more scandalous in the country, where people rise early to see if a new strawberry has happened during the night.

Reginald recalled the lilies of the field, "which simply sat and looked beautiful, and defied competition."   25

"But that is not an example for us to follow," gasped Anabel.

"Unfortunately, we can't afford to. You don't know what a world of trouble I take in trying to rival the lilies in their artistic simplicity."

"You are really indecently vain in your appearance. A good life is infinitely preferable to good looks."

"You agree with me that the two are incompatible. I always say beauty is only skin deep."

Anabel began to realize that the battle is not always to the strong-minded. With the immemorial resource of her sex, she abandoned the frontal attack and laid stress on her unassisted labours in parish work, her mental loneliness, her discouragements—and at the right moment she produced strawberries and cream. Reginald was obviously affected by the latter, and when his preceptress suggested that he might begin the strenuous life by helping her to supervise the annual outing of the bucolic infants who composed the local choir, his eyes shone with the dangerous enthusiasm of a convert.

Reginald entered on the strenuous life alone, as far as Anabel was concerned The most virtuous women are not proof against damp grass, and Anabel kept to her bed with a cold. Reginald called it a dispensation; it had been the dream of his life to stage-manage a choir outing. With strategic insight, he led his shy, bullet-headed charges to the nearest woodland stream and allowed them to bathe; then he seated himself on the discarded garments and discoursed on their immediate future, which, he decreed, was to embrace a Bacchanalian procession through the village. Forethought had provided the occasion with a supply of tin whistles, but the introduction of a he-goat from a neighbouring orchard was a brilliant afterthought. Properly, Reginald explained, there should have been an outfit of panther skins; as it was, those who had spotted handkerchiefs were allowed to wear them, which they did with thankfulness. Reginald recognized the impossibility in the time at his disposal, of teaching his shivering neophytes a chant in honour of Bacchus, so he started them off with a more familiar, if less appropriate, temperance hymn. After all, he said, it is the spirit of the thing that counts. Following the etiquette of dramatic authors on first nights, he remained discreetly in the background while the procession, with extreme diffidence and the goat, wound its way lugubriously towards the village. The singing had died down long before the main street was reached, but the miserable wailing of pipes brought the inhabitants to their doors. Reginald said he had seen something like it in pictures; the villagers had seen nothing like it in their lives, and remarked as much freely.

Reginald's family never forgave him. They had no sense of humour.

Question 2

(Suggested time 40 minutes. This question counts as one-third of the total score for Section II.)

Among the many poets who have expressed their opinions about education are William Wordsworth and Howard Nemerov. As a romantic poet, Wordsworth envisions and describes the ideal and true education as one centered on experience and living with nature. Nemerov, a modern poet, also has a very specific attitude about education that he reveals in the following poem. Read his poem carefully. Then, in a well-written essay analyze how Nemerov uses poetic elements and techniques to convey his complex viewpoint about education that is similar and/or different from that of Wordswoth.

In your response you should do the following:

- Respond to the prompt with a thesis that presents an interpretation that requires defense and support.
- Select and use evidence to support your line of reasoning.
- Explain how the evidence supports your line of reasoning.
- Use appropriate grammar and punctuation in communicating your argument.

To David, About His Education (1990)
by Howard Nemerov

The world is full of mostly invisible things,
And there is no way but putting the mind's eye,
Or its nose, in a book, to find them out,
Things like the square root of Everest
Or how many times Byron* goes into Texas,   5
Or whether the law of the excluded middle
Applies west of the Rockies. For these
And the like reasons, you have to go to school
And study books and listen to what you are told,
And sometimes try to remember. Though I don't know   10
What you will do with the mean annual rainfall
On Plato's Republic,† or the calorie content
Of the Diet of Worms,§ such things are said to be
Good for you, and you will have to learn them
In order to become one of the grown-ups   15
Who sees invisible things neither steadily nor whole,
But keeps gravely the grand confusion of the world
Under his hat, which is where it belongs,
And teaches small children to do this in their turn.

Question 3

(Suggested time 40 minutes. This question counts as one-third of the total score for Section II.)

Frequently a work of literature will concern itself with a major transformation in a character. This transformation could be actual or symbolic. Either from your own reading or from the list below, choose a work of fiction in which such a transformation occurs. Then, in a well-written essay analyze how the complex nature of the transformation relates to the character and theme of the work. Do not merely summarize.

In your response you should do the following:

- Respond to the prompt with a thesis that presents an assertion that requires defense and support.
- Select and use evidence to support your line of reasoning.
- Explain how the evidence supports your line of reasoning.
- Use appropriate grammar and punctuation in communicating your argument.

Frankenstein	*The Importance of Being Earnest*
Metamorphosis	*The Color Purple*
Native Son	*The Awakening*
A Doll's House	*Things Fall Apart*
The Poisonwood Bible	*Invisible Man*
Twelfth Night	*Pride and Prejudice*
Othello	*Gulliver's Travels*
I Know Why the Caged Bird Sings	*The Things They Carried*
Sula	*Crime and Punishment*

---

* Lord Byron, a leading English Romantic poet.
† Classical Greek philosophical dialogue about the nature of a just city-state.
§ Declared in 1521 that Martin Luther was a heretic and banned his teachings.

The Joy Luck Club   *The Stranger*
Madame Bovary   *The Scarlet Letter*
Pygmalion

END OF SECTION II

ANSWERS TO MULTIPLE-CHOICE QUESTIONS

Answer Key

1. E	20. B	39. A
2. D	21. D	40. E
3. B	22. A	41. C
4. C	23. C	42. E
5. A	24. B	43. A
6. E	25. E	44. D
7. A	26. C	45. C
8. C	27. D	46. D
9. D	28. B	47. B
10. C	29. A	48. E
11. B	30. D	49. A
12. E	31. E	50. D
13. D	32. D	51. E
14. A	33. A	52. B
15. E	34. E	53. C
16. C	35. C	54. A
17. B	36. A	55. D
18. D	37. E	
19. A	38. C	

Answers and Explanations

Richard II

1. **E.** This is a terminology question. This is a soliloquy that reveals Richard's thoughts to the audience through his internal monologue that is stated audibly.

2. **D.** References to kingship are part of Richard's real world, and therefore not part of the metaphor. Images of poverty, fortune, and beggars' penury support and develop the thoughts he has in his state of deprivation. Treason also refers to his thoughts, which he hopes will enable him to deal with his imprisonment.

3. **B.** Again, this is basically a vocabulary question. To "hammer" something out is to analyze a problem thoroughly.

4. **C.** The image is one of conception, but Richard's thoughts are going to reproduce and people the world that is in his mind.

5. **A.** Building on the information in the previous question, the only reliable answer is A.

6. **E.** This is a terminology question that requires an understanding of how the term can be used in a work. An example of personification is found in lines 23–24. You can locate direct address in line 15; hyperbole is used in lines 16–17. Lines 25–26 contain an example of simile. Synecdoche is a literary device that has the part representing the whole, and it is not used in this passage.

7. **A.** Lines 23–30 provide the evidence that thinking of others helps to ease one's personal hardship.

8. **C.** The opening two lines establish Richard's imprisonment, and the concluding lines state, "Nor I nor any man," which expands the concept from a specific situation to a universal concept.

9. **D.** Richard realizes that to be truly at ease, he must accept that he has lost everything that previously seemed to bring him contentment. This contradictory concept is an example of paradox.

10. **C.** All of Richard's thoughts about religion, ambition, and contentment lead to the concluding statement beginning in line 38 that he accepts being nothing and is thereby content.

11. **B.** Although "female" and "father" are mentioned, there is no inherent contrast between them.

12. **E.** Lines 3–4 express the literal solitude. Lines 31–32 describe his figurative coping with this solitude.

Beginnings
by Leah Napolin

13. **D.** The answer is found in the last sentence: "I have lived many lives in different times and places." This brief paragraph gives no other information that could lead to and of the other choices.

14. **A.** The entire paragraph creates a sense of curiosity about the narrator's background. But, inserting the phrase "up until probably the last ten," almost forces the reader to ask what happened during those ten years.

15. **E.** This is a question that requires your working knowledge of literary devices and techniques. Make certain to review these terms. Of the choices, only metaphor is used to develop this paragraph. See lines 9 ("strange house") and 12–13 ("large encompassing giant").

16. **C.** "Large encompassing giant" is an example of personification. It compares the house to a living creature.

17. **B.** The last sentences of the second and third paragraphs suggest that the narrator has and will to continue to have a connection to the house of her grandmother. Fear, rejection, envy, and anger are not introduced into this passage.

18. **D.** "So that gave me some role in this affair" is indicative of an individual who accepts being given a role in family affairs.

19. **A.** Here is an example of a piece of punctuation that serves a rather sophisticated purpose. The narrator is describing her grandmother, both physically and emotionally. The long dash indicates the narrator's difficulty, hesitancy, and reluctance to clearly characterize "Mammy's" controlling persona.

20. **B.** The preceding three paragraphs present a physical description of the house. Using "But" allows the narrator to switch from describing

this object to describing the people who inhabit that house. It transitions from reportorial to personal.

21. **D.** The use of "I" does not allow for a strictly objective or reportorial perspective. There is no mention of a death, nor are there any techniques or devices used to suggest bitterness. Relating the dining event and the family interactions with each other supports the idea of an involved memoirist.

22. **A.** The final paragraph is all about the grandmother: her actions and the actions of those around her as they respond to her demands. This is on whom the narrator centers her attention.

23. **C.** The pair of words that correctly apply to the entire passage is frank and thoughtful. Nostalgia could be applied, but it is paired with a word that cannot be correctly used to describe the tone of the passage.

24. **B.** The detailed description of a typical dinner with Mammy and the interactions of all of those gathered around the table provide the opportunity for the narrator to imply and the reader to conclude that this is a family with a multitude of stories.

25. **E.** Lines 44–45 and 50–51 are the telling signs that the narrator was not happy with her mother's passivity.

Love Poem
by John Frederick Nims

26. **C.** You should use the context of lines 7–8 to help you. "Steady" implies a lack of movement and leads you to the best choice, "wavy," which implies motions.

27. **D.** The entire poem lists the beloved's faults, yet the speaker adores her for them. This contradiction is the essence of the ironic title. Choice A is close, but it refers to the situation of the entire poem, not just the title.

28. **B.** It is easy to jump to the conclusion that the lover has broken yet another object. However, A, C, D, and E all support that idea; therefore, they cancel one another out.

29. **A.** You are required to reread the lines prior to the word "only" in order to realize that it provides a contrast. B and C are readily eliminated with a glance, and D and E are not supported by the poem.

30. **D.** Pay careful attention to the word "except." Then use substitution to find the one quality she does not exhibit. The answer is supported in line 15 with "wit," line 1 with "clumsiest," line 14 with "at ease," and line 19 with "gayly."

31. **E.** By definition, an apostrophe is an example of direct address.

32. **D.** Even though there is some exaggeration and humor, they are used to develop the character of the beloved, and a narrative requires elements of a story.

33. **A.** As you can see, it is imperative that you know terminology. To make sense, lines 5 and 6 must be read smoothly to the punctuation rather than to the end of the line.

34. **E.** The tone is revealed clearly in lines 16, 19, 23, and 24. The speaker adores his beloved.

35. **C.** This is a question that is almost too easy. Use your information from questions 30, 31, and 34 to help you recognize that all the other choices are negative.

36. **A.** As toys bring joy and delight, so, too, does the lover bring pleasure to the speaker's life. She holds toys and the speaker in her hands.

37. **E.** The clocks and solar system represent time and space. (See metonymy in Chapter 8.) "Wrench" indicates a breakdown of a system (e.g., "throwing a wrench into the system").

38. **C.** A straightforward, factual question. Again, you need to know your terms.

39. **A.** This is a poetic term and example question. The two metaphors are that palms are "bulls" and "burs in linen."

40. **E.** This is a subtle question which asks you to hear the sound of the line. All the open "O" sounds reinforce the idea of floating. None of the other given devices is present in this line.

As I Lay Dying
by William Faulkner

41. **C.** One of the universal symbols of freedom is flight. To refer to "wild geese going north" is to reinforce Addie's desire to be free.

42. **E.** "I" indicates a first person narrator point of view. The phrases "little dirty snuffling nose," "damp and rotting leaves," and "it was worst then" are indicative of conflict, setting, and tone. What is *not* mentioned in this first paragraph is a central event.

43. A. These lines are primarily composed of dialogue, so it is here that you should look for your answer. Vocabulary, similes, and syntax all point to colloquial (informal, conversational) diction.

44. D. The similes found in these two sets of lines are examples of figurative language. The other lines are factual and reportorial.

45. C. The concepts and images associated with alienation are found in phrases containing "secret," "blood strange," "cemetery," and "got no people." C, on the other hand, is cause and effect.

46. D. There is no evidence of any of the other choices in the passage. The very last line begins with the word "so." It is indicative of a matter-of-fact result of Anse being in the right place at the right time.

47. B. In this passage, Addie's conversation and interaction with Anse always place him in a subservient, uncomfortable position. See lines 27–28 and 31–33 to support the idea of her dominance.

48. E. Lines 17 and 46 indicate a straightforward cause and effect that just so happens to lead to Addie marrying Anse. Ambivalence, irony, setting, and highlighting an event are *not* references of the given phrase.

49. A. The "it" in this question is used the second time in the same way. See lines 4–6: The early spring, longing, potential, and desire to be free as wild geese lead to the conclusion that Addie has a restless nature.

50. D. Lines 1–15 give you the direct answer. ". . . and I would think with each blow of the switch: Now you are aware of me!"

51. E. A careful reading of the passage will lead you through Addie's experiences and thoughts about living and dying, about being alone, about being in a relationship, and about being free. Therefore, you need to recognize that, for Addie, hope and liberation is not in her future.

52. B. The second paragraph gives you the correct answer. It directly refers to the father.

53. C. Contrast demands difference. The only appropriate choice, therefore, is "rotting leaves . . . new earth." Rotting and new are the contrast here.

54. A. Paragraphs 1, 2, and 4 allow the reader into Addie's psyche. The one characteristic *not* associated with her seeking quiet is hatred.

55. D. This is another universal symbol. The associations with spring, especially early spring, center around renewal, regeneration, hope, fertility, and the continuance of life.

Rating the Essay Section

Rubrics for "Reginald's Choir Treat" by Saki

A high-range score (5, 6):

- Presents a prompt with a defensible assertion and indicates a line of reasoning.
- Identifies the two views of life presented in the story.
- Recognizes which view is preferred by the author.
- Effectively and coherently analyzes Saki's craft.
- Is cognizant of satire.
- Recognizes the humor in the allusions.
- Understands the irony and tone of the essay.
- Delineates Reginald's character.
- Cites appropriate textual references.
- Presents advanced insight and complexity.
- Strongly adheres to topic and uses connective tissue.
- Demonstrates an ability to manipulate language in a mature style.

A mid-range score (3, 4):

- Refers accurately to the prompt with a defensible assertion and probable line of reasoning.

- Presents the two philosophies.
- Refers accurately to Saki's craft.
- Infers the narrator's preference of lifestyle.
- Presents less-developed discussion of the two views of life.
- Adequately links elements of the discussion.
- May miss the satire of the story.
- Concentrates on the obvious rather than on the inferences and implications.
- Organization is adequate.
- May exhibit a few errors in syntax and/or diction.

Sample Student Essays

Student Essay A

In the short story "Reginald's Choir Treat" Saki contrasts two philosophies of life. One is a daring, cynical, and whimsical approach to life, like Reginald's. The other is a conservative, intellectual, religious, reforming approach to life like Anabel's. The author's sarcastic tone with a hint of diffidence indicates that he agrees with Reginald's cause, but he pities the fact that few people can relate to or understand "pioneers." Saki contrasts and shows the irony of both Anabel and Reginald's actions and perspectives about life to help the reader understand the two philosophies. However, even Anabel's philosophy shares some similarities to Reginald's and is more appealing to Saki's story than that of Reginald's family, which lives a modest, pedestrian, and uncompromising life, with no tolerance for the whims of Reginald.

Reginald does not fit in with his family's lifestyle. He questioned the universe and pleased himself with unconventional fantasies. Anabel is a gifted vicar's daughter who leads a charitable life and tries to be worldly at the same time. She attempts to make Reginald more religious and to coax him with her womanly charms but is unsuccessful. Saki ironically has her traveling to a French resort to pick up a good French accent from the Americans living there. She also persuades Reginald to lead a more virtuous life like herself and then ironically leaves Reginald to complete one of her charitable obligations without her. In a dialogue between the two main characters, Saki uses conversation to contrast Reginald with Anabel's perspectives. She speaks against the "sin of an empty life," and Reginald recalls the artistic "simplicity of the lilies" that simply sit and look beautiful. The greatest humorous irony of the story is Reginald turning religious charity work in the form of a choir outing into a whimsical pagan festival which is an allusion to the mythological Bacchus, the god of wine and pleasure. He shows his carefree and sarcastic approach to life by giving choirboys "tin whistles" and parading them through the streets with symbols of Bacchus. Another irony is that he has children honor Bacchus (god of wine) with a temperance hymn familiar to them, and that the parade which was intended to be gay turns out to be a lugubrious procession with the "miserable wailing of pipes."

A sign that Saki sides with Reginald's unappreciated actions over those of Anabel, or especially those of his family, is in the story's conclusion. Reginald's family never forgives him, and Saki adds that they felt this way because "they had no sense of humour."

5

10

15

20

25

30

This makes it clear that the unfortunate and almost bitter ending is their flaw and not Reginald's because they should have appreciated the humor of the situation.

Saki shows that he shares some of Reginald's philosophy with his frequent use of irony and sarcasm. He shows that people who share Anabel's philosophy will not be able to reform those whimsical pioneers like Reginald. But, they should be amiable and attempt to appreciate the sense of humor in the actions of those like Reginald. If not, they will be doomed to live an ill-humored, mundane life like that of Reginald's family.

Note: With specific reference to the 6-point rubric, we will use the following abbreviations to indicate into which column the comment would fall: **T** = **thesis, E = evidence, C = complexity, S = sophistication**.

This is a high-ranking essay for the following reasons:

- Introduction contains a clear thesis with a defensible assertion that sets up the organization of the essay. T
- Contains a clear opening, which sets up the organization of the essay. T
- Clarifies distinction between the two views and the characters (lines 5–10, 11–14). E/C
- Establishes Saki's attitude. C
- Introduces sarcasm and defends it (lines 3–5). E
- Contains strong textual references. E/C
- Draws appropriate conclusions based on the evidence presented (lines 34–37). C
- Addresses the writer's craft. E/C
- Juxtaposes the two characters and their opposing views (lines 18–20). E/C
- Provides a perceptive interpretation of a grammatical detail (lines 29–31). S
- Strongly adheres to topic using transitions and echo words. S
- Is direct and accurate. S
- Organization, syntax, and diction are adequate. S

This is an essay that can be categorized as high. Its strong textual references and understanding of the subtleties allow it to be in the high range even though there are some lapses in syntax.

Student Essay B

Saki's short story "Reginald's Choir Treat" contrasts two different philosophies of life. Each philosophy is represented by different characters. Conformity is represented by Anabel and nonconformity is represented by Reginald. In this story, Anabel and Reginald's parents try to make Reginald conform to the rest of society. Yet, his choir treat demonstrates that their goal failed. Through his use of tone, dialogue, and contrast, Saki indirectly shows his support of Reginald's nonconformity.

Saki uses a sarcastic tone, particularly towards Anabel and the other conformists. The first line of the story has an adage from Reginald: "never be a pioneer. It's the Early Christian that gets the fattest lion." This saying sets the sarcastic tone for the rest of the story. Later on, in his description of Anabel, Saki notes that, "if you abstain from tennis and read Maeterlinck in a small country village, you are of necessity intellectual." Likewise, in his description of Reginald's family, Saki points out that the rest of his family used "primroses as a table decoration." Saki is mocking all the

conformists because of their desire to conform to society. He uses this sarcastic tone to
demonstrate his partiality towards Reginald's free nature.   15

Saki also uses a contrast between Reginald and Anabel. The only direct
description of Reginald is that "[He], in his way, is a pioneer." On the other hand, the
author describes many details about Anabel. He calls Anabel, "the vicar's one extravagance."
Yet, in this case, Saki uses the pronoun "it" to refer to Anabel's fanciful name,
demonstrating his distaste for her. He sarcastically relates that "Anabel was accounted   20
a beauty and intellectually gifted" because "she had been twice to Fecamp to pick up a good
French accent from the Americans staying there." Saki presents the notion that many
believe the conformists are better than the nonconformists and uses Anabel to refute that
notion. Despite these accolades Saki has attributed to her, he mocks her and her philosophy.

Similarly, Saki uses dialogue to demonstrate his favoring nonconformity. The   25
conversation between Reginald and Anabel revolves around trying to convince Reginald to
abandon his nonconformity. She tries to do so by insulting him. Anabel tells him that
"[He is] really indecently vain in [his] appearance." For a woman who is supposed to be
smart and sweet, she does not display any of those qualities here. Her nasty nature
towards Reginald in this dialogue further emphasizes Saki's distaste for her and   30
her philosophy.

Obviously, Saki views individual expression as important and nonthreatening.
He recognizes that the best weapon to fight conformity is humor.

This is a mid-range essay for the following reasons:

- Clearly presents a thesis related to the prompt and the organization of the essay (lines 1–6). T
- Establishes the characters of Reginald and Anabel. E/C
- Recognizes and discusses sarcasm (lines 10–11). E
- Presents dialogue as indicative of character (lines 25–30). E
- Makes inferences and understands satire. E/C
- Presents author's preference and defends it (lines 7, 13–15). E/C
- Draws threads of the essay together and synthesizes technique with interpretation (lines 32–33). C/S

The syntax and diction shortcomings do not allow this essay to be rated in the high range.

Rubrics for the Poetry Essay

A high-range score (5, 6):

> KEY IDEA

- Effectively and coherently analyzes the poet's attitude toward education.
- Effectively and coherently analyzes the similarities and differences between Nemerov and Wordsworth.
- Indicates a fluency with poetic analysis.
- Identifies and analyzes appropriate references to support an interpretation.
- Exhibits strong line of reasoning.
- Draws mature inferences.
- Responds to subtleties in the poem.
- Writer's syntax and diction demonstrate a mature style.

A mid-range score (3, 4):

- Adequately addresses the prompt.
- Identifies and discusses the writers' techniques.
- Adequately discusses the similarities and differences between Nemerov and Wordsworth.
- Presents an adequate discussion of the poet's attitude.
- Displays acceptable writing skills.
- May not be sensitive to inference and tone.
- Focuses on the obvious and may not recognize the subtleties in both poems.
- Writing may have a few errors in syntax and/or diction.

Student Essay A

If weirdly possible, Wordsworth and Nemerov would probably have a heated conversation about education. While they would both agree that being taught and learning are important and necessary, they would probably disagree about where the lessons should come from, they may agree about the purpose and direction of education, and the value of education. Nemerov's "To David, About His Education" poetically promulgates his views about education which are facilitated through the poem's structure, tone, and imagery.

"To David, About His Education" suggests that what the world sees as important parts of life are learned through books rather than Wordsworth's experience and nature. In the opening lines of the poem, Nemerov makes the case that the world's "invisible things" can only be learned in books. Lines 2–3 call for "putting the mind's eye / or its nose, in a book" to receive a proper education for learning these "invisible things." Continuing, the speaker states that studying from books is a more effective way to learn but cannot procure a benefit to the method. He questioningly states, "You will have to learn them / in order to become one of the grown-ups" (14–15), not to any kind of an enlightened, educated person. This begins to place a doubt in the reader's mind about the real value of book learning.

Perhaps in line with with Wordsworth's belief in an education based soley on experience and living in nature, "To David, About His Education" presents examples of the intellectual pursuit of an education in which the images are of ridiculous facts and esoteric information, such as "the square root of Everest" (4) or the humorous "calorie content of the Diet of Worms" (13). The images are hyperbolic examples of the studies in an education through books. According to the speaker, only this kind of an education will produce the answers to such questions presented by "mostly invisible things." And, the reader may be led to ask whether or not this kind of information is of any value.

An answer to this type question is created by the tone established in the poem which is tongue-in-cheek or a bit sarcastic. Using parallel examples (4–13) that enumerate almost useless facts and information, the speaker describes the results of book learning to his son, but he does not praise these results. Rather, he seems to put it down in lines 15–19, "In order to become one of these grown-ups / Who keeps invisible things neither steadily nor whole, / But keeps gravely the grand confusion of the world." Nemerov is sarcastically saying that education has value, but for what and for whom?

So, it would seem Wordsworth and Nemerov have more in common than one would originally conclude. Both see the value of education, as most of the modern world does. Their differences most likely lie in the how, not the why.

Note: With specific reference to the 6-point rubric, we will use the following abbreviations to indicate into which column the comment would fall: **T = thesis, E = evidence, C = complexity, S = sophistication.**

KEY IDEA

This is a high-ranking essay for the following reasons:

- Contains a sophisticated and complex thesis and introduction to the task at hand (lines 1–7). T
- Clearly and concisely identifies the attitude of the poet toward education and supports it with references to the text (lines 10–11, 23–25). E/C
- Perceives implications arising from the poem (lines 12–16, 22–24, 32–34). C
- Uses connective tissue well (paragraphs 2, 3, 4, 5). S
- Analyzes the purpose of the imagery and tone (paragraphs 2, 3, 4). C

This spare essay falls into the high range because it is packed with appropriate detail and effective and coherent analyses and interpretation that is clearly related to the thesis and indicates a wider application.

Student Essay B

As shown in his poem "To David, About His Education" Howard Nemerov would disagree with William Wordsworth about how one should be educated. Wordsworth believes that true education is only gotten through experience and living in nature. But, from the very opening line of his poem, Nemerov makes it clear that a proper education is achieved through school which is something almost everyone would agree with. This is made obvious 5 by Nemerov's tone and imagery.

Throughout the poem Nemerov illustrates that he is very educated. At times, it seems as if Nemerov has a sarcastic, almost cynical approach toward school, with his mocking of things taught in school, such as "the square root of Everest" and "how many times Byron goes into Texas." He also uses humor in the line "calorie content / Of the diet of Worms." Seeming to 10 realize the underlying benefits of a proper education, Nemerov points out that "such things are said to be good for you." However, he also states in lines 10–13 that "I don't know / What you will do with the mean annual rainfall / of Plato's Republic."

Nemerov uses a very unusual sarcasm in this poem, as he applies two or more academic subjects which may have nothing in common except that they are both taught in school, and 15 he is able to tie them together to make sense, almost in joking manner. Statements such as "the law of the excluded middle applies west of the Rockies" illustrate this method, as does the "calorie content of the Diet of Worms." Although Diet of Worms has nothing to do with eating, Nemerov connects the two almost as if his brain has been overloaded with useless 20 information, similar to the way a student might accidentally confuse the material of multiple subjects he is studying. Nemerov fully understands the value of an education "in order to become one of the grown-ups."

Nemerov and Wordsworth have blatantly opposing opinions about the best method of education. While Wordsworth believes that an education through Nature is more valuable 25 than spending hours reading books, Nemerov understands that in order to be accepted by society, a knowledge of academic subjects is vital.

This is a mid-range essay for the following reasons:

- Presents a clear thesis that addresses the prompt and indicates a line of reasoning (paragraph 1). T
- Adequately illustrates a facility with analysis with respect to imagery (paragraph 2) and tone (paragraph 3). E/C
- Provides adequate evidence to defend interpretations (paragraphs 2, 3). E/C
- Transitions logically lead from one claim to another. S
- Support is adequate but needs more analysis of purpose. E/C
- Lacks implications for a wider view and applicaton. S

This is a mid-range essay with clear analysis, topic adherence, and support. Details chosen are obvious and limited in scope with a few lapses in syntax and diction.

Rubrics for the Free-Response Essay

A high-range score (5, 6):

- Clearly states the thesis with a defensible assertion and presents a line of reasoning.
- Effectively and coherently addresses the nature of the transformation.
- Effectively and coherently discusses the effects of the transformation on character and meaning.
- Insightful choice of details from an appropriate novel or play.
- Differentiates between actual and symbolic transformations.
- Focuses on the results of the transformation with regard to character and theme.
- Thoroughly discusses a specific character in context.
- Strongly adheres to topic.
- Demonstrates mature writing style.

A mid-range score (3, 4):

- States a clear thesis with a defensible assertion and probable line of reasoning.
- Adequately identifies and discusses the transformation.
- Adequately addresses the transformation's effect on the character and theme.
- Results of transformation are presented with less-developed discussion and/or analysis.
- Relies on obvious details to support the prompt or discussion.
- Adequately adheres to topic and uses connective tissue.
- Demonstrates some errors in syntax and diction.

Sample Student Essays

Student Essay A

In the novel <u>The Color Purple</u> by Alice Walker, the heroine, Celie, grows and develops tremendously as an individual. Throughout the course of the story, Celie undergoes major spiritual and psychological transformations. In essence, Celie is reborn. The novel's themes of the power of faith, a united sisterhood, and rebirth are all emphasized by Celie's dramatic character evolution.

The novel begins with Celie writing a letter to God, telling him how her father has been raping her. Only fourteen years old, Celie is naive and still somewhat immature. She doesn't understand what her father is doing to her, and even more

5

unfortunately, she doesn't have anyone to confide in. Thus, the reader senses Celie's
immense isolation as she shares her confusion with, and only with, God.   10

Celie's life takes on a turn for the worse when she is sent to live with her
arranged husband, Mr.—, who beats her and doesn't appreciate her. She does
all of his work for him and his children, and again she has not a friend to turn to.
However, when Mr.—'s son, Harpo, marries Sophia, Celie comes into contact with
another woman. Celie doesn't really understand Sophia because she is a   15
strong-willed, independent person who actually stands up to men. Thus, the
reader senses the weakness in Celie's character when she advised Harpo to beat
Sophia. Celie has been abused her whole life, and to her, being beaten is part of
being a woman. She is totally numb to abuse; she even imagines herself to be
a tree when being abused. This is her way to escape and void all feelings, to be   20
indifferent to the pain.

Naturally, she is envious of Sophia's strength and character, and so she
feels a beating would do Sophia good. When Sophia discovers that it was Celie
who told Harpo to beat her, she is both furious and hurt. Sophia confronts Celie,
and this a pivotal point in the novel. Celie realizes that she meant enough to   25
Sophia for her to be upset, which means that Celie has actually affected another
person. The two women quickly mend their relationship and begin a quilt to
symbolize their friendship. This ties into the theme of sisterhood because now
Celie has a friend, and the unity that the two share becomes an amazing force
throughout the novel.   30

Celie's character undergoes the strongest transformation after meeting
another "sister," Shug Avery. The circumstances under which Shug and Celie
become friends are incredible, for Shug is Mr.—'s mistress. However, their
unlikely bond is the main cause of Celie's rebirth. It was Shug who first
expressed appreciation to Celie for helping her get better after a serious illness. No   35
one had ever thanked Celie before, but Shug was so gratified for her care that she
wrote a song for Celie. This small act of appreciation becomes the turning point in
Celie's life. She now feels she is no longer as numb as a lifeless tree.

Shug's influence leads Celie to go from being a passive victim to becoming
an assertive, vibrant, independent woman. Shug was the one who makes Mr.— stop   40
beating Celie, as well as the one who found Celie's lost sister Nettie's letters which Mr.—
had been hiding. Shug even inspires Celie to begin her own pants-making business,
giving Celie total economic independence and creative freedom. Thus, the theme of
rebirth is emphasized. Walker stresses how the human soul is an unbelievably
powerful force, and how it contains the strength to emerge victorious despite adversity.   45

Shug Avery is also responsible for giving Celie a new spiritual outlook on life.
She explains to Celie that God isn't necessarily an old, white-bearded man. Shug's
view is that God is everything and is everywhere. The title becomes significant when
Shug tells Celie that God becomes angry if you walk past the color purple in a field and
don't notice it. This is a significant step in Celie's spiritual life because she now doesn't   50
feel that God is a man who is indifferent and deaf to her prayers. She has renewed her

belief, and the theme of the power of faith is reinforced, for Celie's faith has remained strong.

The Color Purple is a perfect example of a work of literature where the character undergoes a dramatic transformation. Celie changes from a numb, unassertive victim to being an aggressive, creative, vibrant, and independent woman. The unity of her female confidants and her unending faith allowed her to undergo such a deep transformation.

Note: With specific reference to the 6-point rubric, we will use the following abbreviations to indicate into which column the comment would fall: **T = thesis, E = evidence, C = complexity, S = sophistication**.

This essay is within the high-range parameters for the following reasons:

- Presents a clear, strong thesis with a a defensible assertion and indication of the line of reasoning. T
- Presents clear, appropriate evidence/support for thesis. E
- Incorporates connected meaning with every point made. E/C
- Thoroughly presents Celie's character. E/C
- Provides pivotal moments and details to illustrate the prompt. C
- Organization allows presentation to build chronologically and from the merely physical to the metaphysical. S
- Indicates both a perceptive reading of the novel and an understanding of some of its complexities. S
- Strongly adheres to topic. E/C/S
- Uses good connective tissue. S
- Demonstrates mature manipulation of language. S

This is a solid high-range essay that clearly indicates a reader who not only "got" the novel but also "got" the tasks demanded of the prompt.

Student Essay B

Set in the malevolent, shadowy era of the Cold War, Ian McEwan's The Innocent centers on a fervent young Brit working for a covert anti-Soviet intelligence agency. His youthful good nature, manners, and naiveté are what make Leonard Marnham "the innocent." The new threat constantly slithering around the corner is the dreaded red snake of Communism, ensnaring and asphyxiating the world with its wicked omnipotence. Leonard travails scrupulously and surreptitiously for its willful opposition and relies on his innocence throughout his occupation and life. When suddenly thrust into a spiral of new and exciting, but vaguely frightening experiences exploring the life he never lived, something immense in Leonard changes. This flagrant transformation is momentous and permanent.

The most vital characterization of the protagonist is his underlying innocence, which is repeatedly and implicitly emphasized throughout the novel. The reader and revolving characters are drawn into Leonard's

ingenuousness until he chooses to walk a path unknown to him which
results in his surrendering his innocence. This transformation begins
when Leonard becomes enraptured by the discovery of his own sexuality.
He is an innocent in the purest sense of the word. Maria, his young,
German lover, uncorks a surge of forceful new sensations and emotions   20
in Leonard. This unleashing of unbridled passion allows him to give in to
urges that ultimately push him over the edge. His exploration of sexuality
brings new found masculinity and confidence. Leonard officially enters
manhood and undergoes a tremendous transformation of temperament.
His behavior is increasingly unrestrained. At a crucial turning point,   25
Leonard willfully imposes himself on Maria, ignoring all cries of distress
of his lover. It is then that the reader becomes fully aware of Leonard's
grave potential to give rein to his basest nature.

Following this traumatic incident with Maria, Leonard distinctly
apologizes and makes a conscious effort to reform himself. The two scarred   30
companions reconcile only superficially and suffer perceptible losses of
intimacy. The plot is complicated by the appearance of Maria's inebriated
and disgruntled husband who attacks Leonard. After a crushing blow to
his genitals, Leonard unleashes a shocking display of malice and murders
and mutilates his assailant.   35

When Leonard callously forces himself onto Maria, we see his
capability for harsh insensitivity, resulting in severe damage. But when
Leonard slaughters Otto, and severs all his limbs, in order to fit the body
into a suitcase, with the intent of eschewing penalty, it is all but too clear
that Leonard Marnham is no longer the shy, unripe innocent the author   40
introduced us to.

In reference to Leonard's inhumanity the author uses irony to convey
the idea that human actions during this time period were largely inhumane.
McEwan's assessment of humanity and essentially his thesis by writing
The Innocent is that man is inherently evil, requiring only the slightest   45
corruption (such as Leonard's entrance into manhood and the decadence
exemplified by society) to unveil his intrinsic iniquity.

This essay is within the mid-range parameters for the following reasons:

- Presents a clear thesis with a defensible assertion and probable line of reasoning. T
- Uses specifics from the text to illustrate points (paragraphs 2 and 3). E
- Organization builds to a strong conclusion. S
- Adheres to topic well. S
- Does not provide a balanced characterization of Leonard. E/C
- Does not provide proof of Leonard's innocence other than his sexuality. E/C
- Demonstrates a willingness to stretch with regard to syntax and diction. S
- Demonstrates a clear voice. S
- Exhibits instances of awkward word choice (lines 7, 12, 37). S

- Exhibits instances of awkward sentences (lines 9–11, 25–27). S
- Veers dangerously close to plot summary. E/C

It is obvious that this is an eager, intelligent, and thoughtful reader and writer. However, the results of the transformation on Leonard are not as fully developed as the prompt demands. It is only at the end of the essay that the transformation is connected to theme.

Appendixes

Suggesting Reading Guide
General Bibliography
Glossary
Websites

As you probably know, a standard curriculum for AP Lit does not exist. Instead, teachers are urged to present material that will be appropriately challenging and enlightening while providing the opportunity for literary analysis. There are several ways of organizing the literature you study in an AP Literature and Composition course. Regardless of specifics, a broad selection of literature, covering many centuries and many styles, should be offered. Be confident that your teacher and course will meet the needs of the AP requirements.

We've developed several ways for you to reflect upon your own background. Once you have a clear overview of what you do know, you will be able to assess your particular strengths and weaknesses. You will also see the interrelationships of the literature you've studied and the commonalities and differences you will draw on to write your essays.

One approach to organizing your studies is chronological. This is the traditional survey of literature from "Beowulf to Virginia Woolf to Thomas Wolfe." This broad-based study provides you with many samples from different time periods and offers a context grounded in history. Another approach is the thematic one. Works are grouped by common ideas and are variations on a theme through time and genre. Often, it is obvious that certain works share a common sensibility. Generally, these characteristics are classified together as a literary movement. By connecting form and function, this type of reflection will broaden your understanding and analysis.

What follows is a bibliographic overview of literary movements.

Classicism

The classical writer generally exhibits or is concerned with the following:

- Universality
- Noble ideas
- Dignified language
- Restraint
- Clarity
- Objectivity
- The importance of structure
- An edifying purpose

Suggested classical works and authors:

Homer	*The Iliad, The Odyssey*
The Bible	"Genesis," "Exodus," "Matthew"
Sophocles	*Antigone, Oedipus Rex*
Euripides	*Medea*
Aristotle	"On the Nature of Tragedy"
Plato	"The Apology," "The Allegory of the Cave"

Molière	*Tartuffe, The Misanthrope*
Racine	*Phaedra*
John Milton	"L'Allegro," "Il Penseroso," "On His Blindness," *Paradise Lost* (excerpts)
Alexander Pope	"An Essay on Man," "An Essay on Criticism," "The Rape of the Lock"
Jonathan Swift	*Gulliver's Travels*
Voltaire	*Candide*

Make a list of classical works you have read: Cite title, author, and major thoughts about each.

_____

_____

_____

_____

Realism

KEY IDEA

The realistic writer generally exhibits or is concerned with the following:

- Truth and actuality
- Detail
- Character portrayal
- Psychology
- Objectivity
- Lack of sentimentality

Suggested realistic works and authors:

Chaucer	*The Canterbury Tales*
Fyodor Dostoyevsky	*Crime and Punishment*
Leo Tolstoy	*Anna Karenina*
Anton Chekhov	*The Cherry Orchard*
Ernest Hemingway	*The Sun Also Rises*
Henrik Ibsen	*Hedda Gabler, A Doll's House*

Make a list of realistic works you have read: Cite title, author, and major thoughts about each.

_____

_____

_____

_____

Romanticism

The romantic writer generally exhibits or is concerned with the following:

- Emotions and passion
- Imagination and wonder
- The variety and power of Nature
- The individual
- Freedom and revolution
- Dreams and idealism
- Mystery and the supernatural
- Experimentation with form
- Spontaneity

Suggested romantic prose works and authors:

Anonymous	*Beowulf*
Bocaccio	*The Decameron*
Rabelais	*Gargantua*
Cervantes	*Don Quixote*
Shakespeare	*Hamlet, King Lear*
Goethe	*Faust*
Hawthorne	*The Scarlet Letter*
Brontë	*Jane Eyre*
Hugo	*Les Miserables*

Suggested romantic poetic works and authors:

Multiple authors	The Ballads—Scottish and British
Shakespeare	Sonnets
Robert Burns	"To a Mouse," "John Anderson, My Jo," "A Red, Red, Rose"
William Blake	"A Poison Tree," "The Sick Rose," "London," "The Chimney Sweep"
William Wordsworth	"Tintern Abbey," "My Heart Leaps Up," "London, 1802," "The World Is Too Much With Us," "I Wandered Lonely as a Cloud," "Ode on Intimations of Immortality," Preface to the Lyrical Ballads
Samuel Taylor Coleridge	"Kubla Khan," "The Frost at Midnight," "The Rime of the Ancient Mariner"
Lord Byron	"Sonnet on Chillon," "When We Two Parted," "Maid of Athens," "The Isles of Greece," "She Walks in Beauty"
Percy Bysshe Shelley	"Ode to the West Wind," "To a Skylark," "Ozymandias"
John Keats	"On First Looking Into Chapman's Homer," "Ode to a Nightingale," "Ode on a Grecian Urn," "When I Have Fears That I May Cease to Be"
Alfred, Lord Tennyson	"Ulysses"
Robert Browning	"My Last Duchess," "Pippa's Song," "Soliloquy of the Spanish Cloister"

Make a list of romantic works you have read: Cite title, author, and major thoughts about each.

_____

_____

_____

_____

Impressionism

The impressionist writer generally exhibits or is concerned with the following:

- Appeals to the senses
- Mood and effects
- Vagueness and ambiguity
- Momentary insights
- Impressions of setting, plot, and character
- Emphasis on color and light
- Emotions and feelings
- Sensations into words

Suggested impressionistic works and authors:

Henry James	*The American*
Joseph Conrad	*Heart of Darkness*, *The Secret Sharer*, "The Lagoon"
Katherine Mansfield	"Bliss"
Kate Chopin	"Story of an Hour," *The Awakening*

Make a list of impressionistic works you have read: Cite title, author, and major thoughts about each.

_____

_____

_____

_____

Expressionism

The expressionist writer generally exhibits or is concerned with the following:

- Subjective responses
- Inner reality
- Abstract and mystical ideas

- Symbols and masks
- Man and society in chaos
- Creation of new worlds

Suggested expressionistic works and authors:

James Joyce	*Dubliners*
Eugene O'Neill	*Desire Under the Elms, The Hairy Ape, The Iceman Cometh*
T. S. Eliot	"The Hollow Men," "The Love Song of J. Alfred Prufrock"
Franz Kafka	*Metamorphosis, The Trial*

Make a list of expressionistic works you have read: Cite title, author, and major thoughts about each.

_____

_____

_____

_____

Naturalism

The naturalist writer generally exhibits or is concerned with the following:

- Realism to its extreme
- Fact and detail
- Social awareness and reform
- A broad spectrum of subjects, both positive and negative
- Man as animal in society
- Scientific impartiality

Suggested naturalistic works and authors:

Tennessee Williams	*A Streetcar Named Desire, Cat on a Hot Tin Roof*
Frank Norris	*The Octopus*
Stephen Crane	*Maggie, A Girl of the Streets*
Upton Sinclair	*The Jungle*

Make a list of naturalistic works you have read: Cite title, author, and major thoughts about each.

_____

_____

_____

_____

A note about literary movements: These are the movements you will find emphasized in the Western canon of literature. However, be aware that there are other literary movements that are currently recognized. Among them are the:

- Symbolist—an outgrowth of romanticism
- Existentialist—concern with man's alienation
- Absurdist—takes existentialism one step further into the realm of fractured reality
- Magical realism—modern genre that moves between the objective world and the world of fantasy

GENERAL BIBLIOGRAPHY

Recommended Poets

In addition to those referred to throughout this book, the following poets are representative of the poets you will encounter on the exam.

Matthew Arnold

Fatimah Asghar

W. H. Auden

Jay Bernard

Hera Lindsay Bird

Elizabeth Bishop

Gwendolyn Brooks

Billy Collins

Sophie Collins

e. e. cummings

Tishani Doshi

Rita Dove

T. S. Eliot

Lawrence Ferlinghetti

Robert Francis

Allen Ginsberg

Robert Graves

Donald Hall

Robert Hayden

Seamus Heaney

Luke Kennard

Galway Kinnell

Maxine Kumin

Zaffar Kunial

Hollie McNish

Pablo Neruda

Sharon Olds

Mary Oliver

Wilfred Owen

Linda Pastan

Safiya Sinclair

Edna St. Vincent Millay

Hannah Sullivan

May Swenson

Wislawa Szymborska

Dylan Thomas

Natasha Tretheway

Kevin Young

Recommended Authors

Chinua Achebe: *Things Fall Apart*

Aeschylus: *Oresteia*

Margaret Atwood: *The Handmaid's Tale, Oryx and Crake*

Jane Austen: *Pride and Prejudice, Sense and Sensibility*

James Baldwin: *Go Tell It on the Mountain, Another Country*

Saul Bellow: *The Adventures of Augie March*

Charlotte Brontë: *Jane Eyre*

Emily Brontë: *Wuthering Heights*

Albert Camus: *The Stranger*

Willa Cather: *My Antonia, One of Ours, Death Comes to the Archbishop*

Anton Chekhov: *The Cherry Orchard*

Kate Chopin: *The Awakening*

Sandra Cisneros: *The House on Mango Street*

Joseph Conrad: *Heart of Darkness, Lord Jim, The Secret Sharer*

Stephen Crane: *The Red Badge of Courage*

Don Delillo: *White Noise*
Charles Dickens: *Great Expectations, A Tale of Two Cities*
Juno Diaz: *The Brief Wondrous Life of Oscar Wao*
Isak Dinesen: *Out of Africa*
Fyodor Dostoyevsky: *Crime and Punishment*
Theodore Dreiser: *An American Tragedy, Sister Carrie*
George Eliot: *Silas Marner, Middlemarch, Mill on the Floss*
Ralph Ellison: *Invisible Man*
Euripides: *Medea*
William Faulkner: *As I Lay Dying, The Sound and the Fury*
Henry Fielding: *Tom Jones*
F. Scott Fitzgerald: *The Great Gatsby*
Gustave Flaubert: *Madame Bovary*
E. M. Forster: *A Passage to India*
Thomas Hardy: *Jude the Obscure, Tess of the D'Urbervilles, Mayor of Casterbridge*
Nathaniel Hawthorne: *The Scarlet Letter*
Joseph Heller: *Catch-22*
Ernest Hemingway: *The Sun Also Rises*
Homer: *The Iliad, The Odyssey*
Khaled Hosseini: *The Kite Runner*
Zora Neale Hurston: *Their Eyes Were Watching God*
Aldous Huxley: *Brave New World*
Henrik Ibsen: *A Doll's House, Ghosts, Hedda Gabler*
Kazuo Ishiguro: *The Remains of the Day*
Henry James: *The Turn of the Screw, The American*
James Joyce: *A Portrait of the Artist as a Young Man, Dubliners*
Franz Kafka: *Metamorphosis, The Trial*
Ken Kesey: *One Flew Over the Cuckoo's Nest*
Barbara Kingsolver: *The Poisonwood Bible, Animal Dreams*
Maxine Hong Kingston: *The Woman Warrior*
D. H. Lawrence: *Sons and Lovers*
Chang-Rae Lee: *Native Speaker*
Cormac McCarthy: *The Road, Blood Meridian, All the Pretty Horses*
Gabriel García Márquez: *One Hundred Years of Solitude*
Herman Melville: *Moby-Dick, Billy Budd*
Arthur Miller: *Death of a Salesman, The Crucible*
N. Scott Momaday: *House Made of Dawn, In the Presence of the Sun, In the Bear's House,
    The Way to Rainy Mountain*
Toni Morrison: *Beloved, Song of Solomon, The Bluest Eyes*
V. S. Naipaul: *A Bend in the River*
Gloria Naylor: *Women of Brewster Place, Linden Hills*
Tim O'Brien: *The Things They Carried*
Eugene O'Neill: *Desire Under the Elms, Long Day's Journey into Night*
George Orwell: *1984*
Alan Paton: *Cry, the Beloved Country*
Jean Rhys: *Wide Sargasso Sea*
Jean Paul Sartre: *No Exit, Nausea*
William Shakespeare: *Hamlet, King Lear, Macbeth, Othello, Twelfth Night*
George Bernard Shaw: *Major Barbara, Man and Superman, Pygmalion*
Mary Shelley: *Frankenstein*

Sophocles: *Antigone, Oedipus Rex*
John Steinbeck: *The Grapes of Wrath, Of Mice and Men, Cannery Row*
Tom Stoppard: *Rosencrantz and Guildenstern Are Dead*
Jonathan Swift: *Gulliver's Travels*
Amy Tan: *The Kitchen God's Wife, The Bonesetter's Daughter*
Leo Tolstoy: *Anna Karenina*
Mark Twain: *Adventures of Huckleberry Finn*
John Updike: *Rabbit Run*
Voltaire: *Candide*
Kurt Vonnegut: *Slaughterhouse-Five*
Alice Walker: *The Color Purple*
Edith Wharton: *Ethan Frome, The House of Mirth*
Oscar Wilde: *The Importance of Being Earnest*
Thornton Wilder: *Our Town*
Tennessee Williams: *A Streetcar Named Desire, The Glass Menagerie*
Virginia Woolf: *To the Lighthouse*
Richard Wright: *Native Son*

allegory A work that functions on a symbolic level.

alliteration The repetition of initial consonant sounds, such as "Peter Piper picked a peck of pickled peppers."

allusion A reference contained in a work.

anapest A metrical pattern of two unaccented syllables followed by an accented syllable ($\breve{}\ \breve{}\ \acute{}$).

antagonist The force or character that opposes the main character, the protagonist.

annotation To make personal notes on a text in order to get a better understanding of the material. These notes can include questions, an argument with the author acknowledging a good point, a clarification of an idea, theme, etc.

apostrophe Direct address in poetry. Yeats's line "Be with me Beauty, for the fire is dying" is a good example.

aside Words spoken by an actor intended to be heard by the audience but not by other characters on stage.

assonance The repetition of vowel sounds in non-rhyming words in close proximity.

aubade A love poem set at dawn which bids farewell to the beloved.

ballad A simple narrative poem, often incorporating dialogue that is written in quatrains, generally with a rhyme scheme of *a b c d*.

blank verse Unrhymed iambic pentameter. Most of Shakespeare's plays are in this form.

cacophony Harsh and discordant sounds in a line or passage of a literary work.

caesura A break or pause within a line of poetry indicated by punctuation and used to emphasize meaning.

catharsis According to Aristotle, the release of emotion that the audience of a tragedy experiences.

character One who carries out the action of the plot in literature. Major, minor, static, and dynamic are types of characters.

climax The turning point of action or character in a literary work, usually the highest moment of tension.

comic relief The inclusion of a humorous character or scene to contrast with the tragic elements of a work, thereby intensifying the next tragic event.

commentary To present an explanation with evidence about a specific text based on the prompt, the audience, and the intended line of reasoning.

complexity The presence of tension, conflict, differences, changes, emotions, and human foibles in a specific text.

conflict A clash between opposing forces in a literary work, such as man vs. man; man vs. nature; man vs. God; man vs. self.

connotation The interpretive level of a word based on its associated images rather than its literal meaning.

convention A traditional aspect of a literary work, such as a soliloquy in a Shakespearean play or a tragic hero in a Greek tragedy.

couplet Two lines of rhyming poetry; often used by Shakespeare to conclude a scene or an important passage.

dactyl A foot of poetry consisting of a stressed syllable followed by two unstressed syllables, ($\acute{}\ \breve{}\ \breve{}$).

denotation The literal or dictionary meaning of a word.

denouement The conclusion or tying up of loose ends in a literary work; the resolution of the conflict and plot.

deus ex machina A Greek invention, literally "the god from the machine" who appears at the last moment and resolves the loose ends of a play. Today, the term refers to anyone, usually of some stature who untangles, resolves, or reveals the key to the plot of a work. See the conclusion of Euripides's *Medea* for an example or the sheriff at the end of *Desire Under the Elms* by O'Neill.

diction The author's choice of words.

dramatic monologue A type of poem that presents a conversation between a speaker and an implied listener. Browning's "My Last Duchess" is a perfect example.

elegy A poem that laments the dead or a loss. "Elegy for Jane" by Roethke is a specific example. Gray's

"Elegy in a Country Church Yard" is a general example.

enjambment A technique in poetry that involves the running on of a line or stanza. It enables the poem to move and to develop coherence as well as directing the reader with regard to form and meaning. Walt Whitman uses this continually.

epic A lengthy, elevated poem that celebrates the exploits of a hero. *Beowulf* is a prime example.

epigram A brief witty poem. Pope often utilizes this form for satiric commentary.

euphony The pleasant, mellifluous presentation of sounds in a literary work.

exposition Background information presented in a literary work.

fable A simple, symbolic story, usually employing animals as characters. Aesop and La Fontaine are authors who excel at this form.

figurative language The body of devices that enables the writer to operate on levels other than the literal one. It includes metaphor, simile, symbol, motif, hyperbole, and others discussed in Chapter 8.

flashback A device that enables a writer to refer to past thoughts, events, episodes.

foot A metrical unit in poetry; a syllabic measure of a line: iamb, trochee, anapest, dactyl, and spondee.

foreshadowing Hints of future events in a literary work.

form The shape or structure of a literary work.

free verse Poetry without a defined form, meter, or rhyme scheme.

hyperbole Extreme exaggeration. In "My Love is Like a Red, Red Rose," Burns speaks of loving "until all the seas run dry."

iamb A metrical foot consisting of an unaccented syllable followed by an accented one; the most common poetic foot in the English language, ($\smile$ $\prime$).

idyll A type of lyric poem which extols the virtues of an ideal place or time.

image A verbal approximation of a sensory impression, concept, or emotion.

imagery The total effect of related sensory images in a work of literature.

impressionism Writing that reflects a personal image of a character, event, or concept. *The Secret Sharer* is a fine example.

irony An unexpected twist or contrast between what happens and what was intended or expected to happen. It involves dialogue and situation, and it can be intentional or unplanned. Dramatic irony centers around the ignorance of those involved while the audience is aware of the circumstance.

line of reasoning The logical sequencing of claims that present support of a thesis statement. This is accomplished by showing the relationship between and among the thesis and the claim developed in each of the body paragraphs.

lyric poetry A type of poetry characterized by emotion, personal feelings, and brevity; a large and inclusive category of poetry that exhibits rhyme, meter, and reflective thought.

magical realism A type of literature that explores narratives by and about characters who inhabit and experience their reality differently from what we term the objective world. Writers who are frequently placed in this category include Gabriel García Márquez, Günter Grass, and Isabel Allende.

metaphor A direct comparison between dissimilar things. "Your eyes are stars" is an example.

metaphysical poetry Refers to the work of poets like John Donne who explore highly complex, philosophical ideas through extended metaphors and paradox.

meter A pattern of beats in poetry. (Answers to questions in poetry review: 5, 3, 2, 2, 4)

metonymy A figure of speech in which a representative term is used for a larger idea. ("The pen is mightier than the sword.")

monologue A speech given by one character. (Hamlet's "To be or not to be . . . ")

motif The repetition or variations of an image or idea in a work which is used to develop theme or characters.

narrative poem A poem that tells a story.

narrator The speaker of a literary work.

octave An eight-line stanza, usually combined with a sestet in a Petrarchan sonnet.

ode A formal, lengthy poem that celebrates a particular subject.

onomatopoeia Words that sound like the sound they represent (hiss, gurgle, bang).

oxymoron An image of contradictory terms (bittersweet, pretty ugly, giant economy size).

parable A story that operates on more than one level and usually teaches a moral lesson. (*The Pearl* by John Steinbeck is a fine example. See *Allegory*.)

paradox A set of seemingly contradictory elements which nevertheless reflects an underlying truth.

For example, in Shakespeare's *Much Ado About Nothing*, the Friar says to Hero, "Come, Lady, die to live."

parallel plot A secondary story line that mimics and reinforces the main plot. (Hamlet loses his father, as does Ophelia.)

parody A comic imitation of a work that ridicules the original.

pathos The aspects of a literary work that elicit pity from the audience.

personification The assigning of human qualities to inanimate objects or concepts. (Wordsworth personifies "the sea that bares her bosom to the moon" in the poem "London, 1802.")

plot A sequence of events in a literary work.

point of view The method of narration in a work.

protagonist The hero or main character of a literary work, the character the audience sympathizes with.

quatrain A four-line stanza.

resolution The denouement of a literary work.

rhetorical question A question that does not expect an explicit answer. It is used to pose an idea to be considered by the speaker or audience.

rhyme/rime The duplication of final syllable sounds in two or more lines.

rhyme scheme The annotation of the pattern of the rhyme.

rhythm The repetitive pattern of beats in poetry.

romanticism A style or movement of literature that has as its foundation an interest in freedom, adventure, idealism, and escape.

satire A mode of writing based on ridicule, which criticizes the foibles and follies of society without necessarily offering a solution. (Jonathan Swift's *Gulliver's Travels* is a great satire that exposes mankind's condition.)

scansion Analysis of a poem's rhyme and meter.

sestet A six-line stanza, usually paired with an octave to form a Petrarchan sonnet.

sestina A highly structured poetic form of 39 lines, written in iambic pentameter. It depends upon the repetition of six words from the first stanza in each of six stanzas.

setting The time and place of a literary work.

simile An indirect comparison that uses the word, "like" or "as" to link the differing items in the comparison. ("Your eyes are like stars.")

soliloquy A speech in a play which is used to reveal the character's inner thoughts to the audience.

(Hamlet's "To be or not to be . . . " is one of the most famous soliloquies in literature.)

sonnet A 14-line poem with a prescribed rhyme scheme in iambic pentameter. (See Chapter 9 for a comparison between Shakespearean and Petrarchan sonnets.)

sophistication In the support of the thesis and development of the line of reasoning, the writer demonstrates a mature control of language and/or the ability to connect the text and prompt to a broader context, perspective, or argument.

spondee A poetic foot consisting of two accented syllables ($'$ $'$).

stage directions The specific instructions a playwright includes concerning sets, characterization, delivery, etc. (*See Hedda Gabler* by Ibsen.)

stanza A unit of a poem, similar in rhyme, meter, and length to other units in the poem.

structure The organization and form of a work.

style The unique way an author presents his ideas. Diction, syntax, imagery, structure, and content all contribute to a particular style.

subplot A secondary plot that explores ideas different from the main storyline. (In *Hamlet*, the main storyline has Hamlet avenging the death of his father. The subplot has Hamlet dealing with his love for Ophelia.)

subtext Implied meaning of a work or section of a work.

symbol Something in a literary work that stands for something else. (Plato has the light of the sun symbolize truth in "The Allegory of the Cave.")

synecdoche A figure of speech that utilizes a part as representative of the whole. ("All hands on deck" is an example.)

syntax The grammatical structure of prose and poetry.

tercet A three-line stanza.

theme The underlying ideas that the author illustrates through characterization, motifs, language, plot, etc.

tone The author's attitude toward his subject.

tragic hero According to Aristotle, a basically good person of noble birth or exalted position who has a fatal flaw or commits an error in judgment which leads to his downfall. The tragic hero must have a moment of realization and live and suffer.

trochee A single metrical foot consisting of one accented (stressed/long) syllable followed by one unaccented (unstressed/short) syllable (´ ˘).

understatement The opposite of exaggeration. It is a technique for developing irony and/or humor where one writes or says less than intended.

villanelle A highly structured poetic form that comprises six stanzas: five tercets and a quatrain. The poem repeats the first and third lines throughout.

There are literally thousands of sites on the internet that are in some way related to the study of college-level English. We are not attempting to give you a comprehensive list of all of these websites. What we are going to do is to provide you with a list that is most relevant to your preparation and review for the AP Literature and Composition exam. It is up to you to log on to a site that may be of interest to you and to see for yourself just what it can offer and whether or not it will be of specific benefit to you. Don't forget that you have a dedicated AP website from McGraw Hill that can be of great help to you as you work your way through the AP English Literature course and as you prepare for the exam in May. Go to the Cross-Platform Prep Course: www.xplatform.mhprofessional.com and enter your access code printed on the back cover.

Note: These websites were available and online at the time this book was revised. Please be aware that we cannot guarantee that a site you choose to explore will be operating when you go to that URL.

Because this is an Advanced Placement exam for which you are preparing, why not go to the source as your first choice? The College Board's AP site is called AP Central:

- **http://www.collegeboard.com/apc**

Related to British Literature:

- Romanticism: **http://www.uh.edu/engines/romanticism/poets.html**
- British history: **http://www.bbc.co.uk/history**
- Study guide: **http://www.studyguide.org/brit_lit_timeline.htm**
- Ultimate Shakespeare site: **http://playshakespeare.com**

Related to American Literature:

- Authors, timelines, literary movements: **http://public.wsu.edu/~campbelld/amlit/sites.htm**
- Literature: Voice of the Shuttle: **http://vos.ucsb.edu**

Of General Interest:

- Purdue Online Writing Lab: **http://owl.english.purdue.edu**
- For links to other websites for English literature: **http://www.kn.att.com/wired/fil/pages/listaplitma.html**
- For terms, exercises, tips, and rules from a primate with attitude, go to Grammar Bytes: **http://chompchomp.com**
- For help with rhetorical and literary terms, there are three useful sites: **http://mcl.as.uky.edu/glossary-rhetorical-terms**, **http://andromeda.rutgers.edu/~jlynch/Terms/**, and **http://humanities.byu.edu/rhetoric/**
- For access to the world of arts and letters, including newspapers, literary magazines, and blogs: **http://artsandlettersdaily.com**

- To download free e-books: **www.bartleby.com**
- For a directory to free downloadable e-books as well as articles, reviews, and comments: **www.e-booksdirectory.com**
- For WebNotes, a useful tool that allows you to compile and organize information from multiple web pages and share findings: **www.webnotes.net**

Each of these websites will lead you to many more. You will have to take the time to explore the various sites and to make your own evaluation as to their value to you and your expectations.

We suggest you use your favorite web server or search engine and type in ADVANCED PLACEMENT ENGLISH (AP), or ADVANCED PLACEMENT (AP) LITERATURE. (Our favorite search engine is www.google.com.) From that point on, you can "surf the net" for those sites that suit your particular needs. You will have to take the time to explore these various domains and to make your own evaluation of their value to you and your expectations. Perhaps, you might even decide to set up your own AP Lit website or chat room.

5 Steps to Teaching AP English Literature and Composition

TEACHER'S MANUAL

Michael Hartnett

AP English Literature Teacher
Jericho High School, Jericho, New York

Thanks to Greg Jacobs, an AP Physics teacher at Woodberry Forest School in Virginia, for developing the 5-step approach used in this teaching guide.

Introduction to the *Teacher's Manual*

Since the AP English Literature exam is the culminating, evaluative tool for your students' high school English career, it would be wonderful if it could be truly representative of all that you have covered in the course. But it is only a 3-hour test. Therefore, it must be general, and it must be wide-ranging enough to provide equity and opportunity for every student who takes the exam. What the test makers assume about the students who take the AP English Literature exam is a common background of terminology and skills. It is the intention of *5 Steps to a 5* to provide a resource for terminology and skills, exam clarification and explanation, and practice when needed.

Currently, teachers have no shortage of resources for the AP English Literature class. No longer limited to just the teacher and the textbook, today's teachers can utilize online simulations, apps, computer-based homework, video lectures, and so on. In all probability, you will consider using many of these resources in your class. Even the College Board, itself, provides so much material related to the AP English Literature exam that the typical teacher—and student— can easily become overwhelmed by an excess of teaching materials and resources.

As one of your major resources, this book is an asset for your class because it explains in straightforward language exactly what a student needs to know for the AP English Literature exam and provides a plan students can use to review for the test. In addition to test prep, the text presents activities to introduce, develop, and enrich the skills on which the AP English Literature course is based.

The 5 Steps of Teaching English Literature

This *Teacher's Manual* will take you through 5 steps in approaching and teaching AP English Literature. These 5 steps are:

▶ **Prepare a strategic plan for the course**

▶ **Hold an interesting class every day**

▶ **Evaluate your students' progress**

▶ **Prepare students for the AP exam**

▶ **Become a better teacher every year**

What follows is a discussion of each of these steps, providing suggestions and ideas that I have successfully used in my classes. I hope that you find in this *Teacher's Manual* materials and ideas that will be useful and beneficial to you and to your students.

STEP 1

Prepare a Strategic Plan for the Course

The AP English Literature and Composition Course Exam Description (CED) should be your AP Literature bible. The AP Literature CED proposes six Big Ideas as a foundation for the course. It provides a comprehensive description and analysis of each of these Big Ideas and specifies which CED units of study are related to each of the Big Ideas.

The chart below briefly describes the six Big Ideas, along with the corresponding units of study found in the CED. The chart also shows how *5 Steps to a 5: AP English Literature* can easily be used in conjunction with these Big Ideas, presenting a sampling of chapters, with page numbers, related to the individual Big Ideas.

BIG IDEAS	UNITS RELATED TO THE BIG IDEA	*5 STEPS TO A 5*
Character: Characters in literature allow readers to study and explore a range of values, beliefs, assumptions, biases, and cultural norms represented by those characters.	1, 2, 3, 4, 6, 7, 9	Chapter 8, pp. 128–129
Setting: Setting and details associated with it not only depict a time and place, but also convey values associated with that setting.	1, 3, 4, 7	Chapter 8, p. 127
Structure: The arrangement of the parts and sections of a text, the relationship of the parts to each other, and the sequence in which the text reveals information are all structural choices made by a writer that contribute to the reader's interpretation of the text.	1, 2, 3, 5, 6, 7, 8, 9	Chapter 8, pp. 126–127, 135–136
Narration: A narrator's or speaker's perspective controls the details and emphases that affect how readers experience and interpret a text.	1, 3, 4, 6, 7, 9	Chapter 8, pp. 126–131
Figurative Language: Comparisons, representations, and associations shift meaning from the literal to the figurative and invite readers to interpret a text.	2, 4, 5, 6, 7, 8	Chapter 8, pp. 132–134
Literary Argument: Readers establish and communicate their interpretations of literature through arguments supported by textual evidence.	1, 2, 3, 4, 5, 6, 7, 8, 9	Chapter 5, pp. 71–79

Scope and Sequence

In order to plan your course, obtain your school's calendar for the year. Make sure that it includes all the early release days, teacher workdays, holidays, and state testing dates. Next, find out the date for the AP English Literature and Composition exam in May. Now you are ready to plan your course.

The following plan allows for varied and more fluid paths than the one presented in the CED. The six Big Ideas in the CED are so embedded in works that AP English Literature teachers can have more course design freedom than is advisable in other AP courses. The alternative presented here encourages the teacher to integrate longer works, poems, and short prose works into individual units, rather than to separate each from the others with units strictly according to type as presented in the CED. Such integrated units of longer works, poems, and short prose encourage students to develop a nimbleness in thought and analysis, so they can move seamlessly from one text to another, no matter the scope, scale, or style.

An Alternative Scope and Sequence for AP English Literature

A note before you begin: While some teachers prefer to read fewer full-length works, I strongly suggest planning to integrate as many full-length works as possible. In a society with so many distractions, students generally have had limited exposure to broad and diverse texts. The best way for students to have the literary foundation to take on the challenges of the AP English Literature exam is to read works ranging from classical to 21st century, drawing from a variety of cultures and styles. If your school allows for summer assignments, having students come in with at least two larger novels under their belts to start the school year will set the tone and establish expectations for the course.

The following outline is based on a 4-quarter school year that has approximately 10 weeks per quarter. The class meets 5 times a week at 40 minutes per class = 200 minutes per week.

1st Quarter (35–40 classes)

Students should read at least three full-length works (more if the sizes of the works allow), with a work distributed on day 1 and a new full-length text assigned on the day the previous work has been read (100 pages per week is a good standard). That reading, with accompanying response assignments, will be the basis of all homework. Poetry analysis can take place in those periods when students are completing reading assignments; poetry discussions work well in weeklong mini units.

10–15 CLASSES: BROADER LITERARY ANALYSIS

- ▶ Narrative technique
- ▶ Thematic development
- ▶ Character analysis
- ▶ Narrative structure
- ▶ Setting
- ▶ Literary argumentation

10–15 CLASSES: CLOSE READING ANALYSIS

- ▶ Annotation
- ▶ Figurative language
- ▶ Literary techniques
- ▶ Thesis development
- ▶ Literary argumentation

15 CLASSES: POETRY ANALYSIS

▶ Annotation

▶ Poetic structures

▶ Types of poetry

▶ Poetry interpretation

▶ Poems for comparison

▶ Literary argumentation

2nd Quarter (35–40 classes)

The same general structure continues for each quarter. However, now students can draw on the works of the previous quarter and use the skills gained to develop further sophistication.

10–15 CLASSES: BROADER LITERARY ANALYSIS

▶ Authorial manipulations

▶ Psychological analysis

▶ Motif development and variations

▶ Setting as character

▶ Literary argumentation

10–15 CLASSES: CLOSE READING ANALYSIS

▶ Employment of tone

▶ Establishment of mood

▶ Variation of sentence structure

▶ Thesis development

▶ Literary argumentation

15 CLASSES: POETRY ANALYSIS

▶ Focus on diction and syntax

▶ Nuances of punctuation

▶ Tone shifts

▶ Use of ambiguity

▶ Literary argumentation

3rd Quarter (35–40 classes)

While the same breakdown of full-length works and poetry should continue, the approach should pivot more directly toward the exam with in-class multiple-choice and essay (prose, poetry, and free response) assignments given regularly. As the exam draws nearer, the teacher may have to pull back on full-length texts to focus students on the close textual reading necessary for the AP English Literature and Composition exam.

4th Quarter

THE EXAM . . . AND BEYOND

The AP English Literature and Composition exam is given in the first or second week of May. The remainder of the course is your choice.

STEP 2

Hold an Interesting Class Every Day

Bell Ringers

Many AP English Literature teachers open their class with a quick activity designed to engage students with a discussion among themselves. This allows for the class to begin as soon as the bell rings and gives the teacher time to take attendance. In fact, studies have shown that breaking the intellectual and verbal silence in the first 5 minutes makes it more likely that students will participate during the rest of class. So a good class opener facilitates the goal of ensuring that every student speaks and writes every day.

Here are some ideas of what you can use for class openers, or bell ringers:

▸ Use the "5 Minutes to a 5" section of the *5 Steps to a 5 Elite Edition*, which provides 180 activities and questions, each about 5 minutes long, that are related to specific skills that make up the AP English Literature course. The chart that follows shows which openers in "5 Minutes to a 5" pertain to each of the Big Ideas of the course.

▸ You could have a Lightning Round or Question of the Day—something easily accessible to get students to know each other: For example, you might ask, "Who is the better character: Hamlet or Jane Eyre?" Or you could use something more pedagogically nutritious, such as: "Which is a more revealing line: 'How can we know the dancer from the dance?' or 'What to make of a diminished thing'?"

▸ Alternatively, you can begin class with a brief excerpt from the text you are using that day; this can be discussed in class as a type of intellectual warm-up exercise, or you can have students expound on it in a 2-minute daily journal entry.

The following activities are found in the "5 Minutes to a 5" section of the *Elite Edition of 5 Steps to a 5 English Literature*. These short activities are ideal to use as class openers.

BIG IDEAS	ACTIVITIES IN THE *ELITE EDITION*
Character	Days 24, 37, 94, 102, 114–117, 119, 121–125, 127–132, 141, 152–164
Setting	Days 78, 80–86, 88–89, 105, 139, 146, 148
Structure	Days 24, 26, 47–50, 60, 76–77, 108, 143, 172
Narration	Days 13, 39, 58, 69–75, 79, 109–113, 142, 145, 159–164, 174–175
Figurative Language	Days 27–30, 32–33, 35, 37, 43, 46, 53, 61, 91, 170
Literary Argumentation	Days 11, 62, 65, 68, 92–99, 133–137, 164–165
Multiple Choice—OK, this isn't one of the Big Ideas, but sometimes you just need to find multiple-choice questions	Days 14–26, 30, 40, 43, 51, 56-59, 78, 80–81, 88–89, 109–113, 119, 121–122, 127–128, 130, 132, 141, 150–151

Questioning Techniques as the Centerpiece of Engagement

The design of the AP English Literature exam compels students to become stronger readers and writers. Teachers have wonderful opportunities to guide students through close textual reading and to provide a steady stream of subtle, nuanced approaches to language that students can apply to their own compositions.

Teachers can use every work of literature—whether it is a poem, a short story, a full-length work, or a short prose excerpt—as an opportunity for students to read carefully and to annotate texts. After the students annotate a text, teachers can provide a series of questions that can simultaneously expand the students' understanding of a given work and better prepare them for the AP exam. The "5 Minutes to a 5" section offers many examples of how to proceed with such questions, so teachers should feel comfortable not only drawing on these mini lessons as models, but also adapting and expanding them to suit the long-term needs of the course. A combination of multiple-choice questions and open-ended questions that compel more expansive responses allows for students to develop recognition skills and interpretation skills.

Modeling is an essential technique to build student skills toward student interpretive independence. While Wordsworth argues that "we murder to dissect," teachers really must demonstrate how a reader can attack a poem or a passage. Most students will not be ready to examine literature in a sophisticated way until they see the teacher explore the texts through many layers of questioning. Multiple examples of such modeling, especially with poetry, may be necessary. The ultimate goal is for students to take ownership of the questions, so that the students become the ones doing the asking. When students begin asking these questions themselves, they are demonstrating recognition of what the texts can offer and are able to pivot toward developing rich and varied responses to these questions.

Multiple Choice

Regular practice with multiple-choice questions is important to performing well on the AP English Literature and Composition exam. At the end of each unit (or once a month), you should introduce one prose passage and one poetry passage, each with multiple-choice questions. Use the passages and multiple-choice questions provided in the AP Classroom so that you are sure that they are authentic AP questions. Students will gain practice and build confidence from the beginning of the year so there will be less need for last-minute review just before the test.

Making Literature a More Interesting Class

To make literature a more interesting class for your students, you might try some of these ideas:

► Incorporate at least one play in class, so class members can perform scenes. Some of my more successful classes have been student performances of the climaxes of *Oedipus Rex*, *Hamlet*, and *Hedda Gabler*.

► Use short film clips judiciously in classes to provide variety and counterpoint to your literary analyses. For example, a teacher can apply the theme in *Frankenstein* of a creation that gets out of the control of the creator in works as varied as *The Blade Runner, My Fair Lady, Jurassic Park*, and *Clueless*. Even clips from the 1931 *Frankenstein* movie can serve as an example of this creation gone out of control, as the film is dramatically different from the original Mary Shelley novel. The misappropriation of logic in *Candide* can be reinforced by the witch scene in *Monty Python and the Holy Grail*.

► Seek to offer students a great variety of topics, so they can provide brief individual commentaries/presentations to the class. For example, here are 25 topics for *The Stranger* by Albert Camus:

1. Rituals and symbols
2. Religion
3. Meursault's mother's death
4. The writing style
5. Humor
6. Sleep
7. Sky and light
8. Meursault's daily life
9. Salamano and his dog

10. Raymond Sintes

11. Meursault's friendships

12. Meursault's open-mindedness

13. Commitments

14. Marie

15. The beginning of Chapter 5, Part I

16. The shooting in the sun

17. Meursault's captivity

18. The trial and the law

19. The role of chance

20. The chaplain and Meursault's speech

21. Existentialism

22. The structure of the novel

23. The first-person narrative

24. What Camus omitted

25. The title

Each of these topics should include a series of prompts to help students organize their responses.

▶ **Use art to both broaden and deepen the meaning of literary works.** For example, the depiction of women in 19th-century European art adds a layer of understanding to the feminist outlook of Charlotte Brontë in *Jane Eyre*, as do the silhouette images of Kyra Walker in the novels of Toni Morrison, such as *The Bluest Eye* and *Song of Solomon*. In contrast, the illustrations over the past 300 years for Jonathan Swift's *Gulliver's Travels* shed light as much about the perceptions of specific eras as about the novel itself.

▶ **Look to focus a particular critical lens on specific works.** This approach can allow the class to break free from traditional examinations of theme, plot, setting, and character. For example, both teachers and students can be well served by psychological analysis for Franz Kafka's *The Metamorphosis*, political contextualizing for Barbara Kingsolver's *The Bean Trees*, or colonial influences for Chinua Achebe's *Things Fall Apart*.

▶ **Use music to both broaden and deepen the meaning of literary works.** For example, contrast a Scottish ballad like "Barbara Allen" with a Bob Dylan folk ballad. Have students match an author's style with musical forms. For example, students have often synced the operatic and orchestral-like passages of Herman Melville's *Moby Dick* with classical music (the brief excerpts in the *Idiot's Guide to Classical Music* is a useful source).

▶ **Use the approaches of Poetry Out Loud performances so that students look to memorize and perform poetry.** These dramatic recitations provide a break from the close textual analysis central to interpretation while offering other avenues of investigation. For example, students in their performance can emphasize pacing and cadence, draw on the use of sound devices like assonance, consonance, and onomatopoeia, and employ variations in tone.

Homework Versus What Must Be Done in Class

The centerpiece of homework for AP Literature is reading, reading, and more reading. To be able to expose young minds to some of the great works of literature is one of the great pleasures of AP Literature. Quizzes on the readings are the best and most efficient way of making sure students have done the assigned reading. Teachers should be flexible when students have not completed the book on the assigned due date in that the value of students eventually reading a great work of literature is greater than meeting the deadline. Furthermore, I often give students the opportunity to supplement their quiz grades with close reading responses from these texts. Again, the value of students individually revisiting passages is a valid reason to improve grades.

While I have occasionally assigned an essay that students can write at home, I put much greater value on any essay that students complete during one period in class. Yes, students might still have drawn from outside sources (Schmoop, Sparknotes, Ragnotes, Enotes, etc.) in preparation for an essay or quiz, but the in-class work remains the most authentic. I make an effort to counteract these outside sources by quoting passages from a site like Schmoop or Sparknotes and asking students what the site left out or inadequately addressed. When I give students my own study guide with my own quirky questions (with specific page numbers from the book), students tend to steer away from those outside sources and back to the text.

STEP 3

Evaluate Your Students' Progress

Early evaluations can be smaller in scope and lesser in expectations than later ones. In terms of scope, that may mean students initially write three-sentence responses when addressing a theme or literary technique. Multiple-choice assignments and quizzes based on poems and passages can be brief (perhaps five questions). For both of these scaled-back written responses and multiple-choice questions, teachers can draw from the "5 Minutes to a 5" section for models and materials. Initially, grades should be given for completion rather than evaluation since the brevity of the assignments could lead to wild evaluation swings (two incorrect answers in five would result in 60%). As the scale expands for the written (500 words) and multiple-choice responses (10–25 questions), the evaluations can begin in earnest, reflecting AP-style questions and graded with AP-style rubrics.

As the school year progresses, the goal is to make sure students integrate literary technique in more sophisticated and subtle ways. Early in the year, the teacher should provide more examples and guidance about literary technique in the texts, with that assistance for students steadily receding for each literary work, whether a large novel or a small poem. Chapter 10 in this book can serve as a guide to this incremental approach.

Along with essays and multiple-choice questions, presentations should be an essential component for evaluations. Often the course is better served by most of these presentations being brief, say 2 minutes, so that those classes can have many student speakers, essentially acting as a symposium about a work.

While I make up all my quizzes and essays, I constantly draw on old AP exams as models. The diagnostics and practice exams presented in this book can serve to reinforce the daily lessons, at times offering formative assessment to gauge student progress; at others, offering clear evaluation. For the AP practice exams, students should definitely go over incorrect answers, since that approach has been the most successful in students improving on the multiple-choice section. More on how to approach these corrections in Step 4.

Grading of essays can evolve over the course of the year. That means a first essay that might receive an A could receive a B if it were the fifth essay of the year. The rubrics in the beginning of the year can be softer, gentler versions of the AP rubrics. As the teacher models analyzing poems and passages, provides sample essays, and scaffolds lessons, those rubrics will conform more stringently to the actual AP rubrics.

What is less successful is harsh early essay grading. While it is a technique sometimes used by teachers to show growth, this harsh early essay grading can really undermine the teacher's desire to be supportive in the student's development. A teacher cannot expect students to know what they have not yet been comprehensively taught. A more effective approach is to emphasize a particular skill to incorporate in an essay for the teacher to evaluate. While in this scenario deductions can still take place, they are less likely to have the severity that can be demoralizing as students look to build up their compositional skills.

The skills required to interpret poetry and prose are rich and broad. The teacher should look to keep expectations realistic of students about what they can achieve until the approaches are modeled and students have had the opportunities to practice. That said, by halfway through the course, the teacher's expectations should adhere to the AP rubrics, giving students opportunities to hone their skills, so they will be ready for the May exam. For the last 6 weeks before the exam, students should be writing weekly essays that are graded and should receive weekly at least one section of a multiple-choice exam. Before then, such evaluations can be monthly (early on) and then biweekly.

STEP 4

Get Students Ready to Take the AP Exam

While some elements of discrete knowledge (such as learning literary terms) are valuable in preparation for the AP English Literature exam, the exam is primarily skill-based. Therefore, well before the exam, the teacher looks for students to have numerous encounters with larger works of literature, so that the structures, ideas, and techniques within them can be analyzed. Students should begin their direct preparation for the AP English Literature exam once the first full-length work has been completed, with an AP free-response essay serving as the culminating activity. Such free-response essays should regularly serve as assignments for each full-length work.

As far as the prose and poetry essays go, that writing process should be eased into, especially for poetry. A series of poetry annotations and close textual analysis discussions should build into introductory paragraphs, followed by a steady incorporation of how authors employ literary techniques to expand meaning. During these poetry lessons, multiple-choice questions mirroring those on the exam should be used. These approaches should develop toward a series of AP poetry essays written in the third quarter.

A similar approach should be taken with the prose, although teachers generally can progress more quickly given students' greater familiarity with the structures, especially if the students have already taken the AP Language and Composition exam. In the final month before the exam, students should receive increased in-class exposure to both the essays and the multiple-choice questions for the exam.

While the need for test prep is duly acknowledged, the reviews, diagnostics, and practice exams work better as integrated elements within specific units. A free-response essay as the culmination of a unit focused on a novel or a play offers both AP practice and an opportunity for students to crystallize their ideas about a particular work. Test prep can be drudgery. By integrating the multiple-choice passages and essays into literary units, the bludgeoning from one test after another just before the actual AP exam can be avoided.

As students embark on taking practice tests, they should continue to use some of the previously discussed approaches to help them grow as readers and writers. That means that teachers should initially provide only the answer key to the multiple-choice sections of the practice exams. That way, students can go back to the questions and see if they can figure out why the correct answers are better than the ones they selected, finding the evidence in the text. Teachers can encourage these corrections by returning points on exams or providing extra credit. In addition, teachers should reinforce the need for students to annotate the essay passages, so they can organize their thoughts and cite specifics from the texts.

Become a Better Teacher Every Year

The AP English Literature teacher focuses on two essential elements: how the analysis can dig deeper while the material grows broader. The first-time AP English Lit teacher may need to start with fewer full-length works than what might be ideal to establish a rich literary foundation. The first-time teacher of the course should be primarily committed to introducing students to the multilayered process of literary analysis using a broad variety of styles, genres, and cultures.

With each passing year, teachers should add more works to the curriculum, making room by condensing the lessons in the previously taught works and distilling the methodology to the fullest engagement of core elements. Each new year is an opportunity to explore additional works with students, opportunities that will not only broaden the nature of analysis, but also serve as counterpoints to traditional canonical works. Finally, the teachers will look for new ways to help students hone their craft as writers as they move beyond what a text means to how the author goes about enriching that meaning.

The best materials that teachers can use are the student essay samples provided by the College Board, with the accompanying scoring and analysis. Those materials provide the most authentic, practical, and persuasive means for students (with some guidance from the teacher) to figure out their own approaches to addressing the prompts and texts. Similarly, the released multiple-choice sections with answer keys and diagnostic guides can help students apprehend specific elements of close textual analysis.

Additional Resources for Teachers

Literally thousands of websites are related to the study of college-level English. I have tried to list the websites that are most relevant to the preparation and review for the AP English Literature and Composition exam. *Note:* These URLs were live at the time this book was revised. However, there is no guarantee that they will continue to be operational.

▶ Because this is an Advanced Placement exam you are preparing for, go to the source of the exam as your first choice: **http://apcentral.collegeboard.com**.

▶ Make certain to become a member of the AP Literature English Instructors Discussion group (**https://apcommunity.collegeboard.org/group/apenglish/home**) hosted on AP Central (you can join by application and invitation). It is an invaluable resource.

▶ For online conversations with AP English Literature instructors, you may want to investigate/join these Facebook AP English Literature teachers groups (by application and invitation):

▷ AP Literature and Composition Teachers (**https://www.facebook.com/groups/ap.lit.teachers**)

▷ AP Literature and Composition (**https://www.facebook.com/groups/186856038378257**)

▶ McGraw Hill's Cross-Platform site (**https://mhprofessional.benchprep.com/**) can be very helpful as you work your way through the AP English Literature course and prepare for the exam in May.

FOR LITERARY INTERPRETATION AND ANALYSIS

▶ Explore All Things Poetry (**https://poemanalysis.com/**) is a solid website that offers a general reinforcement of poetry interpretation and close textual analysis.

▶ Glossary of Rhetorical Terms (**https://mcl.as.uky.edu/glossary-rhetorical-terms**) provides help with rhetorical and literary terms.

FOR THE ESSAY COMPONENTS

▶ BGSU Firelands Writing Lab (**https://www.firelands.bgsu.edu/tlc/writing-lab.html**) is chock-full of information.

▶ Purdue On-Line Writing Lab, otherwise known as OWL (**https://owl.purdue.edu/writinglab/the_writing_lab_at_purdue.html**), is a helpful online writing center with a huge set of links.

▶ Owens Community College Writing Center, "Sentence Variety" (**https://www.owens.edu/media/writing/sentvar.pdf**), has activities to create variety and interest in student's writing.

▶ Grammar Bytes (**http://chompchomp.com**) provides terms, exercises, tips, and rules from a primate with attitude!

AP English Literature Tool Box

In the tool box you will find a list of literary works you can use for teaching AP English Literature.

List of Literary Works Useful in AP English Literature

Beyond the works offered in *5 Steps to a 5*, the following is a list of useful short poetry and prose works for the AP English Literature and Composition course (limited to 20 for poetry and 20 for prose). The selections here offer a variety of styles, approaches, time periods, and perspectives. The list ends with five novels to consider integrating into your curriculum. A good way to gather other options is to look at the lists of suggested literary works given for the free-response essays of AP exams over the past 20 years.

WORKS OF SHORT POETRY

▶ "Blackberry Picking," "Mint," and "Digging," by Seamus Heaney. Poetry essay

▶ "Wild Iris" and "The Untrustworthy Speaker," by Louise Glück. Poetry essay

▶ "Hawk Roosting" and "The Thought Fox," by Ted Hughes. Poetry essay

▶ "Kingdom Animalia" and "Consider the Hands That Write This Letter," by Aracelis Girmay. Poetry essay

▶ "Still I Rise" and "Caged Bird," by Maya Angelou. Poetry essay

- "The Lanyard" and "The Afterlife," by Billy Collins. Poetry essay

- "This Is Just to Say" and "Spring and All," by William Carlos Williams. Poetry essay

- "Those Winter Sundays" and "The Whipping," by Robert Hayden. Poetry essay

- "A Far Cry from Africa" and "After the Storm," by Derek Walcott. Poetry essay

- "Holy Sonnet 10" and "Holy Sonnet 14," by John Donne. Poetry essay

- "Warning" and "Fables—Cutting off One's Ears for Someone Else Is Wrong." by Jenny Joseph. Poetry essay

- "Fern Hill" and "Do Not Go Gentle into That Good Night," by Dylan Thomas. Poetry essay

- "There Will Come Soft Rains," by Sara Teasdale. Poetry essay

- "A Smile to Remember," by Charles Bukowski. Poetry essay

- "Break of Day in the Trenches," by Isaac Rosenberg. Poetry essay

- "Who Said It Was Simple" and "Power," by Audre Lorde. Poetry essay

- "The Second Coming" and "Sailing to Byzantium," by William Butler Yeats. Poetry essay

- "Because It Looked Hotter That Way," by Camille T. Dungy. Poetry essay

- "On His Blindness," by John Milton. Poetry essay

- "The People Upstairs" and "Lines Indited with All the Depravity of Poverty," by Ogden Nash. Poetry essay

WORKS OF SHORT PROSE

- "The Story of an Hour," by Kate Chopin. Prose essay

- "Reunion," by John Cheever. Prose essay

- "A Clean, Well-Lighted Place," by Ernest Hemingway. Prose essay

- "Girl," by Jamaica Kincaid. Prose essay

- "Sticks," by George Saunders. Prose essay

- "Home," by Gwendolyn Brooks. Prose essay

- "Miss Brill," by Katherine Mansfield. Prose essay

- "A Blunder," by Anton Chekhov. Prose essay

- "The Dinner Party," by Mona Gardner. Prose essay

- "The Continuity of Parks," by Julio Cortázar. Prose essay

- "Pilón," by Sandra Cisneros. Prose essay

- "Snow," by Ann Beattie. Prose essay

- *One Hundred Years of Solitude* (first paragraph), by Gabriel García Márquez. Prose essay

- *The Haunting of Hill House* (first five paragraphs), by Shirley Jackson. Prose essay

- *Midnight's Children* (first three paragraphs), by Salman Rushdie. Prose essay

- *Sula* (first two paragraphs), by Toni Morrison. Prose essay

- *A Bend in the River* (first seven paragraphs), by V. S. Naipaul. Prose essay

- *In the Time of Butterflies* (first four paragraphs), by Julia Alvarez. Prose essay

- *The Metamorphosis* (first five paragraphs), by Franz Kafka. Prose essay

- *Invisible Man* (first three paragraphs), by Ralph Ellison. Prose essay

NOVELS

- *The Brief Wondrous Life of Oscar Wao*, by Junot Diaz. Free-response essay

- *A Gesture Life*, by Chang-rae Lee. Free-response essay

- *The Poisonwood Bible*, by Barbara Kingsolver. Free-response essay

- *White Teeth*, by Zadie Smith. Free-response essay

- *All the Light We Cannot See*, by Anthony Doerr. Free-response essay